DIARIES AND LETTERS
OF MARIE BELLOC LOWNDES
1911–1947

Mrs Belloc Lowndes

DIARIES AND LETTERS
OF
MARIE BELLOC LOWNDES
1911–1947

Edited by
SUSAN LOWNDES

The Heart of Marie Belloc Lowndes
will always be to me the warmest
spot in London.

GAYNOR MADDOX

1971

CHATTO & WINDUS

LONDON

Published by
Chatto & Windus Ltd
40/42 William IV Street
London W.C.2

*

Clarke, Irwin & Co. Ltd
Toronto

ISBN 0 7011 1790 7

Printed in Great Britain by
T. & A. Constable Ltd., Hopetoun Street, Edinburgh

CONTENTS

ACKNOWLEDGEMENTS

I offer my thanks to those who have given me permission to include letters in this volume: Mr Alexander R. James for the letter of Mr Henry James (*Copyright* 1971 Mr Alexander James); Mr Laurence Whistler for that from his brother, Mr Rex Whistler; Mr Douglas Brown for the letter of his father, Sir Frank Brown; Mr Denning Miller for the letter from his mother, Mrs Duer Miller; Miss Jennifer Gosse for that from her grandfather, Sir Edmund Gosse; Mrs Denis Gwynn for the letter of her mother, Lady Lavery; Mrs Norman Butler for that of her aunt, Mrs Richard Fuller; Mr L. P. Hartley for his help, and my cousin Mrs Reginald Jebb for the letter of her father, Mr Hilaire Belloc; the Hon. Mrs Keith Rous for that from Mrs Hamlyn; the Administrators of the Estate of the late Christopher Hassall for Sir Edward Marsh; Mrs Veronica Anderson for the letter from Mr J. C. O'G. Anderson. I am especially grateful to Professor Gordon Haight of Yale University who did invaluable research for me with regard to the Americans mentioned in the text, Major Eric Dutton who read the MS, Mr W. Simpson who consulted several newspaper files, and Mr J. H. Martin.

The Society of Authors as the literary representatives of the estate of Miss Katherine Mansfield; Mr Frank Magro, the literary executor of Sir Osbert Sitwell; Mr Joseph P. Hennessey, executor of the estate of Mr Alexander Woollcott; Messrs Lloyds Bank Ltd as trustees of the Thomas Hardy Estate; Messrs Colbourne, Bush and Bartlett for the trustees of Mr H. Hamilton Fyfe; Mr J. C. Medley, literary executor of Mr Charles Morgan; Mr P. S. Crane, executor of Mrs B. L. B. Warde; Messrs Jonathan Cape Ltd on behalf of the executors of the Ernest Hemingway estate for the extract from *A Moveable Feast*; all receive my warm acknowledgement for their gracious permission as do those I have been unable to trace.

I thank my sister, Elizabeth Iddesleigh who, as our mother's literary executor, provided the material without which this book could not have been assembled, and I also thank Mrs Maureen Bogue Castanha who typed out for me the original diaries, many of them heavily corrected, in my mother's far-from-clear handwriting.

SUSAN LOWNDES

LIST OF PLATES

Out of the War (Gentleman Anonymous)
Cressida, No Mystery (Love's Revenge)
One of Those Ways
Love is a Flame (Benn's 9d Series)
The Reason Why (Benn's 9d Series)
Duchess Laura, Certain Days of her Life
Duchess Laura, Further Days of her Life (U.S.A.)
Letty Lynton
The Story of Ivy
Jenny Newstead (An Unrecorded Instance—U.S.A.)
The Chianti Flask
Another Man's Wife
The House by the Sea (Vanderlyn's Adventure—U.S.A.)
Who Rides on a Tiger
And Call it Accident
The Marriage Broker (The Fortune of Bridget Malone—U.S.A.)
The Christine Diamond
Reckless Angel (U.S.A.)
Lizzie Borden (U.S.A.)
She Was Afraid
The Injured Lover
Motive (Why it Happened—U.S.A.)
She Dwelt with Beauty (Posthumously)

Short Stories
Studies in Wives
Studies in Love and in Terror
Why They Married
Some Men and Women
What of the Night (U.S.A.)

Plays
What Really Happened
With all John's Love
Why be Lonely

The Second Key
The Empress Eugenie

Memoirs
I, Too, Have Lived in Arcadia
Where Love and Friendship Dwelt
The Merry Wives of Westminster
A Passing World
The Young Hilaire Belloc (U.S.A. Posthumously)

Anonymous
The Life and Letters of Charlotte Elizabeth, Princess Palatine
The Empress Frederick (The Kaiser's Mother)
King Edward the Seventh
Kitchener of Khartoum
Edward Grey
Queen Alexandra

Under Pseudonyms
Noted Murder Mysteries, by Philip Curtin
Not All Saints, by Elizabeth Rayner (Novel)

FOREWORD

MARIE BELLOC LOWNDES had wished from her earliest years to be a writer. Born Marie Belloc, the only daughter of a French father and an English mother, she and her brother Hilaire spent their early years in France. After their father's death, the children lived between the two countries with their mother, Bessie Parkes Belloc, poet, writer and friend of George Eliot, Elizabeth Barrett Browning and other contemporary figures. The romantic story of her marriage at the age of thirty-seven was told by her daughter in a book, *I, Too, Have Lived in Arcadia*, which was published in 1941.

The vitality which was such a marked characteristic of Marie Belloc Lowndes came from the robust, integrated life of the French family with whom she felt she had more in common than with her English forbears. This vitality was shown in the deep and highly intellectual interest she took in those around her, which was an enormous asset to her as a novelist.

When we, her daughters, came to examine her papers, we found her diaries, often with long gaps, owing to her constant writing commitments, and we decided that they could be of interest to a larger circle. Her great absorption in the political and literary worlds of her day and the account of the years of the Second War, cast many sidelights on those times.

A generous, revealing talker, Mrs Belloc Lowndes had a searching knowledge of the human heart. Her many novels of crime, immensely popular in her lifetime, were based on the fact that our life is, or was, conducted on the assumption that murder will not be committed and they depict the reactions of ordinary persons to sudden violence in their own circle. Some sinister happening is dropped, like a stone thrown into a pool. The reader soon knows who is guilty, and so watches the reactions of the people in the story, with an ever deepening sense of horror and suspense.

Mrs Belloc Lowndes did not consider it to be the business of a novelist to inculcate moral lessons, but like most serious students of life she was a realist, and believed that 'who breaks, pays' is true regarding the fundamental laws of conduct. She had the power of endowing her characters with life and her work shows her understanding of human nature both in the heights of self-sacrifice and the frailties and wickedness of which it is capable, and she was acutely aware of the part that money

I

plays, not only in ordinary life, but particularly in the planning and commission of crime.

Born into the Catholic Church, Marie Belloc Lowndes was a profound believer, though she seldom spoke of her religious convictions. She was a person of such integrity that her friends soon became aware of her limitless understanding and she had the rare gift of constantly making new and often younger friends all through her life. She confirmed her many friendships by her gift for letter writing. The big pages in her flowing hand, always written with a quill pen, filled with lively information, comment, and it must be acknowledged, often with the wildest rumours, were eagerly welcomed and treasured, so that we have been fortunate in having a wide selection from which to choose.

Intensely interested in literature and the art of writing, Mrs Belloc Lowndes was a good friend to many young authors whose work she admired and who were downcast by their initial lack of success. When Mr Graham Greene as a young man published *The Man Within*, Marie Belloc Lowndes at once realised that a major writer had appeared. Hugh Walpole, Frank Swinnerton, Margaret Kennedy, Pamela Frankau, E. M. Delafield, James Hilton, L. P. Hartley and many now forgotten writers, owed a great deal to her early encouragement.

"America is my second home", Marie Belloc Lowndes used to observe after her annual visits to that country in the thirties. She dearly loved the originality and vividness of American speech and writing, and several of her closest literary friends were from the States.

Marie Belloc married F. S. A. Lowndes, who was on the staff of *The Times* until his retirement in 1938, two years before his death. His work in Fleet Street allowed his wife to lead, in her own words, "the life of a happy widow". She describes her marriage in the Epilogue to her book, *A Passing World*. Marie Belloc Lowndes was aware of how fortunate she was in being the wife of so imaginative, unselfish and intelligent a man as was Frederic Lowndes.

Their very different backgrounds—F. S. A. Lowndes was the son of a country parson—somehow contributed to their contentment, for Marie Belloc Lowndes was a brilliant interpreter of the French mind and character. She was fascinated by the differences in outlook of Britain and France and considered the French to be far more realistic, and noted with amusement that there is no French equivalent to the term, 'wishful thinking'.

Short and vivacious, Marie Belloc Lowndes was once described by an American friend as 'a small bird perched on the window sill'. She spoke English with a slight French accent and possessed, to a remarkable degree, the art of conversation, of which both the Diaries and Letters give a vivid indication.

In August 1947, she fell ill. It was the 15th, her fête day in France which brought back happy recollections of the French home she loved so well. Her elder daughter drove her down to her husband's house in Hampshire, and there on November 14th she died, having received the Last Sacraments of her Church. The priest who came to administer them was the Roman Catholic Chaplain to Broadmoor Criminal Lunatic Asylum. During her short illness, he had become a friend and she was much moved by the love and understanding attitude he showed towards his flock.

ELIZABETH IDDESLEIGH and
SUSAN LOWNDES MARQUES

CHAPTER I

HOW I BEGAN MY WRITING LIFE

This autobiographical account is a personal introduction to the Diaries and Letters which make up the rest of the book, for it shows Marie Belloc Lowndes' industry and powers of work and how she succeeded in her determination to become a writer.

The real beginning of my writing life was when my mother's little house in Great College Street became unexpectedly vacant in 1888. I persuaded her to try the experiment of living there for a winter, as I hoped to obtain a commission for a book dealing with some phases of French history.

Cardinal Manning, an old friend of my mother, asked me to come and see him, and was shocked when he heard that I had only received £16 for all the rights in my first book which took me four years of hard work. It was called *The Life and Letters of Charlotte Elizabeth, Princess Palatine*.[1] My French family showed their good feeling and their good sense by concealing from my mother how horrified they felt that I should have been allowed to read the famous letters of that vigorous, extremely coarse-minded old lady, of whom Thackeray wrote what remains and always will remain by far the best description in his *History of the Four Georges*.

The Cardinal offered to give me an introduction to W. T. Stead[2] for whom he had a great regard and affection. I eagerly accepted, though till then I had had no thought of even attempting to do journalistic work.

W. T. Stead was then editing *The Pall Mall Gazette*, and some years before I met him, he had caused an immense sensation by printing in his paper a series of articles called *The Maiden Tribute of Modern Babylon*. These papers exposed the fact that children could be, and constantly were, procured for immoral purposes. This horrible traffic was well known to all philanthropists and those who would now be called social workers. Such people were always trying to put an end to the traffic, but they completely failed, largely owing to the fact that a child was not regarded as being mentally capable of taking the oath. Thus the accusation made by a child against a man, went for nothing.

Whether Mr Stead was well- or ill-advised in the methods pursued by him to expose and end this traffic in little girls, is an open question. The

---

[1] *The Life and Letters of Charlotte Elizabeth, Princess Palatine*. Pubs. 1889.
[2] William Thomas Stead: 1849-1912. Assistant Editor to John Morley of *The Pall Mall Gazette* 1880-3 and Editor 1883-9. Founded *Review of Reviews* in 1890. Died in Titanic disaster.

fact remains that it was owing to what he did that British girls are now protected up to the age of sixteen by an Act of Parliament.

Cardinal Manning had been one of his most determined supporters and defenders, though to a man of his refined and fastidious mind, anything like sensational journalism must have been abhorrent.

I went with the Cardinal's introduction to the office of *The Pall Mall Gazette*. Mr Stead, at that time, was completely absorbed in the then indifferent conditions of the sailors in the British Navy, and here, again, he did a great work which was fully acknowledged by all those concerned. He said he would accept me as a contributor, and he introduced me to Edmund Garrett, a member of his staff. He asked this man to look after me, and teach me how to write for the press.

Edmund Garrett was the first young Englishman I ever knew really well, and I was fortunate in having the friend he soon became. He was closely related to the remarkable family of which one member was Dr Elizabeth Garrett Anderson[1], and another the wife of Henry Fawcett.[2]

I have wondered, since, how Edmund Garrett drifted into journalism, and especially into the very trying form of afternoon-paper journalism. He was even then very delicate, and had to be at the office of *The Pall Mall Gazette* at, I think, seven o'clock each morning. We became real friends, though I was quite unlike any English girl he had ever known, and, above all, quite unlike the ideal of young womanhood which obtained in his immediate circle. Such culture as I possessed was either entirely French, or had been instilled into me by my mother. Of education in their sense, I had had none.

As I look back, I know Edmund Garrett was interested, though not passionately as I was, in literature. He was a strong Liberal, and had political ambitions. As was natural he held very advanced views concerning the Rights of Women, and that was a strong bond, being the only subject concerning which we saw eye to eye. From his point of view, only a human being who was either a fool or a knave could become, or remain, a Roman Catholic, though he was too kindly and too well-mannered to discuss the subject of my religion.

For the first time since the death of my English grandmother when I was nine years old, I felt happy in England. Everything in London was

[1] Elizabeth Garrett Anderson: 1836-1917. First Englishwoman to qualify in England as a Medical Practitioner.

[2] Henry Fawcett: 1833-1884. The blind M.P. for Brighton (Lib.), Postmaster-General. m. Millicent Garrett, sister of Dr Elizabeth Garrett Anderson.

of absorbing interest, including art, politics, and even music. I took a lively, sympathetic interest in the relations of men and women. The women belonging to my mother's early life, however advanced they may have been in theory, had been conventional in practice. But from the moment I began earning my own living I unwittingly broke several English rules.

In those days no English girl of any class would ever have thought of going to a young man's rooms, unless strictly chaperoned; in fact she would not have gone there at all. Yet I used to go to tea with Edmund Garrett, and in his rooms I met other young men who probably thought me as odd and unusual as he did.

This conduct of mine became known to two cousins of Edmund. He was much attached to them both and they were devoted to him. I think it must have been at their suggestion he took me to see them. The visit was not a success. I at once realized they did not like me and were afraid either that he would fall in love with me, or that I would try and make him do so with a view to marriage. Even now I smile when I reflect how amazed those two ladies would have been if they could have seen into my mind.

Being a French girl, I knew I should marry some day. Every French girl I had ever heard of, with a few historical exceptions, either married or became a nun.

Edmund Garrett had a strong contempt for the kind of girl he described in a letter as one "who lived at home doing nothing and waiting to be married". In those days few educated women, with the exception of those engaged in teaching, did any work. I was one of the few, though I, after all, lived at home. Edmund was surprised and disturbed at my interest in clothes, and I remember in this connection an incident which comes back to me over the years.

Mr Stead, who was singularly kind-hearted, would now and again make some excuse to send me to Paris. On one occasion I came back provided with a new frock and hat which I had bought with my own money and which, therefore, must have been got off the peg in one of the great Paris shops. I foolishly called Edmund Garrett's attention to them, and afterwards he wrote to me, "If you think that dress and hat pretty, what must you think of the way my cousins dress?" Now the Miss Garretts paid no heed to passing fashions, and wore what they regarded as artistic clothes.

These were sometimes made of materials which recalled the gloomy Morris wallpapers. I thought them hideous so I tried not to answer

9

Edmund's half question. But when we met he persisted in wishing to know, so that at last I told him the truth. I said that in my view every woman ought to dress as far as she could afford to do so in the fashion, and that I considered the two ladies' dresses very unbecoming. He wrote me a long letter pointing out that this was an astonishing point of view on the part of the kind of person he supposed me to be.

There then took place an episode which I look back on with regret. A civil servant, who though a young man, was a widower, was coming home on leave, I think from India, when we met in the Paris-Calais train. He fell in love with me at first sight, and instructed his cabman to follow my cab. He called at our house the same evening, found out my name and wrote, asking if he could call on me and my mother. He soon asked me to marry him and on the eve of his leaving England, I very foolishly consented to a half-engagement. He wrote to me regularly for a long time, then his letters became few and at last stopped. I think he fell in love again, probably with a married woman, for he did not remarry and he died while still a young man.

Mr Stead was one of those people in whom those about them instinctively confide, and I must have told him something of my own and my mother's anxiety concerning my brother. Hilaire had just spent what was called his *volontariat* in the French army. It only lasted for one year because he was the only son of a widow. When he came back to England he seemed neither a Frenchman nor an Englishman. The whole of his childhood and boyhood had been English, then, when he was sixteen, had come the break, and for a short period he had thought of joining the French Navy. But he soon found that he would be quite unsuited for such a life. Some foolish acquaintance then suggested that he might become a farmer, and he lived on a farm for a short while. But this proved a complete failure. He was already writing some of the verse which has since found its way into anthologies, but no one, excepting our mother and myself thought anything of them. However, I persuaded him to send his verses to Mr Stead and he received a most encouraging letter.

I first came across Spiritualism when I was doing some work for W. T. Stead. Though in a sense he was a credulous man, inclined to believe anything he was told, he had a great knowledge of life, and was a brilliant journalist. A most extraordinary thing happened, with which I was to a certain degree associated.

W. T. Stead was that really rare being, an extremely kind man. He was not merely good natured, he would put himself to enormous trouble to help people, and that though he hardly knew them. His private charities were endless, and he had a large number of pensioners—men and women living on his generosity.

One of these I will call Mrs Davidson. Mrs Davidson was well-known to him and his staff in the days when he was editing the *Review of Reviews*. She was a small, fragile woman of about thirty, and she was certainly the most eccentric human being I have ever come across. At a time when everyone who walked about London was dressed in dark colours, unless actually on the way to a garden party or some summer function of that kind, Mrs Davidson was always clad in white. She would wear a white dress in the depths of winter and with it a large white hat.

When she came across Mr Stead, she was undoubtedly on the verge of starvation, owing to the fact that an allowance of fifteen shillings a week, made by her late husband's family had come to an end. Like many people of that type she was very anxious to work, though quite unaware that her extraordinary appearance made it very difficult for her to get any kind of job. Mr Stead, not being in a position to give her work, which was what she wanted, made her an allowance of one pound a week. She was a proud woman and had therefore hit on the idea that she might make herself useful in the office, by making the tea and clearing up the office. This, his staff resented very much, as they believed she gossiped about them to him. As he was an extremely busy man she could not have done this, even had she wished. When she found he was interested in Spiritualism, she revealed that she had an astral body. On more than one occasion she described to Mr Stead places where he had been and what he had done there. However, he took no real interest in her stories as I think he though her slightly crazy, as indeed I did myself.

Mr Stead lived at Wimbledon with his wife and six children. One Sunday they were all at Chapel—he was a fervent Dissenter. Suddenly the congregation saw a woman in white come into the Chapel and walk up the aisle. Mr Stead, and William Stead, his eldest son who worked in his office, at once knew her for Mrs Davidson. One of them opened the pew door, and tried to hand her a hymn book. She did not, however, come into the same pew as the Stead family.

Everyone who was in the Chapel noticed her, partly because of her appearance, and also because she came in after the service had started. Mr Stead supposed her to be in some trouble, and whispered to his wife that they must have her back to their mid-day meal. But at the end of the service he found to his astonishment that she had already left. He and Willie hurried down to the station to look for her, but they did not find her. They were the more bewildered as in those days all the trains that could be stopped, were stopped, while people were supposed to be at Divine Service, and she would have had a long wait for the first train to London.

Within a day or two of this occurrence I was in the office of the *Review of Reviews* and Mr Stead asked me if I would mind looking up Mrs Davidson, as she had not been in the office for a few days, and he wanted to know if she had come to see him in Wimbledon because she was in trouble.

I went to her very poor lodgings, and there I was told by her landlady that she was extremely ill and had been so for some days. There followed a serious investigation, and Mr Stead was much excited at the thought that it might have been her astral body in the Chapel. The doctor was most indignant at being associated with what he thought must be some sort of "stunt", and declared in the most positive way that the woman could not possibly have got up, and was in no condition to walk even a yard.

The mystery was never solved. Willie Stead, who had no belief in occultism, was convinced she had been in Wimbledon in the flesh. He told me he had not a doubt of it. On the other hand, there were three people—the landlady, another woman in the house, and the doctor, who all asserted that she could not have left the house.

The second instance which has remained vividly in my mind is of a very different nature, and in a way much less extraordinary, though I consider it far from simple. There wandered one day into the office of the *Review of Reviews* an extremely pretty woman in search of work. She was English, but explained that she had been married to an Indian, and her name was Mrs Shan Toon. She had gone out to the East, and had then drifted back, and had written a novel round herself. She had done many things: one of them was opening a beauty parlour for pet dogs, but what she longed to do was to go on writing. As usual, Mr Stead bestirred himself to get her work, and gave her an introduction to Oscar Wilde, who at the time was editing a paper for Cassell. I kept in touch with her at Mr Stead's request for some months. She then vanished, probably abroad, and for rather over thirty-five years I never gave poor Mrs Shan Toon a thought.

Then came the curious story of the Oscar Wilde script. I was vividly interested in it, because I had known Oscar Wilde and his wife well. It seems to me inconceivable that the ladies who took down the script could ever have heard of Mrs Shan Toon. Still less that they could have associated her in any way with Oscar Wilde. I feel certain that nothing was written of her in the magazine he was editing, because I subscribed to his magazine and because I was at the time in touch with Mrs Shan Toon, and trying to help her in any way I could. To my mind, the fact that the name appeared in the script proves Oscar Wilde's survival after death. Apart altogether from the question of Mrs Shan Toon, the language of the script—particularly the last terrible passage in which he describes his dreadful condition—seems to me what spiritualists call "strongly evidential".

My mother's acquaintance with Sir William and Lady Wilde in Dublin in the mid-sixties formed a very real link between myself and their son Oscar, and I was encouraged both by him and by his wife Constance of whom I quickly became very fond—to come to her Sunday At Homes. The house was filled with a medley of agreeable people of all kinds. Oscar, unlike many notable wits, was just as amusing and delightful at home as he was in other people's houses, and it was natural to those who journeyed to Chelsea to be drawn to No. 16 Tite Street by the host's brilliance and exuberant charm. He was also extraordinarily kind, always eager to do anyone a good turn. Constance was most courteous and pleasant and would take trouble to introduce those whom she thought shy or friendless, to some agreeable person.

I remember receiving from her a note asking me to come early, because she was expecting two Irish girls who knew no one in London, and she was anxious I should make friends with them and help them in any way I could. The two little boys, Cyril and Vyvyan,[1] were often present at these Sunday gatherings. This was unusual as in those days it was the English custom to keep children in the nursery when their parents entertained. As I remember them, they were pleasant little boys with good manners.

Constance Wilde was exceedingly pretty in a delicate English way. When I first knew her she must have been about thirty, even a little more, yet she looked like a girl. She had beautiful hair of chestnut brown and, when at home, dressed simply and in the type of frock which was beginning to be known as a teagown. But when she accompanied her husband to such functions as private views, which then played a very great role in London, she would appear in what were regarded as very peculiar and eccentric clothes. She did this to please Oscar and not to please herself.

[1] The boys' names were changed to Holland after the case. Cyril was killed in the 1st War. Vyvyan, man of letters wrote *The Son of Oscar Wilde*. Pubs. 1954. Died 1957.

13

I recall seeing her at a private view at the Grosvenor Galleries when she wore a green and black costume reminiscent of an old picture of an 18th Century highwayman. It made a considerable sensation, and instead of looking at the pictures on the walls, a great many people were asking each other if they had seen Mrs Oscar Wilde. I think she very much shrank from that sort of publicity, but undoubtedly Oscar enjoyed it. Indeed, he used to design these costumes and he delighted in her wearing them.

I occasionally dined with them and was there within a very short time of the tragic breakup of their joint lives. I have kept a letter from Constance in which she says "We should both be so pleased to come and meet your friends—Oscar sends his love—but as you may have seen in the papers we are very worried just now, and I do not feel we can go out at present".

I believe it to be true, for I was told it by a friend who did everything in her power to help them both, when came their day of shame and misery, that Constance was completely ignorant of Oscar's other life. To her he had always been the courteous, affectionate and indeed, devoted, husband whom the more simple of her friends, myself amongst them, envied her, and the more fearful must have been her awakening when it be remembered that, at the time Oscar Wilde was arrested, he had become the most popular playwright of his day.

I have little doubt that he had her in his mind when he put into the mouth of one of his characters in *An Ideal Husband* the words: "Women are not meant to judge, but to forgive us when we need forgiveness. Pardon, not punishment, is their mission."

Two of her friends—the Lady Mount Temple of that day and the Ranee of Sarawak[1] both showed themselves angels of kindness and of help.

Constance and her children did not go to her relations, who were later to play such an ill-advised part in her life, but she was pressed by them to leave England. She refused to do this because she did not wish to be out of touch with her husband who had just begun his term of two years imprisonment at Reading Gaol.

I was only once in Oscar Wilde's study. It was on the top floor of the house and was filled with books. It was probably the first white room

[1] Ranee of Sarawak: wife of the 2nd Rajah of Sarawak, H.H. Charles Brooke G.C.M.G., who died 1917. She was the daughter of Clayton de Windt and a good friend to W. H. Hudson, the naturalist, and other writers whose work she admired.

seen in London since the days of the eighteenth century when many rooms were painted white. At the top of the house were a number of small rooms, one of which was used as a dining-room. A friend had given him a writing table that had been used by Carlyle. This was not in the top study: it was in a little room on the ground floor.

The drawing room was delightful, surprisingly unlike most of the rooms in which the London world of that day lived. It was light in colour and had a few good Italian pictures. It was also very comfortable. As one entered the door, to the right was a full-length, though narrow, painting of Oscar. I have often wondered where that painting is now. For within a month of Oscar Wilde's condemnation to two years' imprisonment, he was made bankrupt, though there was still plenty of money coming in from his plays. So everything in the house at Tite Street was sold by public auction and, what may be regarded as truly infamous on the part of those it concerned, no effort was made to conduct the auction in a seemly and decent manner. A huge crowd of the lowest type of dealer and curiosity-monger surged through the desecrated rooms. Many things were stolen; the fine portrait I remember entirely disappeared, and a splendid picture by Whistler was bought for six pounds by one of Oscar's friends, the artist William Rothenstein,[1] who afterwards sold it at a high profit for the benefit of Oscar's family. His books—many presentation copies from noted French and British authors—were sold for a song.

Early in 1889 I went to Paris for some time to help Robert Donald[2] with what was to be called *The Pall Mall Gazette Guide to the Paris Exhibition*. Then at the end of the year occurred what at the time appeared, from my point of view, a serious misfortune. Mr Stead, who had never got on well with the proprietor of the paper since "The Maiden Tribute" case, suddenly made up his mind to give up the editorship and start a monthly magazine, and he was enthusiastically backed with money in this project by Sir George Newnes. The *Review of Reviews* set out to give a survey of each month's literature, and it was thus the precursor of all the Digests in England and in America.

There was also an original article by the editor and, a certain number of notes on current events, so there seemed no place for me. But I could not help hoping that I should be allowed to deal with French publica-

[1] Sir William Rothenstein: 1872-1945. Painter. Principal Royal College of Art 1920-35.

[2] Robert Donald: 1860-1933. Knighted 1924. Journalist. Editor of the *Daily Chronicle* 1902-18. Served on several public bodies.

tions. These were not many and, with the exception of the *Revue des Deux Mondes*, were unknown in England.

Mr Stead, who was apt to act on impulse, and who at the time had formed a close friendship with Miss Flora Shaw,[1] and was anxious to have her on his staff, decided that she should deal with foreign material. This was a bitter blow to me, but very soon Miss Shaw obtained a position, which she kept for some years, on *The Times*, and the French reviews were then offered to me. I think I was paid at first £50 a year, but in time I received £100 a year. I began writing for other magazines and papers and soon was earning £400 a year.

Robert Sherard, a great-great grandson of William Wordsworth, was most generous in giving me valuable introductions, and that though his work was very much on the same lines as mine. But all through those years when I should have been feeling happy and successful, I was anxious and feared the future. I was always afraid that I was going to lose my work and in a letter written by Bob, as his friends all called him, he rebuked me and said that many a person twice my age would be over-joyed to have my opportunities.

He was shocked at the way I spent the money I earned. He was not aware that I always sent half of it each week to my mother and in one letter he said "I do hope that you will not fool away your £5".

He used to go over my work and always he improved it; he was an extremely clever and cultivated man, and I think his book on Oscar Wilde[2] is much the best, and truest ever written.

For many years I specialized in writing articles dealing with French literature of every kind, but always I longed to write fiction. But everyone about me, and my mother knew many distinguished writers of the day—strongly dissuaded me from leaving off the kind of work I was then doing. One and all declared there were too many novels already. An exception was Robert Browning, who wrote a kind letter to my mother concerning my first story, a little tale published in a Catholic periodical called *Merrie England*, edited by the Meynells.[3] He said that he thought the story had great charm, and showed considerable promise.

[1] Miss Flora Shaw: Author and journalist. Head of Colonial Department of *The Times*. m. 1902 Sir Frederick Lugard.

[2] *The Life of Oscar Wilde*: by Robert Harborough Sherard. Pubs. 1906

[3] Wilfred and Alice Meynell. He being a few years younger than his wife, lived to celebrate her centenary in 1950. Her fame as a poet grows. They befriended Francis Thompson, and many other young writers were helped by them.

I vaguely remember writing a short story which was sent to and accepted by the *Leisure Hour*. The editor sent for me and said he thought it a pity for me to go on with journalism, instead of devoting myself to fiction. But he did not make any concrete proposal to take more of my work, and so his words did not make much impression on me. At this time I became acquainted with almost every contemporary writer, from George Meredith[1] to Bret Harte[2] whom I very often met. He had a generous appreciation of the work of those who were junior to himself and well do I remember his enthusiastic praise of Richard Le Gallienne's[3] *The Book-Bills of Narcissus*. But I never heard Bret Harte speak of his own work. I also met Mark Twain[4] during his sojourn in London. There were dinners given in his honour which I attended.

But of the great Americans I have known in my life, the one who was nearest to my heart for many, many years was Henry James.[5] I was a close friend of Rhoda Broughton[6] the novelist, and Henry James used to go and see her every afternoon when I, at her invitation, always outstayed her other visitors. Whatever the weather, Henry James would come and see her, and when she was not in London he wrote to her daily. Rhoda Broughton had arthritis and she could not walk, but round her, during her visits to London, were gathered some of the most delightful and clever people I have ever known.

I have always felt surprise at Henry James' reputation for aloofness. He had a great many friends, but I think he did not enjoy meeting strangers, and particularly did he shrink from meeting unknown admirers.

[1] George Meredith: 1829-1909. Novelist. *Diana of the Crossways*, Pubs. 1885, and *The Egoist*, 1879, are the best known

[2] Francis Bret Harte: 1839-1902. Born in Albany, New York, his short stories are often based on Californian mining life. He was U.S. Consul in Glasgow 1880-85 and thereafter lived in England.

[3] Richard Le Gallienne: 1866-1947. Writer and man of letters. *The Book-Bills of Narcissus*. Pubs. 1891.

[4] Mark Twain: Samuel Clemens 1835-1910. As Mark Twain, author of *The Innocents Abroad*, 1869. *Tom Sawyer*, 1876, and his masterpiece *Huckleberry Finn*, 1884.

[5] Henry James: 1843-1916. Novelist. Born in New York, he lived in London and at Rye.

[6] Rhoda Broughton: 1840-1920. Novelist who started her career with a reputation for audacious writing. She said of herself, "I began my career as Zola, and finish it as Miss Yonge".

A vivid and true picture of him is given in a book by Elizabeth Robins[1] in which are reprinted the letters he wrote to her.[2] She was said to be the one woman whom he had ever cared for sufficiently to wish to marry. One thing often said concerning Henry James is quite untrue: that he left off being American in feeling. On the contrary, he was proud of being an American and was passionately devoted to his brother, the philosopher William James.[3]

He would occasionally say he was a hermit, and speak as if he lived a life remote from the world. I once heard him say this during a brilliant party at Stafford House, where he was the guest of Millicent, Duchess of Sutherland.[4] A lady who was fond of him once observed, when with apparent sincerity he said that he hardly ever went out, "Then I suppose it is your ghost I meet everywhere!"

There can be no doubt that when at the end of his life he adopted British citizenship, it was because of his deep admiration for the many brilliant young men who had been killed in the first winter of the War, which was also responsible, I think, for his own death. He spent a great deal of his time that autumn visiting war hospitals and stayed in London all during that First War summer, though he was devoted to his country home at Rye.

I once spent a day with George Meredith at Dorking. He took a great fancy to me, partly because I was half French and he wanted me to come and stay for three or four days. His daughter, a very good-looking girl rather older than myself, stopped this, to my bitter disappointment. For like all the people of my generation and my age I had a limitless admiration for Meredith's work. He was an extremely agreeable and polished man of the world with a remarkable voice. He talked to me of French literature. I remember the great admiration he showed for almost all the younger writers. After I had gone he sent me *Beauchamp's Career* with an inscription.

He had all kinds of strange theories: one was that a man and a woman should be married for only ten years. I wrote a short story called

[1] Elizabeth Robins: Author and actress, principally known as an interpreter of Ibsen. *The Magnetic North*, pubs. 1904, is her best known book.

[2] *Theatre and Friendship*, pubs. 1932.

[3] William James: 1842-1910. Wrote *Varieties of Religious Experience*, 1902.

[4] Millicent, Duchess of Sutherland: d. of 4th Earl of Rosslyn. m. 4th Duke of Sutherland in 1884.

According to Meredith[1]—the outcome of such an arrangement. I am afraid that Meredith very much disliked this story, which was accepted at once by the editor of *The Fortnightly Review*.

What made it possible for me, ultimately, to take up fiction in a serious sense was the fact that my husband was left a legacy of two thousand pounds and he suggested we should spend the money while I tried to write novels. My first novel *The Heart of Penelope*[2] was well reviewed, but all it brought me in was nine pounds, though I am sure that William Heinemann did his very best for it. His reader had given it an excellent report, and he had hoped to sell ten thousand copies. He did sell under a thousand, and the subscription for my second book *Barbara Rebell*[3] was only five copies more than the whole sale of my first novel. My first books were studies of character, rather than studies of crime.

The second and third of my books, that is *Barbara Rebell* and *The Pulse of Life*[4] sold as many copies as did certain of my books published after I had become well-known, owing to my having written *The Lodger*.[5]

[1] *According to Meridith* re-published in *Studies in Wives*, a volume of short stories by M. B. L. Pubs. 1909.

[2] *The Heart of Penelope*: by M. B. L. Pubs. 1904.

[3] *Barbara Rebell*: by M. B. L. Pubs. 1905.

[4] *The Pulse of Life*: by M. B. L. Pubs. 1907.

[5] *The Lodger*. Pubs. 1913. Is never out of print. It has been made into a play, an opera and several films.

CHAPTER II

1911-1913

No. 9 Barton Street

Marie Belloc Lowndes and F. S. A. Lowndes moved to 9 Barton Street, Westminster in 1909. They were both much attached to this small Queen Anne house and only left it at the beginning of 1940. Shortly after the move, M. B. L. wrote the following:

Not long after we had settled down at No. 9, Barton Street, I became aware that the house was haunted, although I did not mention my view to anyone except my mother. I constantly heard steps going across the hall and then the sound of the same steps going up the staircase. The first time I supposed they were the steps of my husband coming back from the *Times* office late at night, and when they stopped on the little landing outside my door, I used, if awake, to call out to him. Now and again, if he was very tired he would not open the door and would go straight on to his own room, but almost always, knowing I was awake, he would open my door, come straight into my room and we would have a talk. But again and again, after having heard heavy footsteps on our staircase, I would after a while hear sounds in the hall below and then steps on the stairs. The second time it was my husband.

We had been in the house about a year when I received a letter which must have contained good news, probably concerning some new literary work, for I naturally would not have wished to tell my husband anything unpleasant late at night.

I left my door open and when I heard the front door shut, I put on a dressing-gown and with the letter in my hand, I ran downstairs. Before I could speak, there suddenly fell on our ears a series of loud noises coming from the basement. The clatter was tremendous—it was as if chairs were being thrown about, and we heard drawers being flung open. Remembering that what silver we had was down there, including several small pieces which had belonged to my great-great-grandfather, Joseph Priestley,[1] I thought that burglars had got in and would make away with certain things I greatly valued.

We both rushed to the top of the stairs, Freddie preceding me. As he opened the kitchen door there came absolute silence. He turned on the electric light and we saw with astonishment the kitchen clean and tidy, everything in its right place and our two breakfast trays ready for the next morning. I begged him to say nothing of this astounding occurrence to my children's lady-nurse, or to our maid. As is well known, the visits of poltergeists usually take place when there is a young person in

[1] M. B. L. was proud of her direct descent from Joseph Priestley, 1733-1804. Unitarian minister, scientist and discoverer of oxygen.

23

the house. There was no such person then living in 9, Barton Street; my children were very young—and our one servant was a middle-aged woman.

DIARY

I called on Mrs Adam[1] and had a very interesting talk with her and with her mother, Lady Ashburton.[2] They told me what I thought was one of the most striking true stories I had ever heard. Sir Edward and Lady Strachey,[3] who were very well-bred, old-fashioned people, were dining at home alone one night. Sir Edward came down first. The butler threw open the door and announced a Mr and Mrs ——, Sir Edward not catching the name. He said to himself, "They must be acquaintances of my wife, and she has forgotten to tell me they were coming to dinner", so he greeted them courteously. Lady Strachey came down after a minute or two, and she also said to herself, "They must be acquaintances of dear Edward. He must have asked them to dinner, and forgotten to tell me about it". So she also greeted them kindly.

The butler put two extra places and the four went down to dinner. When the entrée had been served and the servants left the room for a moment, the strange man, looking over at Sir Edward, said earnestly: "Now pray tell us about poor Elizabeth". Sir Edward felt very distressed at the question, and said to himself, "If I reveal that I do not know what the man is talking about, he and his wife will think they ought not to have come", so he said: "The subject is such a painful one that I feel I cannot discuss it". The stranger bowed and in due course they finished their meal and went up to the drawing room. At half-past ten the guests took their leave.

Sir Edward and Lady Strachey then had an explanation together and ringing for the butler, they asked the names of their guests, and whether they had gone away in a cab or in their own carriage. He answered that he could not recollect the name, but that the couple had left in their own carriage, and that the gentleman on leaving had left an envelope with the words: "Give this to your master". The butler then handed Sir Edward a blank envelope. Inside it was another envelope on which was written: "For poor Elizabeth". It contained one hundred pounds in notes. The

[1] Mrs Adam: the Hon. Lilian Theresa Claire Baring, b. 1874 m. 1906 Lt. Col. Frederick Loch Adam, M.V.O., Scots Guards.

[2] Lady Ashburton: widow of 4th Baron and daughter of 9th Baron Digby.

[3] Sir Edward Strachey: 3rd Bart. Lady Strachey d. of John Addington Symonds. Parents of St Loe Strachey, Editor of the *Spectator*.

24

Stracheys made every effort to discover who their mysterious visitors had been. They put advertisements in the papers, but they never found out who the couple were, and they finally gave the money to a hospital.

This story was told apropos of Miss Rhoda Broughton's extraordinary experience two years ago. A man called and asked to see her, saying he was an old friend, but refusing to give his name. Miss Broughton characteristically would not receive him under these conditions. Two days later he called again and left a heavy wooden box covered with black paper. Miss Broughton's faithful maid, Pullen, dragged it in and Rhoda again very characteristically observed: "Pullen, I'm sure it's a bomb, and as I would very much rather you were blown up than I, you can take it into the passage and open it there". Pullen did so, and brought back a beautiful embroidered bag out of which there rolled £150 in sovereigns and a piece of paper on which was written in an unknown handwriting: "I hope this will enable you to take a little holiday under sunnier skies". Within a few days a second sum was sent. Miss Broughton put an advertisement in the *Morning Post* imploring the donor to reveal himself, but she never knew who sent it.[1]

DIARY   *December 2nd,* 1911

Maurice Hewlett[2] called on me. He was here for an hour and a half. I tried to persuade him to go to Greece and hope that he will do so. He told me that Henry James had described the reading of *Hilda Lessways*[3] as "squeezing very slowly a very dirty sponge".

DIARY   *December 3rd,* 1911

I went to a most extraordinary Party at Eliza Aria's.[4] The guest of honour was H. G. Wells. The Ford Madox Hueffers[5] also made their

[1] Years later my mother was driving with Miss Mary Hoadley Dodge and related this story. Miss Dodge replied very shyly that herself was the unknown donor.
[2] Maurice Hewlett: 1861-1923. Novelist, poet and essayist. Wrote *The Forest Lovers* 1898, *The Queen's Quair* 1904, etc.
[3] *Hilda Lessways*: by Arnold Bennett. Pubs. 1911.
[4] Eliza Aria: Journalist. Sister of Julia Frankau who wrote under the name of 'Frank Danby'.
[5] Ford Madox Hueffer: Novelist, Ford Madox Ford. The 'bride' being Violet Hunt who wrote *The Wife of Rossetti* in 1931. M. B. L. profoundly disagreed with her version of Elizabeth Siddal's death.

first appearance as bride and bridegroom. A great many pretty actresses were there. Julia Frankau told me that her new book was to be called *Joseph in Jeopardy*. She has received £1,200 from Methuen and £800 in America. Brett of Macmillan's says it is the best book she has yet done. She doubts whether Methuen will take it when he has read it. I said to her that if it was 120,000 words long, Joseph must be very often in Jeopardy. I had a good talk with Mrs Wells. She told me she had come home the other day to find her two little boys being interviewed about a book Wells has just brought out called *Floor Games for Children*. Wells looks much better in health—quite robust.

DIARY

December 4th, 1911

Dined with Mrs Prothero—she and her husband Rowland[1] alone. We had an intensely interesting talk about Byron, whose letters he edited. It was apropos of a long visit he had had from a young German professor who had written to him as an authority on Byron and asked if he could call on him. The young German had formed a very touching and idyllic view of Byron's relations with Mrs Leigh as a lovely example of fraternal love and it was a terrible shock when Rowland Prothero hinted at the truth. He said: "Horrible! Horrible!" and Prothero said, "Not so horrible as you think when all the circumstances are considered," but it upset the German so much that he allowed the subject to drop.

Later, I said: "You have never spoken so plainly to me as you have tonight about this so you might now tell me why you are so kindly to Byron in the matter?"

"I am kindly," he replied, "because when the affair took place Byron was only twenty-two, and she thirty, and they had never met since childhood, and they were snowed up together in a country house for a month. Also, though you may not agree with me for saying this, I consider when a woman is thirty and a man twenty-two it is her responsibility."

To this Mrs Prothero and I both demurred. "I will tell you something else which is most extraordinary," he went on. "When Mrs Leigh became very hard up, after Byron's death, she actually published in a magazine—having cut out the beginnings and the ends of the letters— the most fervent and passionate of his love letters! They appeared in the

[1] Rowland Prothero: 1851-1937. 1st and last Baron Ernle *c.* 1919. Author of *Letters and Journals of Lord Byron* 1898-1901. *The Psalms in Human Life* 1903.

26

thirties of the last century. I had given the letters as *probably* Byron's to some unknown woman, but to my own, and Lord Lovelace's[1] amazement we found all the originals. Mrs Leigh had only provided copies for the magazine."

Mrs Prothero observed that she could not understand Lady Byron's attitude, writing to Mrs Leigh as "Darling Sis" after she knew the truth. Mr Prothero said: "You forget that Mrs Leigh, who was extraordinarily clever, and with no moral sense at all, had certainly made Lady Byron, who was very stupid, believe that Byron had taken her by surprise, and that in a real sense there had been no criminal relationship. Lady Byron was also exceedingly anxious that Mrs Leigh should not join Byron when he left England for good. There is actual documentary evidence that she paid Mrs Leigh a considerable income on the clear understanding that she was never to see Byron again. There exists an undertaking in Mrs Leigh's handwriting not to see or answer her half-brother's letters without first submitting both his letters and her replies to Lady Byron."

I asked Mr Prothero how it was that he and Lord Lovelace had come to quarrel after he had been given such very free access to all these secret documents. He said that to anyone who had ever known Lord Lovelace, the marvel was that they had not quarrelled before—that, slight as was my acquaintance with Lord Lovelace, I feel to be true. Mr Prothero said with extreme bitterness that Lovelace was just like the noxious insect that stings before it dies. I reminded him, however, that Lord Lovelace had not abused him, Rowland Prothero, as he had done the Murrays in *Astarte*.[2] Mrs Prothero observed "I suppose you felt you could not hint the truth when editing the letters". He shook his head, and I said "How odd that the Murrays won't admit it, even to this day, and that they persist in publishing books to prove the whole story is untrue".

DIARY

February 16th, 1912

Freddie and I dined with Mr and Mrs Ernest Fox[3] at Westminster School. My host gave me an interesting account of his family

[1] Lord Lovelace: 2nd Earl 1839-1906. Descendent of Lord Byron. He possessed all the family papers.

[2] Privately printed. 1905.

[3] Mr Ernest Fox: housemaster of Rigaud's for many years. Their son, Charles was in this House.

connection with medicine. There have been Fox's for six generations doctors, mental specialists, and in Somersetshire and the surrounding counties the expression 'he has gone to Fox's' means he has gone mad—not necessarily that he has gone to Fox's famous asylum. He was most interesting on the Lunacy Commissioners. He said they often make amazing mistakes, and let people out who are as mad as hatters.

He told a strange tale of an uncle of his against whom one of the patients, a very beautiful young woman, brought an action. She declared that he had kissed her in the garden. It was a very serious thing for him, he was a married man, as well as a partner in the asylum. She had Walter Phillimore[1] for her lawyer; he defended himself.

He first put in a plan of the asylum which showed that the strip of garden where she said she had been kissed was overlooked by 150 windows. He also pointed out that as her medical attendant he saw her every day alone and he asked why, if he were wishing to kiss her, he should not have kissed her then. However, she was very pretty, and the jury would almost certainly have given her the case, but fortunately evidence arrived at the last moment that she had been in three other asylums, and in each she had accused the principal of kissing her.

DIARY

March 5th, 1912

I was offered by the Public Prosecutor a ticket admitting me to the trial of the Seddons,[2] a couple accused of having poisoned an old woman who was their lodger, for her money. Although much of the evidence was of a dull nature, watching the prisoners was to me intensely interesting. They were the most respectable, commonplace-looking people imaginable. Seddon, an insurance agent, looked like a superior trades-man and Mrs Seddon like a self-respecting, pretty servant. He appears far older than forty, and she younger than thirty-four.

What I found strange and unnatural in their behaviour was the way in which they constantly talked to one another, and his laughter at any-thing in the proceedings which could be considered as comic, such as the pompous way in which an old gentleman took the oath.

[1] Walter Phillimore: 1845-1929. Well-known counsel and judge. 1918— cr. 1st Baron Phillimore of Shiplake.
[2] A classic murder case.

I went to the Royalty Theatre with Hugh Walpole[1] for the first night of *Milestones*[2]. I thought it one of the best plays I had ever seen, certainly the best first night from the play point of view. I hear that though Bennett is getting the whole of the credit for the play, Knoblock made the scenario exactly as it stands. We met an agreeable American, Mary Bisland, who represents an American publishing firm in London. She gave us an extraordinary account of the mistakes made by publishers. For years she pressed Robert Hitchens[3] on the notice of the people she represents here, and they always said his work was good but hadn't a chance of success. At last she begged them to take *The Garden of Allah*. It was eventually accepted on this lady's strong advice, with a royalty of 10% and no advance. Its success was phenomenal. This was said in order to console Hugh Walpole who is very depressed through having had a letter from his publishers saying that though they greatly admire his book, they do not believe it will sell, and they ask him to give up the advance they had arranged to give him. They grudge a young writer in whose future they say they believe, the sum of fifty pounds.

DIARY

March 15th, 1912

Lunched at 10 Downing Street, sitting between Mrs Asquith[4] and Mr Birrell.[5] Lady Frances Balfour[6] sat next to Asquith. All the talk was of the strike.[7] Mrs Asquith is strongly on the side of the men, Birrell evidently terribly irritated at the whole thing. I thought Asquith looked very ill and preoccupied. He came in only for about a quarter of an hour and the day before had spent fourteen hours practically on end, talking either to the men or to the masters.

[1] Hugh Walpole: 1884-1941. Novelist. Rupert Hart-Davis wrote his biography, 1952.

[2] *Milestones*: by Arnold Bennett and Edward Knoblock.

[3] Robert Hitchens: 1864-1950. Novelist.

[4] Mrs Asquith: Born Margot Tennant, m. 1894 Herbert Henry Asquith, M.P. Prime Minister 1908-16, later 1st Earl of Oxford and Asquith 1925. Wrote *Autobiography of Margot Asquith*.

[5] Rt. Hon. Augustine Birrell: 1850-1933. Author. Chief Secretary to the Lord-Lieutenant of Ireland 1907-16.

[6] Lady Frances Balfour: d. of 8th Duke of Argyll. m. 1879 Col. Eustace Balfour who died in 1911.

[7] A million miners were on strike for three weeks.

March 16th, 1912

Lunched at 'Thirty'.¹ We all talked about the enduring power of love. Some of those present said that love goes in a man when the woman becomes middle-aged. I said that it often amazed me to see how love endured though I admitted that in a certain class—the prosperous commercial class, no man, whatever his age, has any use for a woman, even for her company, after she is, say, forty. That is one of the things that strikes me in one circle I frequent. The moment you know a man at all well, he confides to you quite frankly what a bore he finds his wife's friends—that being a man of sixty talking of women between forty and forty-five.

One of the members recalled the series of vivid letters written by Lady Randolph Churchill (2) when she was in the Hospital Ship *Maine* on the way to the South African War. It is to be regretted they were never re-published in book form, having appeared only in the *Anglo-Saxon Review.*

I remember how amused and touched I was when someone said to me that Disraeli had described Winston's mother in *Lothair* as the 'divine Theodora'. One of Lady Randolph's² best traits, a rarer trait than most kind people would believe, was that she never dropped an acquaintance. If they got into any kind of trouble they were sure of both her kindness and understanding.

Someone then gave us a lively account of Winston Churchill writing his election address surrounded by dogs at Blenheim. This was capped by a lady who said that on someone's mentioning Winston's brother, there came the instant answer: "Has he a brother? I should have thought he was unique!"

April 4th, 1912

When Ford Madox Hueffer sold *The English Review* to Austin Harrison, it was believed that it would lose its prestige. This, however, was far from the case. Harrison had a piece of great good fortune in

¹ Luncheon club to which M. B. L. belonged. See *Merry Wives of Westminster.* Ch. XX.

² Lady Randolph Churchill: widow of Lord Randolph Churchill, d. of Leonard Jerome of New York. Mother of Winston Churchill.

obtaining John Masefield's[1] *The Widow in the Bye-Street*. It had an immense success, and not only largely increased the circulation of *The English Review* but brought it to the notice of many people who had never heard of it.

Maurice Hewlett, who has a great admiration for Masefield, shared my delight in his first volume of verse which dealt with the sea, but he thought the now famous Widow too violent. He has a curious shrinking from violence in verse.

DIARY

April 18th, 1912

Lunched at the 'Thirty'. There was much talk of the *Titanic* tragedy. Lady Dorothy Nevill[2] said that the wreck was a judgement from God on those idle rich people who want all earthly luxuries even on the water. She observed: "I am told they even had a garden!" She was very funny about improper books. She said she had heard that the memoirs of Harriette Wilson had been, as she put it, purged. When we assured her that this was not the case, she immediately said she would read them. Someone said that Lady Granville had destroyed one of the four copies of the Memoirs in existence. She found the book in a cupboard, and thinking it too improper for survival, burnt it.

I had supper with the Murray Smiths[3] and I was much moved and intensely interested on seeing there Charlotte Brontë's desk in exactly the condition she left it when she died, with all her little relics, the pattern of a collar she was working for her baby, the cards she had just had printed, and with them a visiting card of Thackeray's evidently the one he left when he called on her and found her out, a little tiny wisp of Anne's hair, everything muddled up together with wafers, patterns of the wallpaper which she meant to have put up in the house, I think the most pathetic memorials of a human being I ever saw.

Poor Mr Nicholls evidently locked the desk and put it away untouched and unsorted. The desk together with those of Anne and Emily have been sold by his widow and all three are in exactly the same state though, Charlotte seems to have tidied up the other two a little.

[1] John Masefield: 1874-1967. Poet Laureate from 1930.
[2] Lady Dorothy Nevill: died 1913. d. of 3rd Earl of Orford. m. 1847 Reginald Henry Nevill.
[3] Mrs Murray Smith: d. of Dean Bradley and m. to the youngest son of George Smith who founded the *Dictionary of National Biography*. Their house in Queen Anne's Gate Westminster, had belonged to Jeremy Bentham.

Nym Murray Smith was very anxious to have Emily's desk but it went for an enormous sum and to someone who would have bid anything, so they were told—I suspect Lord Rosebery. I know he has a boundless admiration for Emily's work. I felt as I looked at it in that beautiful and luxurious drawing room that I would not have cared to live with such a thing in my room. It seemed to me soaked with tragedy and disappointment.

DIARY

April 20th, 1912

To Furze Hill[1] to stay with Lady Stanley, widow of the explorer[2]. I had an interesting talk with her mother, Mrs Coombe Tennant, who though ninety-one was perfectly clear headed, remembering everything and everybody, and able to read the *Times* without glasses. She had known Flaubert intimately from childhood—there are letters to her in his published correspondence—and she said he was always asking her to meet Maupassant but that she found the latter very heavy, silent, self-absorbed and sullen in manner. At last she begged Flaubert never to ask her to meet him again.

H. M. Stanley chose every wallpaper, carpet and even the crockery in the house. The different parts of the grounds are named after places in South Africa. Dolly Stanley took us to see his grave[3] which consists of a huge stone she found on Dartmoor. It is very grand in the little churchyard where it dwarfs everything else. She has had cut on it a cross, the words: "Henry Morton Stanley" with the date of his birth and of his death, his African name "Bula Matari" and then the one word "Africa".

DIARY

April 22nd, 1912

I am fondly attached to Mrs Theodore McKenna.[4] Her husband is a great City solicitor; she was a daughter of Sir Morell Mackenzie, who was the leading British throat specialist. Unfortunately for himself, he went to Berlin at the request of the Empress Frederick, to see her husband the Emperor Frederick. The extraordinary jealousy, indeed hatred,

[1] Furze Hill, Pirbright, Surrey.
[2] Sir Henry Morton Stanley: 1841-1904.
[3] H. M. Stanley's grave is in the village churchyard of Pirbright.
[4] Mrs Theodore McKenna, Ethel d. of Sir Morell Mackenzie, who went to Germany to try to save the life of the Emperor Frederick.

shown him by the leading German surgeons, struck him with astonishment. He told his side of the story in a book which he called *Frederick the Noble*.[1] It was unlucky for him that the Emperor not only liked him but had a high opinion of his professional skill. The Empress Frederick begged him to stay with her dying husband, and this caused bitter feeling all over Germany.

Sir Morell Mackenzie's experiences in Germany undoubtedly shortened his life. Not only was he expected by the Empress to be on call night and day, but Queen Victoria required him to write her a daily letter telling her the exact truth as to the condition of his patient. He paid dearly for the trust, affection and gratitude shown him by the Empress.

DIARY

April 24th, 1912

I dined at the Savoy with the Theodore McKennas. Went to a ball afterwards and sat between W. L. Courtney[2] and Fred Kerr,[3] the actor, at the ball supper.

As a writer I was much amused when Mr Courtney told me that within the last fortnight he had actually received £5 from a publisher, asking him to give a good notice of a new novel. He tore up the cheque in little pieces, put them in an envelope and sent it back to the sender.

DIARY

May 15th, 1912

Lunched with May Spender[4]—a more amusing party than the last. I sat between Mrs Lulu Harcourt[5] and Lady Horner.[6] With the latter I had a curious talk about love. She said one of the strange things she

[1] *Frederick the Noble*. Pubs. 1888.
[2] W. L. Courtney: 1850-1928. Then editor of the *Fortnightly Review* and later a director of Chapman and Hall.
[3] Frederick Kerr: stage name of Frederick Grinham Keen. At this time a well-known West End actor and formerly manager of the Royal Court Theatre.
[4] Mrs Alfred Spender: wife of Alfred Spender, Editor of the *Westminster Gazette* from 1896-1922.
[5] Mrs Lulu Harcourt: d. of Walker Hayes Burns of New York. m. 1899 Lewis Harcourt, then Secretary of State for the Colonies. Cr. 1st Viscount Harcourt 1917.
[6] Lady Horner, O.B.E.: d. of William Graham, sometime M.P. for Glasgow. m. 1883 Sir John Horner K.C.V.O. She was one of *The Souls*.

noticed was the amazing position now attained by young unmarried girls. She spoke as if men valued youth to a very peculiar and exceptional degree, far more so than was the case, say thirty, forty or a hundred years ago. Then, the affairs which married people in society had, were with one another—the girls played no part at all. Now men, both married and single, no longer quite young, delight in the society of girls. They like their conversation and their fresh point of view. I told her that I did not agree. I thought it was true of a small group of girls but quite a small group who, though unmarried, were very much in the world knowing all that went on, able to talk of politics and all the things that the ordinary married woman in that set is interested in. I do not think the sort of man to whom she referred would at all care for the unsophisticated country girl, however nice, fresh and intelligent.

DIARY

May 16th, 1912

Literary Fund dinner. I enjoyed it because I was next to Alice Perrin.[1] Charles Graves[2] who sat the other side of her made an amusing suggestion, namely that we should try and rearrange the tables according to our fancy, putting together the people who ought to be together—such as Marie Corelli[3] and Mrs Barclay, the author of *The Rosary* who were both present.

DIARY

May 21st, 1912

I dined at the Bernard Mallets[4] to meet St Loe Strachey,[5] and Mr and Lady Mary Morrison.[6] I was interested in the latter as a niece of Lady

[1] Alice Perrin: Novelist of Anglo-Indian life. b. 1867, d. of General John Innes Robinson of the Bengal Cavalry, m. 1886 Charles Perrin, M.I.C.E. of the Indian Public Work's Department.

[2] Charles Graves: Assistant editor of the *Spectator* and member of the staff of *Punch.*

[3] Marie Corelli: well-known popular novelist of the day.

[4] Mr Bernard Mallet: was than Registrar-General. K.C.B. 1916. His wife Marie, d. of Henry John Adeane M.P. had been a Maid of Honour to Queen Victoria and an extra Woman of the Bedchamber.

[5] St Loe Strachey: 1860-1927. 2nd son of Sir Edward Strachey. Editor of the *Cornhill* and Editor and proprietor of the *Spectator.*

[6] Hugh Morrison: later M.P. for Salisbury Division of Wiltshire. m. 1892 Lady Mary Leveson-Gower, d. of 2nd Earl Granville.

Georgiana Fullerton and daughter of Lord Granville. St Loe Strachey I thought a kindly, but unimaginative man. He gave us an account of a strike amongst his printers, and it was curious to notice how entirely unsympathetic he was to the working class as a whole. He spoke with great bitterness of the Trade Unions and seemed quite unaware that there might be something to be said on the part of the employee as well as of the employer.

After dinner we had a long talk about crime and he and I agreed as to the consummate ability of Constance Kent[1] who really escaped arrest when there seemed so many suspicious circumstances against her, by her cleverness in not trying to explain inexplicable facts, which almost every criminal tries to do. We agreed that by far the most foolish thing to do is to invent an alibi by means of an imaginary person, a curiously common form of folly on the part of murderers.

DIARY

May 22nd, 1912

The Women Writers' Dinner Committee at Alice Perrin's house. There was a curious discussion as to professional ethics. Someone wanted a young girl asked to the dinner who had written *Letters From a Flapper at the Durbar*. A distinguished woman journalist on the Committee said she would not go to it if this girl were asked, though she did not know her, so there was no personal prejudice. I upheld her on the point that any woman who has disgraced herself professionally should not be asked by us. What a person does in private life seems to me to be none of our business; this was proved by the fact that we are asking half a dozen women who have been very notorious in the last year, but I do not think we ought to ask a novelist who writes pornographic work or a journalist who does work against the whole feeling of what is decent in the profession.

The same night I went to Lady Burghclere's[2] ball at Surrey House, a beautiful and charming sight. In this immense house there are two ballrooms, each so far from the other, that the music of two bands cannot be heard in the respective rooms. I am told that the house is let out at £100 a night and that the chaperones of this year spend all their evenings

[1] Constance Kent: tried for the murder in 1860 of her young step-brother. Imprisoned after confessing to the crime in 1865.

[2] Lady Burghclere: d. of 4th Earl of Carnarvon and wife of the 1st and last Lord Burghclere who d. 1921, President of the Board of Agriculture.

either in Surrey House or the Ritz Hotel, which they find far less pleasant than the old custom of giving balls in private houses.

I had a curious talk with Lord Sanderson[1] on the Malecka[2] case. He told me that he was in the Foreign Office at the time a similar case arose with regard to a Greek Jew who claimed British protection and who had been naturalized. He said, however, the two cases were not at all on all fours and that the Greek Jew's case was a far more straightforward one than Miss Malecka's. I said I thought it put Sir Edward Grey[3] in a very disagreeable position and he replied: "These are the little ways of the *métier* and they are all in the day's work".

DIARY

May 23rd, 1912

Yesterday I went to the *Titanic* enquiry. I found it intensely interesting. I am longing to hear the passengers' evidence for it is quite clear that every officer was trying to shield first the captain, second the company, and third, himself. One of the younger officers went so far as to say that he did not know for certain that any women or children were drowned, and when he was pressed about this he admitted that he knew 1,600 souls had gone down but, declaring that as he never looked at newspapers, he had no idea as to the proportion of women and children.

DIARY

May 24th, 1912

Called on Arnold Bennett,[4] whom I have seen a great deal of this year with his wife Marguerite. I thought him very ill—not so much from overwork—though he has been overworking—as from the mental excitement and strain of his extraordinary success. He told me that he

[1] Lord Sanderson: 1841-1923. Permanent Under-Secretary to the Foreign Office 1894-1906.

[2] Malecka Case. Miss Malecka, a British subject of Polish origin, was tried in Warsaw on a charge of belonging to a revolutionary organisation. She was found 'guilty' on May 10th, 1912 and condemned to four years penal servitude, but was shortly afterwards released.

[3] Sir Edward Grey: 1862-1933. Then Secretary of State for Foreign Affairs. Cr. 1st Viscount Grey of Fallodon 1916.

[4] Arnold Bennett: 1867-1931. Novelist. His fame rests on *The Old Wives Tale* 1908 and *Riceyman Steps* 1923.

had contracts which he must fulfil including one of eight articles of 4,000 words each, for which he is to receive £2,000 serial rights alone. He also has to do three more articles for the series called *What I think of Your America* for *Harpers*, and he desires to do the third *Clayhanger* so as to get it serialized in this country.

DIARY

June 10th, 1912

I had a long talk with Robert Ross. He told me as a great secret that he had only published a third part of *De Profundis* and that the rest told in the greatest detail the story of Oscar Wilde's trial and his relations with Douglas.[1] He has given the manuscript to the British Museum and it is not to be published for seventy years. I said to him: "Then you think Douglas was poor Oscar's *âme damnée?*" He assented.

I asked him about Frank Harris's[2] book. He told me that he was officially supposed to know nothing about it. Harris asked him to read the proofs. "If I do, I shall probably not like something in it, and as Wilde's executor I might have to take action." Apparently Harris's book on Wilde is simply a long account of Douglas's treachery and of the fact— which is pretty well known already—that many things attributed by the prosecution to Wilde in the course of the trial were really done by Douglas.

Every English publisher has refused the book and it will be published in Paris. We spoke a little of Gilbert Cannan.[3] It is sad to see how much he is now disliked. Ross told me that he was once hailed as the most marvellous genius of the age, and that he, Ross, possessed a letter from St John Hankin[4] in which ran the phrase: "Shaw, Barker and Galsworthy all believe Cannan is going to wipe them out".

I much admired the way Ross behaved at the time of the Oscar Wilde affair. Though by no means a rich man, he bought up the Wilde copyrights and transferred them to Wilde's two sons. Ross was amusing concerning a paper published in the *Saturday Review* on Sidney Colvin,[5]

[1] Lord Alfred Douglas: 1870-1945. s. of 8th Marquess of Queensberry.

[2] Frank Harris: 1865-1931. Notorious editor and publisher. Author of *My Life* 1926, banned for many years in the UK.

[3] Gilbert Cannan: b. 1884, Novelist and dramatist. m. J. M. Barrie's wife, Mary Ansell.   [4] St John Hankin: playwright.

[5] Sir Sidney Colvin: 1845-1927. Keeper of prints and drawings at the British Museum. Author. Editor of R. L. Stevenson's *Letters and Works.*

D   37

which was then making something of a stir in the literary world. There was much discussion as to who had written the article which was a most malicious and indeed a cruel attack, while pretending to be a eulogy, for Sidney Colvin had just left the British Museum. Ross said that he felt certain that the paper had been written by Edmund Gosse,[1] for some weeks ago Gosse said to him "I wonder if you remember that Meredith once said of Colvin, 'He is the eternal spinster'."

DIARY

July 26th, 1912

I hear the King has stopped away from Goodwood because of the Morocco affair. It is significant that the *Westminster Gazette* which is the Government organ, Spender being in the closest hourly touch with Grey, has no reference to the crisis at all beyond a note stating that a great deal of fuss is being made about it.

Freddie agrees with me that the situation is very serious. I telephoned to a friend and heard that the Admiralty has sent orders to all the ports saying that the fleet is not to carry out the manœuvres arranged, before the crisis arose. Hilary,[2] who telephoned to me, thinks that the real trouble is that Agadir is a port of small importance to France, but of very great importance to Germany, and that it is really a matter for the British Cabinet to decide whether Agadir is worth war or not. He says that the Germans never put forward the preposterous proposals that they are credited with and that they really want Agadir in order to have a port handy in case they ever go to war with England.

DIARY

July 27th, 1912

I am a great admirer of Lafcadio Hearn,[3] and when dining with the Du Cros[4] today I was sitting next to Mr Diosy who told me many

---

[1] Sir Edmund Gosse: 1849-1928. Librarian to House of Lords. Noted critic. Author of *Father and Son*, pubs. 1907. Kt. 1925.

[2] Hilaire Belloc: 1870-1953. Poet and author. Marie Belloc Lowndes' brother. He was called Hilary by his family and intimate friends.

[3] Lafcadio Hearn: 1856-1904. Lived in Japan and married a Japanese woman. Author of several books on Japan. Edward Laroque Tinker wrote largely about him in the United States.

[4] Alfred Du Cros was M.P. for Bow and Bromley 1910.

interesting things about that writer. Mr Diosy possesses a great number of letters from Hearn, but he says they are too intimate for publication. Then he told me how he discovered a half-sister of Hearn by a strange accident. She lived at Bedford and had come up to London to hear a lecture at the Japan Society on Lafcadio Hearn. When it was finished she came up to Mr Diosy and said "I have been much interested, for my maiden name was Hearn". Diosy thought little of this fact, till she went on "My father was a military surgeon". He then pricked up his ears and heard her add: "And his first wife was a Greek". He put her and her half-brother in touch with one another.

DIARY

July 28th, 1912

Yesterday I lunched at the Pall Mall Restaurant to meet Mrs W. J. Locke,[1] the wife of the novelist. She said he made all his money in America and gave a very funny account of what it is like to be the wife of a popular novelist. The other day a complete stranger rushed up to her and folding her in her arms, exclaimed: "You are the only woman I have ever envied!" "She was quite an old lady," she added drily.

DIARY

August 23rd, 1912

I was much amused to hear at lunch that a hostess wrote to Mr Humphrey Ward: "I hope that you remember that you are dining with us tomorrow, and of course if there is a *Mrs* Humphrey Ward, we shall be very pleased to see her too." Humphrey Ward was so outraged at this that he wrote a curt note saying that he had forgotten the engagement and had, therefore, made another one.

This story was, however, capped by the Ranee. An Italian lady of rank was asked to a luncheon party and put next to Mr John Cross, the widower of George Eliot. She said to him: "I suppose that you, like all the people here at this luncheon, are a famous writer". "No," he said, "but I have the honour to be very closely connected with literature

---

[1] Aimée Locke became a great friend of M. B. L. Her husband W. J. Locke, originally an architect, wrote a large number of popular novels including *The Beloved Vagabond* 1906.

through my wife". The lady, in a tone of delight, cried: "Now I know who you must be—you are the husband of Victoria Cross!"[1]

DIARY

August 27th, 1912

I met Lady Dorothy Nevill and Miss Nevill at lunch. She gave me a most curious account of the child of the unhappy Princess Sophia which she had by her brother the Duke of Cumberland. Queen Charlotte made her ride down the High Street of Windsor the day after the child was born to show the Windsor people—who, of course, knew all about it—that it was not true. The child, who was a boy, was adopted by a relation of Lady Dorothy's and brought up in Dorsetshire, where, in due course, he became the famous huntsman, Johnny Garth. He was a remarkable man.

DIARY

November 27th, 1912

Dined with the Hugh Bells[2] and sat next to Lord Moulton.[3] Lord Moulton and I had, as usual, a very interesting talk about crime, and he promised to ask me to meet Edward Clarke,[4] the last survivor of the counsel engaged in the Bravo[5] case.

We discussed the Lamson[6] crime; he is convinced that Dr Lamson did not give his brother-in-law the poison in the capsule which he brought and administered to the lad for a cold. He thinks he put it in the currants of a cake. He says that the skin of a currant is almost as resistant as india-rubber, and that the poison used was so deadly and immediate that the boy would have died at once instead of lingering, as he did, for many hours in agony. He thinks that Lamson concluded they would

[1] Victoria Cross: a best-selling novelist of the early years of the century.
[2] Sir Hugh Bell: 1844-1931. 2nd Bart. Was an ironmaster and colliery owner. His second wife was a novelist and playright.
[3] Lord Moulton of Bank. A Life Peer.
[4] Sir Edward Clarke: Leading K.C. for many years. Took part in Penge and Bartlett murder cases and the Baccarat case.
[5] The murder of Charles Bravo by antimony in 1876 at Balham, remains one of the great unsolved mysteries.
[6] Lamson Crime. Dr George Henry Lamson convicted of murder and hanged in 1882.

say it was in the capsule and that the scientific witnesses called on his side, should he ever come to trial, would be able to prove this impossible. It was Hawkins,[1] the judge, who hit on the true solution.

DIARY

November 29th, 1912

I dined at Lord and Lady Glenconner's[2] to meet the Prime Minister and Mrs Asquith. I sat between Mr Asquith and Mr Mark Napier. Mr Napier struck me as one of the most original and amusing men I had seen for a long time. He is a great friend of Hilary's. He told me he had three times been to Naples, but only left it twice. This meant that he had been born there! He was born on Vesuvius. I told him that his mother must have been a plucky woman. He said, "No, not plucky, but temerarious". We began talking of the Divorce Commission. He said that marriages were only made to be broken.

Mr Asquith and I talked about crime, a subject in which he takes as great an interest as I do, and my heart warmed to him very much when I discovered that busy and worried as he now is, he yet finds time to follow the extraordinary and mysterious disappearance of Mrs Nowill.[3]

I asked him about the Bravo case: he thinks Mrs Bravo was guilty, which I do not. We spoke of French History. He is firmly convinced that Madame Henriette was poisoned, and he started a theory, new to me, but which I regard as very likely a true one—namely that Louis XIII was the child of Consini and not of Henri IV. Certainly his descendants were more Italian than French in their tastes, their habits and even their appearance.

What to me is very startling and terrible, is that the intelligent criminal has nothing in his appearance, manner or, I fear, nature, making him any different from those about him. To me, with regard to murder, the word that should be used is not 'Who?' but 'Why?'

[1] Sir Henry Hawkins: 1817-1907. Cr. Baron Brampton. Famous as a Criminal Court Judge.

[2] Lord Glenconner: 1st Baron 1911, M.P. Lord High Commissioner to General Assembly of Church of Scotland in 1911, 1912, 1913 and 1914, d. 1920. His wife was Pamela Wyndham who in 1922 as a widow married the 1st Viscount Grey of Falloden.

[3] Mrs Nowill disappeared from an hotel at Newquay on November 23rd. Her body was found in the sea at Newquay on December 2nd.

January 7th, 1913

Lunched at The Give and Take.[1] Ellen Thorneycroft Fowler,[2] Mary Cholmondeley, and Mrs Bailey,[3] were there. We talked of English prudery, and how hard it is that while a novelist can allow unmarried lovers in a novel do anything—*The Rosary*[4] was the novel in question— you must not let a man hold a married woman's hand without the average reader being shocked. We went on talking of *The Rosary* and its wonderful success, and I said I felt sure this was owing to the suggestiveness of certain scenes.

DIARY

January 21st, 1913

Lunched with Lady Allendale[5]—a very pleasant party—Lord Reay[6] and Weenie Ridley[7]. There was a great deal of talk about the new Delhi and the way in which Mr Edwin Lutyens[8] would do the work. With the exception of the hostess who is apparently very fond of him, they all thought it would have been better to employ Indian architects.

DIARY

January 29th, 1913

I had a long talk with Henry James this afternoon at Rhoda Broughton's. He spoke of Edith Wharton.[9] He said that when she was

[1] A woman's luncheon club, started by Miss Mary Cholmondeley, author of *Red Pottage.* It met once a week during the session.

[2] Ellen Thorneycroft Fowler: Novelist and poet. d. of 1st Viscount Wolverhampton, m. Alfred Laurence Felkin, H.M. Inspector of Schools.

[3] Mrs. Bailey: daughter of 4th Baron Lyttelton and wife of John Bailey, distinguished man of letters, chairman of the National Trust.

[4] *The Rosary:* a best seller by Florence Barclay, pubs. 1911.

[5] Lady Allendale: wife of 1st Viscount and d. of 5th Marquess of Londonderry. [6] Lord Reay: 12th Baron.

[7] Lady Ridley, wife of Rt. Hon. Sir Edward Ridley, Judge of the High Court. Novelist and M. B. L.'s closest woman friend.

[8] Mr Lutyens: 1869-1944; later Sir Edwin Lutyens. The best-known architect of his generation.

[9] Edith Wharton: d. 1937. American novelist. Author of *Ethan Frome* and *The Age of Innocence.*

lately at her staymaker's the latter said to her: *"Cela n'est pas tout à fait cela"*. Mrs Wharton replied "But I feel very comfortable". The other observed, *"Oui, et ces corsets donnent à Madame de jolies hanches, mais ce ne sont pas les hanches de cette année"*.

DIARY

January 30th, 1913

Dinner with the Reginald Smiths[1] to meet the Misses Findlater.[2] I sat next to Mr George Macmillan. I told him that were I a publisher the author I should now most envy him was Edith Wharton. Then he told me a curious thing. At one time John Murray published her and he, Macmillan, published Gertrude Atherton.[3] Now they had exchanged these two and were very satisfied with the exchange.

Miss Mary Findlater gave me an extraordinary account of her dealings with publishers. The only time they ever made money was out of a little book called *Friends at the Inn* written by Mrs Wiggs (Kate Douglas Wiggin[4]), some other lady and themselves. It brought them in £1,000 and they did the work in a week. She spoke very bitterly about agents.

DIARY

June 30th, 1913

Dinner with the Haldanes[5]: a small party—the host, his sister, and Lord and Lady MacDonnell.[6] We talked after dinner about the Colin Campbell divorce suit. R. B. Haldane said that when at Dinard with the Prime Minister he had been astonished to see in a seamen's church a votive offering put up by Sir William and Lady Butler,[7] with a certain

[1] Reginald Smith: brother-in-law of Henry Yates Thompson, the collector, and proprietor of *The Pall Mall Gazette*.

[2] Jane and Mary Findlater: Authors jointly and separately of several novels of which *Green Graves of Balgowrie* by Jane Findlater is still read.

[3] Gertrude Atherton: 1857-1948. Popular American novelist.

[4] Kate Douglas Wiggin: Author of the best seller *Mrs Wiggs and the Cabbage Patch*.

[5] Lord Haldane: 1856-1928. 1st Viscount and then Lord Chancellor in the Liberal Cabinet. His sister, Miss Elizabeth Haldane C.H., was later the 1st woman J.P. for Scotland and served on several public bodies. Author.

[6] Lord MacDonnell: 1844-1925. 1st Baron. Served in Indian Civil Service.

[7] Lt. General Sir William Butler: 1838-1910. m. 1877 Elizabeth Thompson who was famous as the painter of *The Roll Call*.

date on it. "When we came home," said Haldane, "Asquith and I took the trouble to look up the date and we saw it was the day when the jury delivered their verdict in the Campbell case".

He evidently thought this conclusive proof of Butler's guilt, but the MacDonnells who knew Butler well, and I who have just read a verbatim account of the whole divorce case, strongly demurred from that view. Lord MacDonnell explained that Butler had refused to go into the witness box, he being the only one of the four co-respondents who so refused, as he had only seen the lady three times, he was determined not to mix himself up in what he regarded as a disgusting case, and his absence was most severely commented on by the judge, and there is little doubt that it might have lost Lady Colin Campbell her case.

Haldane could not believe that guiltless, Butler would not have gone into the box. Haldane believed that Butler's spiritual director advised him to refrain from giving evidence, as being a Catholic he would not perjure himself.

We three all exclaimed—the MacDonnells and I—that we did not believe Sir William Butler had a spiritual director, and that very few Catholics had.

DIARY

December 14th, 1913

In the evening I went to Lady Glenconner to meet the Prime Minister and Mrs Asquith. I had a long talk with them, Margot looked very smart. She asked after Hilary and I gathered that she sees him oftener than I do, partly of course, owing to their intimacy with Maurice Baring.[1]

Mr Asquith looked better than I had seen him for a long time. He certainly seemed far more cheerful and less worried than the last time I saw him at Downing Street. We had a long conversation on divorce, apropos of the Divorce Commission. He does not think the recommendations of the majority will be adopted, but considers as do most people I meet, that divorce should be as easy for the poor as for the rich, and that the sexes should be equal in the matter of simple misconduct, etc. But to my surprise he is against divorce for permanent insanity, which I have always thought, for non-Catholics, ought to be a cause for divorce. He says that if that became law, it will lead to an immense increase in the number of people certified.

[1] Hon. Maurice Baring: 1874-1945. 4th s. of 1st Lord Revelstoke, Diplomat, man of letters and prolific writer. Intimate friend of Hilaire Belloc.

CHAPTER III

1915

The outbreak of the 1914-18 War, at a time when M. B. L.'s only son was seriously ill in St Thomas's Hospital, so affected at first her life and that of my father, that she only made a few notes. This Chapter, therefore, starts five months after the declaration of war.

After his recovery, their son, Charles, went to Sandhurst and then joined the Oxfordshire and Buckinghamshire Light Infantry. He went out to Flanders as a boy of 18 in 1916, and survived the war, after being awarded the Military Cross in his first battle, that of Beaumont Hamel, and being twice wounded.

It seems strange and unfeeling to those who lived through the last war, that life in London went on comparatively normally in the First War, in spite of the appalling casualties. People felt that if they stayed at home and mourned, the war would never be won, and the soldiers returning on 48 hours' leave only wanted to forget the horrors of the Front Line in France and to be amused and entertained.

The letter to M. B. L. from a much younger friend who was serving in France, with which this Chapter ends, gives a vivid picture of what the devastated regions behind the line were really like.

DIARY
January 18th, 1915

Dined at the Theodore McKennas where I was told that Mr Gatty[1] had heard from the Duke of Westminster that Winston Churchill says he expects a fleet of *a hundred Zeppelins* to leave for England on the eve of the German Emperor's birthday, January 26th! He expects seventy to be destroyed, but believes that thirty will reach London and he estimates the casualties at 10,000 to 12,000! Several people are so affected by this tale that they have already sent their children away into the country. Theodore told me that the Germans have not got a hundred Zeppelins to send, but that they will certainly send air-craft over next week. It is thought that they will arrive in the night and hover over London until it is light enough to see quite clearly the buildings they desire to destroy.

DIARY
January 21st, 1915

Yesterday I had a two hours' talk with Colonel Colin Campbell[2] who is just back from the Front. He said he had heard more rot talked in the

[1] Charles T. Gatty: Agent to the Duke of Westminster and author of *Mary Davies and the Manor of Ebury*, pubs. 1921.
[2] Col. Colin Campbell: Central India Horse. m. Miss Leiter, sister of the 1st wife of Marquess Curzon of Kedleston.

47

few hours he had been home than in the whole previous six months! He said his friends out there were very cheerful but that he found everyone at home gloomy. That was why the King had been unwilling to leave France—that he had stayed far longer than they had expected, giving as the reason that it was so pleasant to be with hopeful people!

DIARY

January 23rd, 1915

Ethel McKenna gave me a deeply interesting account of what her brother-in-law Reginald McKenna[1] says about the duration of the War. She had seen him the night before last and he told her that he had never been so hopeful about the War as he had been this week, that private information had reached the Cabinet concerning the Germans' stock of ammunition. Apparently during the first few weeks of the War, in a given space of time, each German gun was provided with 100 to 150 rounds. At the present time a German gun, for the same amount of time, is served out with ten rounds. He added that the Allies were also so far running short that they could only provide 50 rounds—that is, five times more than the Germans—but whereas they will be able to keep up this average, and even slightly increase it if necessary, the Germans will gradually drop to nine, eight, seven and six rounds. He said he thought the War would end in July.

DIARY

January 24th, 1915

A friend telephoned at 2.30 and told me that a naval battle was proceeding on the Dogger Bank, that Germany had lost four cruisers and a large number of destroyers—twenty to thirty.

At five o'clock my friend rang me up again, and said the news was confirmed by the Admiralty. I telephoned and told Freddie: he said nothing of the kind had reached the *Times* office.

I was warned to say nothing to Margaret Warrender with whom I was dining, but before I had been in the room with her a minute, she said: "What is the truth about today's naval battle? I hear the *Lion* has been hit, and has gone back to port at 9 knots."

[1] Rt. Hon. Reginald McKenna: 1863-1943, the Home Secretary. Chancellor of the Exchequer later on in the same year.

During dinner Hugh Warrender[1] gave me a most interesting account of a great Greek-French merchant, who has financial agents in every capital. His German agent, who has just returned from Berlin, brought the news that everything was short, the shortest of all being gold.

DIARY

January 25th, 1915

Called on the Websters.[2] He is most unhappy about the literary outlook. He told me the slump continues, the cheap edition of my book *Barbara Rebell* was put off and nothing was moving at all. I did not tell him that Methuen were not going to have my next book. Their offer was incredibly less good than that of Hutchinson and that though they admitted that *The End of Her Honeymoon*[3] had paid off its advance. I said what seemed to distress him very much, that I thought all fiction would be profoundly altered by the War, and I could not see writers going back to the kind of stories which, if not exactly popular, were highly praised before the War. He seemed to think that if a casual allusion to the War were thrown in, it would make them sell. He could not see that England and English life would be deeply affected if not completely changed.

DIARY

January 26th, 1915

I had tea with Sir Philip Sassoon.[4] His mother was a French Rothschild and I was much interested to hear him say that his French relations all believe the War will end in May. He did not himself seem as cheerful about it. He seemed to have the curious opinion that the Germans would have to be driven back from trench to trench till they reached the frontier.

The serious thing will be if, in their eagerness to make peace, the Allies will leave Germany so strong that she will simply bide her time and start again in, say ten, fifteen or twenty years, probably after the death of the Emperor.

[1] Hugh Warrender: younger son of 6th baronet.
[2] Mr Webster was a partner in Messrs Methuen, the publishers.
[3] *The End of Her Honeymoon* by M. B. L. Pubs. 1914.
[4] Sir Philip Sassoon: 1888-1939. 3rd Bart. At this time Unionist M.P. for Hythe Division of Kent and later this year Private Secretary to Field-Marshal Sir Douglas Haig, Commander-in-Chief of British Armies in France.

January 28th, 1915

There were two American attachés at Mrs Ainley's[1] and I felt that all three were very strongly pro-German. My hostess having accompanied a lady to Aix-la-Chapelle, was arrested as an Englishwoman. She was put into what she described as "a very nice, clean, warm prison". As soon as they found she was American-born, and had been educated at Cologne, they behaved to her with the greatest civility, and allowed her to nurse British, French and Belgian wounded. She declared the British people were being deceived and did not know how splendidly the Germans were doing. On the other hand, I was much surprised that in answer to a direct question, she admitted that all the educated Germans she had come across believed they were done for—ultimately.

In spite of German civility to her, she had to make her escape in the guise of a peasant with the connivance of the American Embassy. The American attaché seemed to admire the British Navy, but not to like the British people or the British Government. He asked me if I thought it fair that England should blockade and so starve 'women and children'. I observed that I felt quite sure that were the positions reversed, Germany would certainly try to starve England out.

February 10th, 1915

I had a most interesting talk with Mrs Charles Rothschild[2] who is Hungarian. She gave me an extraordinary account of her journey home the day before England declared war—the dreadful anxiety she felt, as she had with her two quite young children, an English nurse, and *no money*. A German gentleman was very good to her, looked after her and the children, and ended by lending her £25. When she gave him her name and address, he burst out laughing, and said "I little thought that I should ever live to lend money to a Rothschild!" She gave him a cheque, and he said to her "I do not wish to cash this. I shall frame it—

[1] Mrs Ainley: d. of Charles H. Sheldon of New York, wife of Actor-Manager Henry Ainley.

[2] Hon. Mrs Charles Rothschild: d. of Capt. Alfred von Wertheimstein of Nagynarad., Hungary, m. 1907 the Hon. Charles Rothschild.

but no doubt you will sometime send me the money." As a matter of fact, she has since got an aunt of hers in Stuttgart, to pay him back and he wrote her a very nice letter. He was a manufacturer of munitions, and naturally felt quite cheerful about the war.

DIARY

February 12th, 1915

Lunched with Henry James alone. We touched on no controversial subject, but he told me one or two very interesting things. One was that he knew a leading American banker who came over here *at the end of last September*, to meet a Dutch banker with whom he had big business dealings. The Dutchman said to him: "It is very regrettable that the British so underestimate the Germans. They believe them to be on the brink of bankruptcy: as a matter of fact, Germany is in a perfectly sound monetary position."

This same American banker came over quite recently, within the last fortnight, to collect money owing to America from Germany—not, according to Henry James, a very large sum, some two million thalers—and again met his Dutch banker. The latter said to him, "I am afraid there is not the slightest chance of your ever getting your money". The American said: "But of course I shall get it! Remember what you said about Germany's financial condition." "Oh," said the other, "but that was some months ago. Everything has altered now. Germany is on the brink of bankruptcy and is paying nobody unless she is forced to do so."

I dined with the Haldanes, Lord Haldane spoke to me of the attacks made on him with great feeling. He again gave me a long account of his historic visit to Berlin in 1912 and repeated everything that had passed between him and Bethmann Hollweg, and he described the offer only made known to the world by Asquith this last autumn—when Germany asked England to enter into a defensive and offensive alliance by which under all circumstances England would remain neutral whatever Germany did. To that offer Haldane observed: "How would you feel, for instance, if it suited us to have a war with Denmark later?"

Bethmann Hollweg brushed that aside as a preposterous notion, as of course it was. Then Haldane said, "But would you expect us to stand aside if for any reason you violated the neutrality of Belgium?" Bethmann Hollweg observed that this was as inconceivable as that England should attack Denmark!

Haldane then said: "You must be aware it would be impossible for us to stand by and see France crushed to the earth?"

I told Haldane that I felt the account of his visit to Berlin ought to be made public, and that I wondered very much at the Cabinet not seeing the importance of doing it. He said that he thought the attacks on him were dying down, but to that I could not agree.

DIARY

February 13th, 1915

I went to see Julia Frankau[1], who is, I am afraid, tubercular. She thinks she is being cured by a marvellous new treatment of iodine of which she drinks huge quantities. She says it has brought her back to life, and talked with all her old vigour and directness. We discussed at great length the literary position. She thinks that after the War they will want strong, powerful stories. Her son, Gilbert Frankau, believes that everything will be utterly different in the writing world.

DIARY

February 14th, 1915

Dined at the Reginald McKennas—only Barbara McLaren[2] and Harold Baker[3] there. There was a good deal of chaffing about *the Assyrian*, apparently a nickname for Edwin Montagu.[4] My host is evidently very nervous about the submarine attacks which Germany means to begin this next Thursday. Harold Baker told us one odd fact— that the Germans now run a *train de luxe* daily from Lille to Lodz!

DIARY

February 17th, 1915

Arnold Bennett called on me and said he thinks the War will be over in June or July. He has just finished the last volume of his *Clayhanger*

[1] Julia Frankau: wrote several novels under the name of Frank Danby. Mother of the novelist Gilbert Frankau and grandmother of Pamela Frankau.

[2] Barbara McLaren: d. of Sir Herbert and Lady Jekyll. After her first husband's death in the war, m. General Sir Bernard Freyberg, V.C.

[3] Harold Baker: 1877-1960. Liberal M.P. for Accrington Division, Lancashire, 1910-18. Well-known man about town. Nicknamed Bluey.

[4] Edwin Montagu: 1879-1924. Secretary of State for India. m. 1915 Hon. Venetia Stanley.

trilogy—Clayhanger and Hilda married. He has four officers billeted on him and is astonished to find that they are only interested in the War as it affects them. One is a solicitor, the others all professional men too.

DIARY

February 18th, 1915

There were seven at the Thirty Club. I sat between Lady Stanley and Fanny Prothero.[1] Everyone felt very uneasy about the Russian position, but not much was said owing to the presence of the Russian Ambassadress.

There was a good deal of general talk as to the effect of war on human beings. Marie de Rothschild[2] was less reserved than usual about public affairs. She told us that she had heard the Germans had a hundred submarines. Others present combated this idea, and thought that the utmost they now had must be about forty. Marie expressed a fear lest the Russians would have to evacuate Warsaw. An allusion was made to the enormous number of beds now being got ready for the future wounded: not far short of 100,000 are required.

Weenie Ridley told me this afternoon she had seen at lunch an old governess who has been staying in Holland with an ex-pupil married to a Dutchman. This lady said Holland was violently pro-British with the exception of a small Court party. She had met the chief notary of a Dutch town, and he said to her: "I know the Allies will win, for I do a great deal of business with both Germany and England. I can get no money at all from Germany but I am paid by my British clients as if it were peace time."

DIARY

February 19th, 1915

I dined with Lord Haldane. He was most interesting; I never saw him so good natured and in better spirits. He spoke more freely of the German Emperor than I have ever heard him do before. He said he would never be surprised if William the Second became insane, which

---

[1] Fanny Prothero née Butcher: m. George Prothero, Editor of the *Quarterly Review* and brother of Lord Ernle.

[2] Marie de Rothschild: d. of Achille Perugia. m. 1881, Leopold de Rothschild, C.V.O.

E   53

from him was very frank. Haldane observed "I shall never go to Germany again". I said "Yes, you will go there, when Germany is a Republic", whereupon he brightened up and exclaimed, "If Germany is ever a Republic, I *shall* go back".

He said that just before the War the two countries had got on better than they had ever done, but that the military party suddenly got the upper hand: I don't believe the peace party in which he, Haldane, believed, ever counted or even amounted to much as regards numbers. He quoted Jules Cambon's[1] despatch saying that the German Emperor had turned against a policy of peace about two years ago. He said he thought this was true, and that the Emperor had suddenly made up his mind to wage a great and victorious War.

DIARY

February 22nd, 1915

At 10 Downing Street I sat next to the Prime Minister. There were only six people there, including the American proprietor of *The Chicago Tribune* (who has come over to see whether news can be less censored) and Lady Essex.[2] The talk centred round the Dardanelles and many ships were mentioned.

The Prime Minister told us some amusing things about Winston Churchill—how he had wanted to call a ship *Cromwell* and when the King had not thought that a suitable name, Winston suggested *Ironside*! Winston had thought of the splendid old name of *Ark Royal*, one of the Armada ships. This brought us to the *Queen Elizabeth*. Winston would like to call one *The Great Harry*. Mr Asquith does not like the names *Indefatigable* or *Invincible*. I felt sorry I said something about the expeditionary force to Egypt, for he seemed annoyed and surprised I knew about it, but he added the fact that 15,000 Marines are going out. Margot has been having a brandy cure for anaemia of the brain, taking it in tiny doses as a medicine.

DIARY

March 1st, 1915

Dined with the Glenconners, no one else there but Sir Edward Grey. He was extremely cheerful and said that as he grew older he often forgot

[1] Jules Cambon: French Ambassador in Berlin.
[2] Lady Essex: wife of 7th Earl of Essex and d. of Beach Grant of New York.

curious and amusing events he desired to remember. He has a great fund of whimsical humour which makes him very agreeable in what the French call *petit comité*.

At this time I was asked by a Liberal publishing firm to write a short life of Edward Grey. It was felt that the public knew very little about him. I did not consult him in any way, but I did obtain—through Lord and Lady Glenconner, his closest friends—leave to make use of the privately printed life of his first wife written by Mrs Creighton.[1]

To my anger and annoyance the book had only just appeared when I received a furious letter from Mrs Creighton because I had quoted a letter which had appeared in her privately printed book. I wrote to my mother:

"She must be a horrid woman, for I more than amply acknowledged the source. I had the pleasure—and it was a pleasure—of writing and telling her that her book had been given me by Edward Grey with full leave to take anything out of it I thought would help in my really difficult task, for there is nothing more trying than to write an account of a person one knows, who is alive. The better you know them, the more difficult it is."

DIARY

March 3rd, 1915

At Mrs de Rothschild's I sat next to Neil Primrose[2] and Mr Rattigan,[3] a diplomat who had been in Berlin when War broke out, and who was now going to Roumania. He has a pretty wife who seemed much to regret the War as it had interfered with their accepting a shooting invitation from the Crown Prince! Neil Primrose talked a good deal about British prisoners. He had just seen a man who had described to him their very insufficient feeding. They have one cup of coffee with no milk or sugar in the morning, water soup in

---

[1] Mrs. Creighton: d. of Robert von Glehn, widow of Bishop Mandell Creighton, Bishop of Peterborough and then of London. She was cruelly nicknamed the Bundle of Old Bent Pins.

[2] Hon. Neil Primrose: M.P. 2nd son of 5th Earl of Rosebery. Killed in action 1917.

[3] Frank Rattigan: C.M.G. Diplomat. served in First War.

55

the middle of the day, a 2 lb. loaf of bread for two days, a cup of tea at five, meat twice a week in the soup. Practically starvation rations.

DIARY

March 7th, 1915

I called on Rhoda Broughton. Henry James was there and was exceedingly interesting. He had been lunching with Morton Frewen,[1] Winston Churchill's uncle, who gave him an extraordinary account of the preparations which are being made in view of the coming operations. Four hundred aeroplanes have just come from America. He also described a new British airship, not as large as a Zeppelin, but a far more workmanlike bit of aircraft which has on board a peculiar scientific instrument which will enable the airship to see a submarine under water. As a matter of fact the seas are almost clear of enemy submarines owing to the new nets.[2] These nets, which are said to be the invention of quite a young man, are of steel, each mesh being ten feet wide. They have been placed round Zeebrugge so that no more submarines can get out or return.

Henry James read to us a remarkable letter sent him by Edith Wharton, describing a motor car trip made by her from Paris to Verdun. She was the first woman who had been there since the War began. She described the town as practically dead, all non-combatants having been sent away, everyone exceedingly excited concerning coming operations. I thought her letter admirably expressed but she reiterated in it a statement which I feel quite sure was untrue, namely that practically wherever the car stopped, the French officer in command had read one of her books. I doubt if there is a single author, English or French, who could possibly make such a claim. I am quite sure it would not be true, for instance, of Anatole France. It might be so of Old Dumas or of Victor Hugo, should their ghosts return. In this country, the same thing might be true of Kipling, but certainly of no other writer.

[1] Morton Frewen: 1853-1924, of Brede Place, Sussex. m. Clara d. of Leonard Jerome of New York.
[2] This was the paravane, invented by Cmdr. Charles Dennistoun Burney, R.N., C.M.G., M.P. (U) Uxbridge Div. of Middlesex 1922-29. Responsible for construction of R.100. Succeeded father as 2nd Baronet 1929.

Chisbury,[1]
Kingsdown Road,
Epsom
March 10*th*, 1915

No, I do *not* believe in either Zeppelins or an invasion. I did believe in Zeppelins till I took the trouble to investigate the question—They are *very* fragile—They have not even ventured to send them into France. Aeroplanes may come, but they do very little damage.

There is an invasion scare but I don't believe in that either (unless the British Fleet had been really destroyed)—England might lose a big Naval battle and still be far stronger than Germany on the sea. I do think the tide has now turned. Hilary tells me the War is costing £11 a second now, and will soon be £20 a second. Everything is going up, in price, by leaps and bounds.

I am here, for one night, alone with Freddie. We are working terribly hard at the book.

Do not worry at what you see in the *Times*. Colonel Repington[2] does believe in an invasion of 200,000 men landing at different places. I think it is a wild delusion, as long as the Fleet is in being.

DIARY

March 11*th*, 1915

I saw Lord Frederic Hamilton[3] who had just seen Lord Fisher.[4] He, Fisher, says that the forcing of the Dardanelles will be a matter of at least three weeks. Lord Fisher seems very vexed with Winston Churchill who, he says, talks too much as to future plans. There is a rumour—but this did not come through Lord Fisher—that Winston is going to India to succeed Lord Hardinge.[5]

[1] A house M. B. L. and her husband rented for weekends and summer holidays.
[2] Col. Repington: well-known War correspondent.
[3] Lord Frederic Hamilton: s. óf 2nd Duke of Abercorn. Author of *The Days Before Yesterday*, pubs. 1920.
[4] Lord Fisher: 1841-1920. First Sea Lord 1904-10 and 1914-15.
[5] Lord Hardinge of Penshurst: 1858-1944. Viceroy of India 1910-16.

At Rhoda Broughton's, Marie Mallet was full of extraordinary stories. She is terribly anxious, with one son in the Dardanelles in the warship *Vengeance*, and the other in the trenches.

She gave us a terrible account of the mines in the Dardanelles. They have been laid by the Germans at the bottom of the sea in the Narrows. They are controlled from the shore, and the idea is that when a battleship goes over a certain place, a button will be pressed on shore and the ship will blow up.

Mr Liddell gave me a curious account of his duties as the Lord Chancellor's secretary. He opens all the letters from lunatics. They have a right to send unopened letters to the Lord Chancellor twice a month. He says some of the letters that are coming in now are most pathetic, the burden of many of them being, "Only let me out, and I will at once enlist!" He said the war had neither increased nor diminished the number of lunatics. I asked him if he had ever discovered a sane man incarcerated unfairly. He said no, but that they always looked out for such cases, and that he makes a very special note when any new lunatic's letter arrives. He also makes very particular enquiries when a lunatic writes a complaint of physical ill-treatment. He says he believes the medical superintendents are always humane, but that it is very difficult to get the right type of man to be a male nurse, as the work is so depressing. I said it ought to be done by monks and nuns.

At Mrs Langford Brooke's[1] I heard read aloud some letters from the Russian front. The writer is very optimistic, but seems to think no great advance can take place there till May. He gave a very curious account of the astonishingly different types seen in Russian regiments, like men belonging not only to different countries but to different hemispheres.

[1] Mrs Langford Brooke: w. of Col. Henry Langford Brooke of Mere Hall, Knutsford and m. of Lilian, Lady Throckmorton.

March 15th, 1915

Dined at the Yates Thompson's,[1] met a niece of Arthur Balfour. She gave me an interesting account of the Sunday before the War. Winston called on Balfour, told him the Cabinet were going to resign, and that a Coalition Ministry would have to be formed. Balfour strongly advised that the Government should stay in as then constituted. He wired to Lansdowne[2] and Bonar Law[3] who were in the country. They hurried back to town, held a short meeting and composed a message assuring the Government of their support.

March 17th, 1915

I hear Sir Ian Hamilton[4] has gone to the Dardanelles. This is supposed to be a great secret. He started at a few hours' notice, a cruiser taking him to Le Havre, a special train to Marseilles and a French cruiser to the Straits.

At the Leo Rothschilds, Arthur Balfour said Lord Fisher had been very funny concerning the raiding German cruisers. He said the Admiralty had done what it always did—set four tortoises to catch a hare, and finding that no good, sent off *eight* tortoises!

March 23rd, 1915

Bertram Christian[5] gave a lunch in honour of some Serbians. Sat next to my old friend Mr Steed,[6] now on *The Times*. He gave me a most

[1] Mr Yates Thompson: 1838-1928. Sometime proprietor of *The Pall Mall Gazette* and a noted collector. Mrs Yates Thompson, eldest d. of the Victorian publisher George Smith who published Charlotte Brontë's *Jane Eyre*.

[2] 5th Marquess of Lansdowne: 1845-1927. Foreign Secretary 1900-05. Minister without Portfolio 1915-16.

[3] Andrew Bonar Law: 1858-1923. Unionist M.P. Chancellor of the Exchequer 1916-18. Prime Minister 1922-23.

[4] General Sir Ian Hamilton: 1853-1947. G.O.C. in Chief Mediterranean and Commanded Mediterranean Expeditionary Force 1915.

[5] Bertram Christian: director Nisbet and Co. Publishers. At this time was Chairman of the Macedonian and Serbian Relief Funds.

[6] Wickham Steed: 1871-1956. Editor of *The Times* 1919-22, then of the *Review of Reviews*.

dramatic account of all that had immediately preceded the war. According to him, Asquith, Grey, Haldane and Winston were firm for War from the first—the rest wished England to remain neutral. He said that if England had not gone in when she did, she would have to have done so three weeks later, at very great disadvantage. He said all governments always consulted financiers, and what folly it was as financiers are the worst judges of human nature and also of the political future, for they always go by the money standard which is artificial.

DIARY

March 24th, 1915

The Arnold Bennetts dined with me to meet Sir George Riddell[1] and Pamela McKenna.[2] Bennett told me of the vast sums he was making: a hundred pounds for a 1,500 word article in the new Sunday paper. He gets two hundred pounds from American papers for each article he writes of the same length and £3,500 for serial rights of a novel. He has fixed up three serials for £10,000 with an American paper. He gave a funny account of the Editor of *Munsey's* going to see Sir Gilbert Parker.[3] Sir Gilbert received him with hauteur, whereupon the American said: "What you've first got to do is to come off your perch—and listen to what we want. I can only do business on those lines." The great man gave in and got off his perch.

DIARY

April 26th, 1915

I heard that the asphyxiating machinery brought into action by the Germans the last few days was an entire surprise to Sir John French and his staff. The Germans had already thrown gas bombs, but nothing had been attempted on a big scale. The person who told me had seen the officer who had brought back specimens of the gas to the War Office.

It was a most extraordinary sight as seen from the British side, for the

---

[1] Sir George Riddell: 1865-1934. Proprietor of *News of the World* and other publications. Cr. 1st Baron Riddell 1920.

[2] Pamela McKenna: wife of Reginald McKenna and d. of Sir Herbert Jekyll.

[3] Sir Gilbert Parker: 1862-1932. Author. M.P. for Gravesend 1900-18. Was in charge of publicity in America for $2\frac{1}{2}$ years after First War was declared.

Germans who dealt with the new engine of destruction were clothed like divers. The soldiers behind them had their noses plugged with cotton wool and respirators over their mouths, but even so, 1000 perished by their own gas.

I had a melancholy confirmation of what the fighting is costing France just now, for someone I know has not been able to get back from the South of France for four days owing to the stream of ambulance trains which block up the whole railroad to Marseilles. He hopes to come back on Thursday, but if the fighting continues as fiercely, he may be kept down there indefinitely for in addition to the ambulance trains, there are of course troop trains hurrying up reinforcements.[1]

DIARY

April 28th, 1915

The feeling against Winston Churchill is growing in intensity with the one exception of Garvin.[2] No one in the press has a good word to say for Winston. There is one outstanding exception amid all his blunders and that is the great service he rendered to the country by his action just before the War, that is when he kept the Fleet mobilized.

Lady Leicester[3] told me that she had heard that one reason why the German Emperor hates Lichnowsky[4] is that the German Government received some secret information a week before Germany declared war on France stating the British Fleet was all gathered together at a certain point. The Ambassador was asked to find out if this was true. He went to the Foreign Office, and there received an evasive answer. Apparently this evasive answer was given in all good faith, the Foreign Office not being aware what Churchill had done, or rather was doing. The Ambassador believed from the answer that there was nothing out of the way happening in connection with the Fleet, and transmitted this view to Berlin.

When I heard this story I could not help feeling what a dreadful pity it was that the F.O. had not answered: "Yes, it is quite true. And we are doing this as we think the situation abroad is becoming menacing from *our* point of view." Had this happened, it would certainly have given pause even to the German War Party.

[1] People travelled to and from France all through the First War.
[2] J. L. Garvin: 1868-1947. Then Editor of *The Pall Mall Gazette*.
[3] Lady Leicester: wife of 3rd Earl. d. of 2nd Baron Annaly.
[4] Prince Lichnowsky: German Ambassador in London 1912-14.

May 2nd, 1915

I called on Lady Edward Cavendish who talked of the Germans and of how unlike they were to English people both for good and evil. She said that when acting as hostess for her brother, Sir Frank Lascelles[1] at the British Embassy in Berlin, she called late one afternoon on a lady of the Court. The lady expressed the most exaggerated surprise at seeing her, and said, "I wonder you are out today, and at such an hour!" Lady Edward replied, "Why should I not be?" The other said "But are not the Emperor and Empress coming to dine with you tonight?" Lady Edward answered "Yes, but I gave all my orders to the cook, butler and so on this morning, and arranged the flowers that were to be put on the table". We all agreed that English servants would not stand the kind of interference which apparently is usual in great German households. Lady Edward spoke with pity of the Empress who, she said, was a very nice woman.

May 9th, 1915

I lunched with Lady Hall[2] to meet J. L. Garvin and the First Secretary of the Dutch Legation. I thought Garvin less cheerful than I had ever known him. He seemed to think the Russians had had a very bad time and that it would delay the end of the War. There was a great deal of talk about America. He declares that the one thing we ought to hope for is that America will keep out of it, as if she came in she would of course stop making all the things she is now manufacturing for the Allies as she would require them for herself.

Garvin gave me a curious account of the days before the War, described the letter the King was made to write to Poincaré as a most feeble document, said a copy had been seen by the German government, who, by its tenor, decided that Great Britain was not going to declare War. He said the entry of England into the war had upset all the German plans and meant Germany's ultimate defeat, as our Navy will end by strangling Germany. He believes the censorship was not half strict enough and that the *Times* and the *Morning Post* ought to be suppressed

[1] Sir Frank Lascelles: 1841-1920. Diplomat, British Ambassador in Berlin 1895-1908.

[2] Lady Hall: wife of Col. Sir John Hall. 9th Baronet. d. of Henry Duncan and widow of Spencer Alwyne Oliver, D.S.O.

or compelled to drop criticism of the Government, if only for the reason that it heartens up the Germans, who grossly over-estimate the effect of that sort of writing on the English public. He thought Winston Churchill ought to be muzzled, but not expelled from the Cabinet, as it would hearten the Germans so much if any serious changes were made.

M. B. L. TO MISS ELIZABETH HALDANE

> 9, *Barton Street,*
> *Westminster, S.W.*
> *June 8th,* 1915

Dearest E,

It rather looks as if *already* the New Govt. was cracking—over Campbell. Carson is the culprit. How *could* Mr Asquith have in such a stormy petrel. However I hope the difference will be composed—for it would look so *very* bad for it to break up as soon as this.

I wish you could have heard Hilary on your brother the other evening. He is shocked at the lack of patriotism shown by those who let him go, "the one man of real power, and great capacity, they possessed"—and much more to the same purpose. And Elizabeth, I do think it argues very badly for the Party. However, I don't know that you agree with me about this. But sometimes the outsider sees most. The turning point was months ago—when Asquith himself, Kitchener, *or* Grey should have said a sharp, clear word, it could have been done in 3 minutes. But Asquith preferred to keep his head in the sand. Grey was *genuinely* ignorant (of what he *ought* to have known) and Kitchener is evidently a most selfish egoist. However, *I am* beginning to think that *as things are turning out, recent* events may be for the best. There is evidently a public revulsion of feeling about your Brother, and people are shocked at B.[1] being Lord Chancellor. Have you heard that he called out "Order! Order!" in the House of Lords the other day—and certain old peers nearly had a fit!

HENRY JAMES TO M. B. L.

> 21 *Carlyle Mansions,*
> *Cheyne Walk, S.W.*
> *August 17th,* 1915

My Dear Marie,

It is only the deluge of benedictions that has kept me breasting it all these days to such a tune that I find the time to have gone more in

[1] 1st Viscount Buckmaster K.C.: 1861-1934. Lord Chancellor 1915-16.

panting and puffing for simple grateful life—than in really "answering" more good and beautiful words than I think ever fluttered on a poor old modest and denuded head, at such a rate and in such a compass of days, before. I still but gape, fondly and delightfully at my welcomers and well-wishers, and though I pretty well thought I *should* like doing what I have done, I find it agrees with me still better than I have imagined. *Je vous serre bien doucement la main*—with an intended *douceur*. I mean and shall venture to invoke your presence here for a little as soon as I can have any confidence in your being back in town again. I stick fast you see—I think I *taste* my citizenship[1] rather more on this spot—discounted as it truly was when I took it up by something four long years so remarkably like it that I wonder anyone can tell them apart—I myself being all but unable to. I had yesterday a postcard from Hugh Walpole "in Galicia" closely about and *in* the trenches, and under fire as an intimate Red Cross ministrant, and pronouncing the last three months, in spite of his twice having but just escaped capture by the enemy— "Which I dread much more than anything else"—the very happiest of his life. He hopes to get back here in September—when I count upon his being far more interesting and informing than if he had spent this interval otherwise. I hope you keep hold (and add to your stock) of something good, and am

yours affectionately ever
Henry James

J. H. MARTIN[2] TO M. B. L.

Trenches,
Flanders
November 3rd, 1915

My Dear Mrs Lowndes,

Your letter gave me so much pleasure on my first night in the trenches that I hope you will feel that it was not without its reward.

I came up here some days ago by an unforgettable evening march, beginning in the country of comparative peace, and coming straight through our artillery lines to the trenches themselves—all the daylight was spent along those long poplar-lined roads, which have in France a picturesque and lovable stiffness—like a grandfather's chair—but up

[1] Henry James was naturalised a British subject this year.
[2] John Hanbury Martin: Served throughout First War 1914-19. Labour M.P. Southwark (Central Division) 1940-48.

here at any rate now seem about meticulously correct to pedantry! Just after dusk these led us into the most appalling scene of desolation that you can conceive, except of course Jerusalem and Nineveh and the un-earthed Pompeii—a street of little red brick artisan's houses, all deserted and some rather badly damaged, turned suddenly into what had evidently been the main street of a good-sized and rather pretentious town. In the middle of this second street was a cleared path along which we marched, to right and left in unrecognisable confusion was the debris of innumer-able shops and houses, the homes of countless little bourgeois now I suppose in exile, depending on "trading" as some would say, on the philanthropy of the wealthy and soft-hearted English. Only two things that could be certainly identified stood out in the midst of all this chaos —a broken lamp post and a bit of a tramline.

I see I have said all this was to our right and left, though it doesn't matter—it was actually for the most part on one side of the road—the other being taken by a great abbey church or cathedral of which only the bare shell remained. Through the glassless windows the evening light struggled, enough for us to pick our way through the masonry into the Grande Place—here again the whole of one side was held by one of those great "halls" which Flanders abounds in—the outside wall with its broken turrets and shattered carvings—stands or stood, but absolutely nothing else—one house only had survived the various bombardments here—a glaring white place that might have been a hotel or *grand magasin*, and which stood up in the middle of the pathetic ruination of street after street of houses belonging to the poor, whose homes con-tained probably not only all their worldly possessions, but the stock of their trade or business as well—it would have been tragic in broad day light—in that half twilight it was melodramatically dreadful.

CHAPTER IV

1916-1918

As the First War went on and on, endless rumours were heard as to peace overtures and the successes or otherwise of the Allied Armies. London and many parts of England were bombed. M. B. L. and her husband were consumed with anxiety over their son, Charles, at the Front. They sent their daughters on long visits to their grandmother in Sussex, and to various close friends in the country.

Marie was too absorbed and working too hard to keep anything approaching a regular diary. However she constantly saw her friends when they were off duty from their voluntary war work as V.A.D.'s and Ambulance Drivers. Her most intimate friend, Lady Ridley, was occupied in the making of artificial limbs.

DIARY

January 12th, 1916

I am just back from Lady Battersea[1] at Overstrand. It was one of the pleasantest visits I have ever paid because it was so quiet and yet not at all dull, for she is a very agreeable woman and a pleasant companion. The story she told me which interested me the most was one concerning Sir Charles Dilke.[2] Many years before the case, Mrs Mark Pattison[3] with whom she was acquainted, asked herself to lunch. After lunch Sir Charles Dilke came in, this having evidently been arranged between them. There was a funny little incident of a dropped and picked-up geranium. Mrs Cyril Flower, as she then was, was amused tho' a little vexed. She told an intimate friend what had happened, and then forgot all about it.

Soon afterwards Sir Charles Dilke called on her for fourteen consecutive days, always finding her out as it was the height of the London season. On the fifteenth day he came at 2.30 and she was in. He asked to see her alone and for a while they talked about nothing in particular, then suddenly he said "You don't *look* like a cruel woman!"

She answered, "I hope I am not, Sir Charles". He replied "But

---

[1] Lady Battersea: d. of Sir Anthony de Rothschild 1st Bart. and widow of Cyril Flower, 1st and last Lord Battersea. Her gardens at The Pleasaunce, Overstrand, were famous.

[2] Sir Charles Dilke: 1843-1911. The central figure of the divorce case in 1886, which effectively prevented Dilke, then Liberal M.P. for Chelsea, from holding office.

[3] Mrs Mark Pattison: 1840-1904. Wife of the Rector of Lincoln College, Oxford, who when a widow married Sir Charles Dilke in 1885.

you have been very cruel without meaning it, to a noble, beautiful and innocent lady. You told a friend of yours that I had met Mrs Mark Pattison at your house." Then he burst into tears!

Mrs Flower was terribly taken aback, and exceedingly sorry. She explained to him that she had not meant to make mischief, and as a matter of fact, had said very little.

Many years later she was giving a dinner-party to which she had asked Sir Charles Dilke. Just before they sat down a note was brought from him saying he could not come and she would soon know why. In the middle of dinner she told someone of this note, and said she could not imagine what it meant. The person, who was a lady, had a fit of hysterics and had to be helped out of the room. Lady Battersea found that almost everyone there except herself was aware of the reason why Sir Charles had not come, for it was on that day that the scandal had broken.

She told me that Lord Battersea had remained very faithful to his friendship with Dilke, and they had gone on seeing him. I realised that of the two she liked Dilke far better than Lady Dilke. One day Sir William Harcourt[1] came and told her that Lady Dilke intended to ask her Lady Battersea, to present her at Court! She would have been willing to do it, had the Queen been willing.

M. B. L. TO MISS ELIZABETH HALDANE

9 Barton Street, S.W.
February 29th, 1916

Dearest Elizabeth,

I lunched with the Crewes[2] yesterday, and tomorrow I go to Downing St. *Through the telephone* Margot informed me that "The Government are *mad*, quite *mad*. But Henry doesn't care"!!!! I have made friends with Elizabeth.[3] She warms my heart by her *extraordinary* knowledge of books, but I do not think her so very brilliant. She is not a patch on her mother. I fear she is very far from well. I saw her in bed. She longs, one can see, to be married, and so start her own life—poor little thing . . . . . .

---

[1] Sir William Harcourt: 1827-1904. Home Secretary 1880-85. Chancellor of the Exchequer 1886 and 1892-95.

[2] 1st Marquess of Crewe: 1858-1945. At this time he was Lord President of the Council. m. Lady Margaret Primrose, d. of 5th Earl of Rosebery.

[3] Elizabeth Asquith: 1897-1945. d. of Mr Asquith and his 2nd wife, Margot Tennant. m. Prince Antoine Bibesco 1919.

Isn't America strange? I don't like Colonel House.[1] I think he is Mr Facing-Both-Ways.

Poor Henry James.[2] I was really very fond of him. Of late years I saw him *often*.

DIARY

April 12th, 1916

Yesterday my Elizabeth and I went to the most remarkable Poets' Reading I have ever attended. It was held at Lord Byron's beautiful house in Piccadilly, lent by Lady d'Erlanger, in aid of the Star & Garter Home at Richmond.

Mr Augustine Birrell was in the Chair. He looked far from well and overtired—indeed at one moment he fell asleep. I was moved by Mr de la Mare[3] reading five poems of great beauty. Elizabeth was thrilled at seeing for the first time W. H. Davies, a strange tiny poet. He read *Love's Silent Hour* and three others. Hilary read *The Poor of London* and *The Dons*. He got a big reception.

G. K. Chesterton proposed the vote of thanks. Looking back on this afternoon I remember best H. B. Irving declaiming the Waterloo Stanzas from *Childe Harold*. I suppose being an actor gave him a start over poets. I shall keep the programme among my papers.

DIARY

May 25th, 1916

Sat next to Reginald McKenna at dinner. I felt that, like all English politicians, he is much puzzled by the small amount of influence the French Government have over France. It is impossible for any Liberal Politician here, however clever, to face the truth—that is, that just now France is governed by a military oligarchy to whom she owes her very life, while she knows that to the Government she owed the awful unpreparedness in which she was caught in August 1914. However, he did

[1] Colonel House: b. Houston, Texas 1858. At this date was Personal Representative of President Wilson to the European Governments. He later took an active part in the Armistice negotiations, the making of the Versailles Treaty and the founding of the League of Nations.

[2] Henry James had died the previous day.

[3] Walter de la Mare O.M.: 1873-1956. Author and poet. His *Memoirs of a Midget* appeared in 1921.

71

say one very striking thing. I asked him whether he thought Germany was in the state we hear of. He answered: "It is impossible to know what state Germany is in, as the neutrals who come back all tell a different tale—but what to me proves that Germany must be feeling very anxious is her complete cave-in over submarine warfare. During the last fortnight the submarine campaign has practically stopped. No neutrals have been sunk and very few allied ships".

Apropos of the Irish rising, about which people still talk as if it were far more important than the War, Professor Mahaffy[1] became a Home Ruler two years ago. For many years he had spent Easter with the Dowager Lady Londonderry.[2] She wrote to him this year and said, "I am sure you would not care to join my Easter party, as I will have Sir Edward Carson[3] and several other people you might not like to meet; for, after all I feel that this question is a very serious one". He wrote back and said, "I am glad to hear that after a long life spent entirely in the pursuit of pleasure, you have at last come to an age when you are capable of taking *any* question seriously!"

M. B. L. TO J. H. MARTIN

The Guest House,
Overstrand, Norfolk
May 29th, 1916

Your letter just come, your words about the *Red Cross Barge*[4] gave me great pleasure. But in America it has been rejected by one set of publishers as pro-German—by another as pro-Ally. This is a *very* bad time for writers, and I see the time coming when the inhabitants of 9 Barton Street will have to do all their own housework! As it is we are going to start one servant only when we go back. But this sort of thing never troubles me at all. Food is getting *very* dear but I consider food to be the *last* thing people should economise on. In that I am quite French. Most of the millionaires I know are now starving themselves and their households—eating margarine instead of butter or honest dripping.

[1] Sir J. P. Mahaffy: 1839-1919. G.B.E. Provost of Trinity College, Dublin.
[2] Dowager Lady Londonderry: widow of 6th Marquess and daughter of 19th Earl of Shrewsbury.
[3] Sir Edward Carson: 1854-1935: Already famous as a leading Counsel. Became leader of Ulster against Asquith's Home Rule Bill 1913-14.
[4] *Red Cross Barge*: by M. B. J., Pubs. 1916.

Well! there has been an *extraordinary* wave of optimism over London. A belief the War was on the point of *ending*. I believe the reason is that there is no doubt of the desperate straits to which Civilian Germany is reduced, or of the Kaiser's determination to have peace. He is "working" America, Sweden, Spain and the submarine campaign has been practically given up. There is a belief that Germany won't be able to live through the last 3 weeks before the harvest. When the harvest comes it won't give Germany *fats* which is what she needs above all.

We have come here for three weeks. People speak as if we were very temerarious. But so far tho' Zepps cross over they do not drop bombs. But the place is a desert, not one child on the beautiful sands. My two, and their dog, the only live objects. Lady Battersea has most kindly lent us this house.

The following was written by a man in the Admiralty and will amuse you.

> "Absolute evidence have I none—
> But my Aunt's charwoman's sister's son,
> Heard the policeman in Downing Street,
> Say to a housemaid on his beat,
> That he has a brother, who has a friend,
> Who knows to a day when the War will end "

HILAIRE BELLOC TO HIS SISTER M. B. L.

Kingsland,
Horsham
June 9th, 1916

Dearest Mary,[1]

The Navy is convinced that the German Fleet is really knocked out for months, and the more details come in the more that appears to be true. I dined with Charteris[2] in town, who told me that Mr Balfour[3] was now convinced of the magnitude of the success. It is very good news.

---

[1] M. B. L.'s brother called her Mary and not Marie as did all her friends.

[2] Hon. Evan Charteris: 1864-1940. Son of 10th Earl of Wemyss. Author.

[3] A. J. Balfour: 1848-1930. Prime Minister 1902-05. At this time was First Lord of the Admiralty.

73

I will write at greater length when I have more leisure. I am dictating this in the middle of the night on my arrival, on reading your letter.

I have given, in company with Baring and one or two other friends, a statue of St Christopher to the Cathedral.[1] I have got the leave of the Cardinal.[2] No one must be told of this yet. It is quite a small statue, and is to be put up for the sake of the Flying men in the army, who have taken him as their patron.

H. HAMILTON FYFE[3] TO M. B. L.

Galernain Ulitsa 26,
Quartier 6, Petrograd
August 21st, 1916

My dear Mrs Lowndes,

Figure to yourself my surprise on opening the evening paper last night to find a tale in it by Gospozha Bellok-Lownds, called *An Occurrence in Berlin.* I at once read it, and send it to you as a curiosity. I wonder where they got their illustrations.

I have just come back from one of my periodical visits to the Front. Except for aeroplane bombs, there was not great activity in the regions I visited. But we had plenty of *them.* My wife, like a brick, came out to me after I had been in Russia three months, and has stuck it out ever since.

Remember me to Freddie please. Is he a volunteer or a special constable or anything?[4] I proposed myself for a commission a long time ago, but was turned down as 'too old'. I should smile. They may want me yet. For the time being I have to content myself with being a chronicler. Nell joins in kindest thoughts,

Yours ever,
Hamilton Fyfe

[1] An Administrator of Westminster Cathedral caused this small and historic statue to be removed some years ago from its place by the Baptistry.

[2] Cardinal Bourne: 1861-1935, who had been Archbishop of Westminster since 1903.

[3] H. Hamilton Fyfe: 1869-1951. Author and journalist. On staff of *The Times.* Editor of *Daily Mirror* and War Correspondent with French, Russian, Roumanian, Italian and British armies 1914-18. Editor *Daily Herald* 1922-26. m. 1907 Eleanor, d. of William Kelly of the War Office.

[4] F. S. A. Lowndes had joined a Volunteer Force in the City.

September 13th, 1916

Yesterday I had an interesting talk with Sir John Hanbury Williams,[1] the General who has been with the Russian Army since the beginning of the War. He made a great impression on me as I could see he looked at the War from quite another angle from that which people do here, in fact I felt it to be the Russian angle. He is a quiet, clever man, and spoke without any violence or emphasis, but he said he is convinced the War ought to go on until Germany is invaded and until the Germans themselves have had the opportunity of knowing what it is like to have a foreign army in occupation. He said, "I don't say this from any vindictiveness but because I am sure that if this does not happen, Germany will start another war in our own time".

He said the whole of the Russian people were set on the War and its prosecution though there was still a small, very powerful group of pro-Germans, but he believes that these people are entirely actuated by money considerations, in other words, they are in the pay of Germany.

It was quite a mistake to suppose, however, that at any moment Russia was even within sight of making a separate peace. He said, "I mention this because of course it was widely believed here last year". I asked him about the Russian successes recently and he said yes, they were very good, but that after all they were only against Austria and that nothing could be of any use until Germany was tackled. He hopes great things from the advance at Salonika. He agreed with me that Roumania coming in was a good sign as Roumania must know more than we do about what is going on inside Germany.

September 14th, 1916

I asked J. H. Morgan,[2] now Captain Morgan of the War Office, to meet Mr McClure[3] at dinner. McClure gave us a very interesting account

[1] Major General Sir John Hanbury Williams: 1859-1946. Chief of British Military Mission with Headquarters Russian Army in the Field 1914-17. Marshal of the Diplomatic Corps 1920.

[2] J. H. Morgan: 1876-1955. Reader in Constitutional Law to the Inns of Court. K.C. 1926. A.A.G. Military Section of Paris Peace Conference. Author.

[3] S. S. McClure: 1857-1949. American editor and publisher. Founded *McClure's Magazine* 1893 in which *The Lodger* first appeared as a short story in January 1911.

of his adventures in Germany. He repeated with great conviction that Germany was obsessed with an awful terror of Russia, and on my observing that Germany's next move was evidently going to be to try and influence America to propose an Alliance between England, Germany and America, he exclaimed: "Why of course they were right on to that all the time I was there". Both Captain Morgan and I could see very well that McClure deep in his heart rather hoped this was coming to pass, and I think he was surprised at what we both said to him. I observed that quite early in the War—say, at the end of three months, after the Battle of the Marne, it is conceivable that there would have been quite a big party in this country desirous of bringing about such a state of things, but that now, thanks to Germany's own conduct, such a proposal would be received with rage and incredulous disgust.

Captain Morgan said that, speaking for himself, at the beginning of the War he had a far greater dislike and distrust of Russia than he had of Germany, and that this feeling was almost universal among British Liberals, but that now he recognised he had been entirely wrong and for his part would never again either shake hands with a German or sit down in the same room with one. He also said that when he was appointed Commissioner for the Home Office, he had very little belief in the atrocities, or rather he thought that the Germans had simply committed the kind of atrocities which members of all armies commit during wartime. Only a very few days convinced him that this was quite a mistake and he spoke with such force and conviction that he quite startled McClure, the more so that he has a quiet, reserved manner.

There was also a good deal of interesting talk about the man whom Captain Morgan described as "my unfortunate client" Roger Casement[1] He gave us a curious account of F. E. Smith[2] coming to him one day about the now famous "diary". Smith was very upset and nervous because he had discovered that neither Morgan nor another counsel in the case had been shown the diary. He was evidently afraid that he would be blamed for this afterwards. Morgan spoke, as have done all decent people who have spoken to me on the subject, with the utmost contempt of F. E. Smith's action in the matter of the diary—his showing it and

[1] Roger Casement: 1864-1916. British Consular Official. Irish rebel. His trial and execution for high treason still arouses acute controversy.

[2] F. E. Smith: 1872-1930. cr. 1st Earl of Birkenhead 1922. A famous counsel. He was Attorney-General at the time of the Casement trial.

allowing it to be shown round to people in order to prejudice them against Casement.

When Mr McClure had left, I asked J. H. Morgan what he really thought of Casement. He said he genuinely believed him to have been insane and he declared that if he had lived he would probably have been in an asylum within a short time.

M. B. L. TO MISS ELIZABETH HALDANE

9 *Barton Street,*
*Westminster S.W.*1
November 2nd, 1916

The Raid night was *horrid*—I got E. and S.[1] to a big building on the Embankment: then, rather foolishly came back here—as Freddie had refused to leave the house. So I was here through the awful gunfire— 2 hours. Every moment we expected to hear the bombs drop close by or *on* us, for the machines sounded overhead. Our neighbours are really very strange—Tho' I am by way of being on cordial terms with her. She is so grudging in her manner of asking us in on Raid nights that now we never think of going in there—and though I suggested it, F. flatly refused, saying he would rather be bombed at home—than saved by them! So we sat in the hall, while the house shook. We felt *very* stupid and tired all yesterday.

Miss Callaghan,[2] who was with the children in the Embankment building, still looks worn out as she, of course, had to deal all yesterday with terrified mothers who attend the Centre where she works. It is a great comfort they did not come *last* night. If they had done so I should have gone to the Reginald McKennas—Pamela is *very* kind and warmly invited us all to come. Of course, the Burrs[3] are important to me because of Freddie. It is such a comfort not to have him being slowly killed with overwork—yet he remains a member of *Times* Staff, and is there any night he feels like it. We are going to spend the week-end of 17th at Aston Clinton with Lady Battersea.

[1] M. B. L.'s daughters, Elizabeth and Susan.
[2] Miss Harriet Callaghan: Princess Christian Nurse to M. B. L.'s children. Later Superintendent of the Westminster Health Society's Centre.
[3] Charles H. Burr: American business man with whom F. S. A. Lowndes worked for a time.

9 *Barton Street,*
London S.W.
December 8*th,* 1916

Well! this week has been an exciting one and extraordinary tales are going the round. I wish you had been at 'Thirty' yesterday—really very interesting talk. Violet Markham thinks L. G. will last out a good while but that all "the Old Gang" as people are beginning to call them, will gradually crystallise into a Peace Party.

Every hour one hears of new combinations—at first Samuel succeeding McKenna, Montagu remaining at Munitions, Carson at Admiralty, Derby War Office. But S. and M. have resigned, after all, with the others. Some still think P.M. will come back. L. G. was in such a hurry that he kissed hands last night. As things (at War) could hardly be worse, I fear that L. G.'s usual luck will pursue him, and that everything which "comes off" in Greece, etc. etc. will be put down to him. Strange tales are about regarding Margot. I am told on good authority, (private) that she actually wrote to Lord Stamfordham telling him to ask the King to take no notice of Asquith's letter of resignation as "he was not himself when he wrote it". She sent this along by hand and was surprised that it had no result.

It amuses me, or would if we were not at War, to hear some prominent Liberals now mentioning the Marconi business. Wailing over the P.M.'s misplaced generosity over it.

Winston expects something, but will not get it I hear, I don't envy L. G. It is lucky he can't hear what some of his new colleagues say about him.

DIARY

January 21*st,* 1917

I dined with the Carruthers.[1] In addition to the host, there were two other War Office men: a very pleasant Major Foll, the explosives expert, was one of them. After dinner, when alone with Violet, she told

---

[1] Lieut. Col. James Carruthers, M.V.O., D.S.O. European War 1914-18. m. Violet Markham C. H. 1917, granddaughter of Sir Joseph Paxton. She served as member and chairman of a large number of Government committees and boards mainly concerned with woman.

me that she had been offered, and had accepted, a new post, that of organizing voluntary woman labour. She seemed, however, very melancholy about it, said it ought to have been started at least a year ago, that it would mean a mass of untrained human material which could do very little until trained.

Major Foll drove me home. He told me he came of a Huguenot family and gave me a most interesting account of his work. Apropos of the awful explosion at Silvertown the other day and the rumours which were about as to its delaying our coming advance, he said it would not delay it for one minute, that he had stored underground enough high explosives for fifteen months. He has visited every munitions factory in France. He said they are much less careful there in regard to precautions and they never report explosions as they do here.

DIARY

February 8th, 1917

Lunched with the George Protheros where I met Charles H. Burr. All the talk was of America and of Bernstorff's[1] dismissal. Burr said that Bernstorff was a very clever man. This was borne out by M. Fleurien, the French attaché who had known Bernstorff well, and who was there. They both agreed that he was a really great diplomat, wonderfully clever at sending disagreeable messages. Burr gave us a most striking story of the early days of the War in America.

Late in August, 1914, he went in to see Bernstorff and found him sitting in his study with a very curious look, a kind of smile hovering over his face. Burr said to him, "Well, how do you feel?" Bernstorff answered: "I am worried. Just one thing is worrying me very much, and that is what my people will do with the little British Army they have just surrounded and captured; 100,000 prisoners will be a trouble and stuff up the roads during the advance on Paris."

Burr said: "You don't mean that the British Army has been surrounded?" and Bernstorff handed him his official despatch from Berlin announcing the fact. About three weeks later, Burr saw Bernstorff again and said to him: "Say, Bernstorff, are you still worrying about the little British Army?" He said Bernstorff did not like this chaff at all.

There was a long discussion as to why England went into the War,

[1] Count von Bernstorff: German Ambassador to U.S.A. until Germany entered the war.

79

and I listened with intense interest as to what Fleurien had to say about the Cabinet. He, of course, agreed with me that it was Haldane who was one of the very few who did wish for a declaration of War from the first, and that Lloyd George was dead against it. There was a discussion concerning Kuhlmann[1] and of how completely mistaken he had been, though honestly mistaken—largely owing to the fact that he saw the wrong kind of people and also sent home the news that he knew would be acceptable there.

As to the peace party in the Cabinet, so completely deceived were they by Germany up to the last minute, that they thought themselves quite safe in promising to go into War in the—as they thought—impossible event of Belgium being invaded. When the news came in that the Germans *had* crossed the frontier, some of them were so stupefied at the Cabinet meeting that they could not speak.

In the evening I saw Hilary. He said that the United States will do all in their power to maintain their neutrality, but he thinks that they will end by being driven into the War. On the other hand, he hopes the present situation will be prolonged because he believes it will be best for the Allies for America to be in a state of benevolent neutrality rather than at War. He is just off to see Haig[2] and to stay at French Headquarters. He is convinced that by April the submarine menace will be thoroughly in hand.

DIARY

March 5th, 1917

Lunched with the Ian Hamiltons. There was a great discussion concerning Winston Churchill. He is evidently coming back into public life. I said I hoped he would, I had always had a high opinion of him, but everyone else expressed fear lest this should happen. This from people who declared they were warmly attached to him.

Wickham Steed in a French review recounts several things that were till then quite unknown to me. One was that Winston's life was saved by Botha during the South African War. Almost any man would have had

[1] Baron von Kuhlmann: the most influential member of the staff of the German Embassy in London.
[2] Field Marshal Douglas Haig: 1861-1928. cr. 1st Earl Haig 1919. Commander-in-Chief of the British Forces in France 1915-18 then of the Home Forces until 1921.

him shot under similar circumstances. Botha freed him, owing to the fact that at that moment he was not fighting but was looking after the wounded, although he had on him a revolver.

When Winston was First Lord of the Admiralty, Botha did a cure in Germany. Coming back to England he met Winston and said to him: "You ought to be ready. The people with whom I have just been staying are very dangerous. They mean ill by you. They said things to me that they would not have said to any Englishman. Don't be taken by surprise. As for me, the moment I am home, I shall get ready to fight in German South-West."

In my opinion Winston Churchill is not only a great writer, but has a fine character; he inspires confidence by his honesty. He has made large sums of money by his writing, but in England it doesn't do a man good to have two professions, politics and literature. He has a childlike habit of boasting of the big sums he makes.

DIARY

March 9th, 1917

I have just heard a very interesting account of the return of the Danish Minister to England. Before being allowed to travel through Germany he had to get a special permit from the German Minister at Copenhagen. This man, an old friend of his, remarked: "I can give you a permit to go through Germany but you will never be able to get to England for our submarines completely block the Channel".

He had a terrible time going through Germany, there being no food either on the train or at the stations, no heating at all from lack of coal. In the station at Berlin his fur coat was stolen. He got no food in Berlin except what he managed to get at the Danish Legation. When the Duke of Mecklenburg Schwerein was asked by the King of Denmark what he would like for a Christmas present he said: "Any kind of food".

I met yesterday a British officer who had charge for a while of a young U-boat Commander—the one who sunk the seven Dutch ships. He was a pleasant youth of 22. He spoke admirable English and in the course of a long talk he observed: "The War will be over in August but you will not obtain a real victory. It will be a draw, for though we shall be finished by then, you will equally be finished, so it will be a contest of wits round the Conference table."

The Englishman answered very courteously: "I don't know about you, but I can assure you that we shall not be defeated by then." "Oh, yes, you will," replied the young German, "for by then our U-boats will have reduced you to starvation." He showed, however, considerable uneasiness when he saw the buffets at the stations where the train stopped.

DIARY

April 10th, 1917

There has been a spate of very early marriages and I heard of a lady who was asked if she was happy about her youthful son's marriage. She replied, "I don't know what I should feel if it were not wartime, for in that case he would still be at Harrow!"

DIARY

April 15th, 1917

I met General Sir John Cowans[1] at dinner at Lord Haldane's. He was said to be the best Quartermaster-General since Moses. We made friends, and he asked if he could come and see me. This astonished Elizabeth Haldane, who murmured, speaking with more truth than civility "I was told that he only cared for young women!" I whispered back, "Well, he apparently likes one of forty-nine!"

DIARY

September 21st, 1917

This summer Cowans would sometimes run in to see me at Barton Street for a few minutes: when I say "run" he was a big heavy man, who walked very quickly. As Quartermaster-General he helped in every conceivable way the fighting forces.

I only remember once seeing him upset, and he was rather hurt because I could not help smiling at his annoyance. Some amateur photographer in the ranks took a picture of a number of Tommies in France being warmly embraced by a set of pretty French girls. I thought they must belong to a concert party. By an unlucky chance the wives and sweethearts of these men saw the picture in a newspaper and apparently blamed Sir John Cowans for the over-affectionate demonstration.

There are all kinds of jingles going around. After Lloyd George took the reins, Margot Asquith was said to have written these lines apropos of the fact that he had created eighty-nine new Government posts.

[1] General Sir John Cowans: 1862-1921. Served in Egypt and India—Quartermaster-General 1910-19.

"Wait and see,
Said the twenty-three,
Give us time,
Say the eighty-nine!"

DIARY

October 10th, 1917

Philippe Millet[1] is the one of my French relatives to whom I am most attached and whom I regard as an exceptionally brilliant man. Last Spring he told me that Nivelle, of whom the British Cabinet expected great things, was in no sense a great commander. On the contrary, he was an excellent corps commander, but if given the kind of position he was given, he would sacrifice men recklessly. He had been confident that he would break through, but had attacked on too wide a front with insufficient artillery and thousands of men had been sacrificed. Philippe said he had heard that every officer's heart in the French Army had sunk when they heard that Nivelle had been given supreme command. Petain, he said, was far the better man, but had a disagreeable manner and was ill-tempered.

DIARY

November 30th, 1917

I am astonished at the sensation made by the "Lansdowne Letter"[2] in the *Daily Telegraph* yesterday. It is thought that Lord Lansdowne had written it some months ago and it had been a great deal rewritten before publication. It was true that he had first sent it to the *Times* and that he and the editor had corresponded about it. I noticed that most of those who approved of the gist of the letter regretted that it was published when it was, just as the Army had had a bad reverse. The letter filled the Germans with joy.

Someone told me with great bitterness that the writer was now called the "Marquis of Hands Up" and "Lords Lands-Us-Down". The story goes that someone rang up Lord Lansdowne and insisted on speaking to him. It was an old friend who said, "Are we Lansdowne-hearted?" He then added with a shout, "No!"

[1] Philippe Millet: elder son of René Millet and cousin of M. B. L.
[2] "Lansdowne Letter". This open letter from the 5th Marquess of Lansdowne (1845-1927) proposed a negotiated peace.

December 1st, 1917

Lunched at 20 Cavendish Square, the beautiful old house that had been bought for Margot by her father when she married. I had the good fortune to sit next to Mr Asquith and he showed me a paper sent him by the King concerning the record of his son's brilliant bravery. He told me the King is sent an account of the gallant deeds of every soldier who is to receive a decoration, and that he carefully reads every one.

I asked Mr Asquith what he thought of Lord Morley's book.[1] He replied that he had been delighted with the pen portrait of John Stuart Mill but in one sense it was a most untruthful book as it entirely concealed Morley's difficult character. He said Morley had always quarrelled even with his best friends and that his long life had been strewn with broken friendships.

Mr Asquith said that now and again, but very rarely, Morley made up a quarrel. After he had quarrelled with Meredith he found he could not live without him. We both laughed over Morley's acid account of Campbell Bannerman.[2] I suggested that Lady Campbell Bannerman must have been a very remarkable woman. Mr Asquith said she was the ugliest woman he had ever seen, but that she and Campbell Bannerman really cared for one another.

M. B. L. TO HER SON CHARLES[3]

9 Barton Street,
Westminster S.W.
August 27th 1918

We *long* to know how you are getting on. Louis Belloc[4] has just gone out. By the way I *have* just told Granny that you have moved to some

---

[1] Viscount Morley of Blackburn: 1838-1923. Statesman and man of Letters. *Recollections.* Pubs. 1917.

[2] Sir Henry Campbell Bannerman: 1836-1908. Liberal Prime Minister 1905-08. m. 1860 Sarah Charlotte, d. of Major-General Sir Charles Bruce.

[3] Charles Belloc Lowndes: 1898-1948. Served First War, M.C. Second War. m. 1925 Lily Pescatore, d. of Antoine Pescatore, Chargé d'Affaires of Luxembourg at the Court of St James.

[4] Louis Belloc, eldest son of Hilaire Belloc. He was actually killed on August 26th when his aeroplane was seen to go down near Cambrai. His father went on hoping he was a prisoner. After the war a memorial was put up to him in Arras Cathedral.

place where your Regiment is—so you can write how you like. Have you everything you want. How about soap and Keating's Powder?

I met Uncle H. today. He was wearing yellow spectacles—just like Sir Edward Grey—He does not think War likely to end before April or even *June*. A French Saint says it will end before Christmas.[1] Oh! how I wish it would, and that I could have you, my darling boy, home again.

[1] The saint was right.

CHAPTER V

1919-1926

During these years after the First War, Marie Belloc Lowndes wrote continuously. The Lonely House, From the Vasty Deep, What Timmy Did, Why They Married, The Terriford Mystery, *and* Bread of Deceit, *were all published between 1919 and 1925. She also wrote a number of short stories which appeared in the numerous monthly magazines—*The Strand, Pearson's, Woman, Good Housekeeping, *and others.*

England returned to normal life sooner than after the Second War, and literature rather than politics absorbed M. B. L.'s versatile mind. Many young writers found in her a stimulating and encouraging friend. F. S. A. Lowndes went back to The Times *where he was engaged in much more interesting work than hitherto.*

In 1919 their son Charles was sent to Archangel after serving in Dublin. In October 1925, he married Lily Pescatore, the daughter of old family friends.

The Irish troubles clouded all these years and Marie was brought into close touch with them through her friendship with Lady Lavery. The Northcliffes also became warm friends at this time and M. B. L. gives a lively account of a visit she paid to them in the South of France.

DIARY

February 12th, 1919

I was present at a very early committee when Miss Alice Warrender[1] was founding the Hawthornden Prize.[2] She and I were the only women present, but there were six or seven men, all of them distinguished writers. The first prize was given for a long poem by Edward Shanks,[3] called *The Queen of China.*

The question arose as to who should actually present the prize: every man present said that if Edmund Gosse were not chosen to do so he would most certainly do everything in his power to injure the Hawthornden. He was, therefore, approached, and willingly consented. One of the members of the Committee was Edward Marsh.[4]

[1] Miss Alice Warrender: sister of the Misses Margaret and Eleanor Warrender, daughters of 6th Baronet.

[2] Hawthornden Prize: a prize of £100 per annum to be awarded to a work of 'imaginative literature'.

[3] Edward Shanks: 1892-1953. Poet and writer.

[4] Edward Marsh: 1872-1953. Secretary to Winston Churchill. Editor of *Georgian Poetry* and noted art collector. See the admirable biography by Christopher Hassall. Pubs. 1959.

EDWARD MARSH TO M. B. L.

5 *Raymond Buildings,*
*Gray's Inn, W. C.*1
June 16th, 1919

My Dear Marie,

I got a letter from Squire[1] this morning—he hadn't seen the *Times* announcement, and said he thought it was high time to publish something—adding that a circular letter, differently worded from the *Times* thing, should be sent to the other papers. I am answering that I expect the others have copied the *Times* by now, and that I don't see what else there is to say at this stage—but I pass on his suggestion for your husband to consider, as I understand he is so good as to make the "press" part of his province.

Gosse asks for details of the programme. I am telling him that Hewlett has been asked to follow him, and that, so far as I know, we do not contemplate a Chairman as well—isn't it quite unnecessary to have one? I heard from Squire that Gosse would hate a Chairman who spoke for more than 3 or 4 minutes, and we could hardly ask anyone if we had to make such a stipulation! I have asked Gosse to please himself as to the length of his oration, provided it is not less than 20 minutes. Is that right?

Squire votes formally for Shanks' *Queen of China*, and so do I—and as Miss Warrender was prepared to agree, I imagine that is practically settled, as Binyon[2] can hardly start anything else now.

MEMORANDUM BY EDWARD MARSH

June 19th, 1919

The Hawthornden Prize, which Miss Alice Warrender is offering for the encouragement of young writers, is named in honour of her countryman, William Drummond of Hawthornden. In many respects it recalls the Polignac prize, which lapsed on the outbreak of War after having been awarded in successive years to Messrs John Masefield, Walter de la

[1] J. C. Squire: 1884-1958. Kt. 1933. Writer. Acting Editor *New Statesman* 1917-18. Editor *London Mercury* 1919-34. On the Hawthornden Prize Committee.

[2] Laurence Binyon: 1869-1943. C.H. 1932. Author and poet. Keeper of Oriental Prints and Drawings in the British Museum.

Mare, James Stephens[1] and Ralph Hodgson.[2] The present prize is also annual, and the amount, £100, is the same. Any work of imaginative literature, either in verse or in prose, will be eligible, provided it has been published in the twelve months previous to the award, and the author is under forty. The intention is to choose books which both show considerable achievement and give promise of still better work to come. The Committee of Selection will consist of the prizegiver herself, two poets, Mr Laurence Binyon and Mr J. C. Squire, who is also well-known as a parodist and an editor, and Mr Edward Marsh, who edits the anthologies of contemporary verse called *Georgian Poetry* and wrote the *Memoir of Rupert Brooke*.

The first presentation will be made on behalf of Miss Warrender by Mr Edmund Gosse, C.B., at 5 p.m. on Thursday July 10th at the Essex Hall, Essex St, Strand, when Mr Maurice Hewlett will also speak. Invitations will be issued, but will not be necessary for admission, and it is hoped that anyone who is interested will attend the ceremony.

The choice for this year has already been made, but will not be divulged till the presentation takes place.

NOTE

I am rather in favour of adding this. It will (1) choke off people from making suggestions, and (2) create an atmosphere of pleasing suspense.

DIARY

July 10th, 1919

The Hawthornden Prizegiving went off well. The hall was filled. Most of Gosse's speech, which was very amusing, consisted of explaining how almost without exception the great literary prizes awarded in the last fifty years by the French Academy had concerned prose books or poems of no real value, and destined to quick oblivion.

M. B. L. TO HER SON CHARLES

Cowden,
Dollar, N.B.
September 4th, 1919

My dearest Charles,

We had a most interesting time at Cloan as Lord Haldane got advance copies of the memoirs of Ludendorff, von Tirpitz and Bethmann von

---

[1] James Stephens: 1880-1950. Author and poet. Wrote *The Crock of Gold* 1912.   [2] Ralph Hodgson: Poet. Author of *The Bull*.

Hollweg. He read us some chapters—those which described his notorious visit to Berlin 1912. He is very happy, poor man, as they bear out his story of what happened and showed that he did not fall victim to their wiles. In fact, they all speak most bitterly of him, and consider that he was much too loyal to France, and to England's engagement to France.

The German Emperor lately described Lord Haldane as "that snake". There were also at Cloan, Professor Haldane[1] of Oxford and his son John who was wounded in Mesopotamia.

M. B. L. TO HER SON CHARLES

9 *Barton Street,*
Westminster
February 16th, 1920

I think it will interest you to hear that I had the great delight on Saturday of being asked to meet Marshal Foch. The person who kindly asked your father and me was an old lady, Lady DuCane. Her son is a general.[2]

I had a talk with Foch, who asked after Uncle Hilary. I thought he looked remarkably well as regards health—a relief to me as there were rumours that he was really ill.

Have you heard the absurd verse which I heard yesterday—

> A voice from the Colonies arrives—
> "Send wives!—send wives!"
> The whisper floats from homes' dear bowers,
> "Take ours!—take ours!"

FROM LADY BURGHCLERE TO M. B. L.

Cannes,
A.M. France
November 26th, 1919

Pétain has bought a small house on the hills by Cagnes, and means to farm. His stock will consist of 2 cows, 1 pig and several fowls. It is

---

[1] Professor John Haldane: 1860-1936. Younger brother of Viscount Haldane of Cloan. Scientist. His son, J. B. Haldane, became a famous biochemist.

[2] General Sir John DuCane. British Representative with Marshal Foch 1918.

rather like one of Plutarch's heroes, isn't it? It gave me pleasure to think of the victor of Verdun content to live a life of such frugality. There is very little frugality or austerity to be seen elsewhere in this district. The costumes would make Margot look quite frumpy.

EDWARD MARSH TO M. B. L.

5 *Raymond Buildings,*
Gray's Inn
March 2nd, 1921

Winston went off today on his way to Egypt, leaving me to what he called (to Ivor's[1] delight) "Keep the home fires burning". I shall be quite happy here, as there are heaps of first nights! but I should have liked to see Jerusalem, where he is also going.

I am nearly through Brett Young's new book *The Black Diamond,* which I think extremely fine, and easily so far my first favourite for Hawthornden. I only hope it won't get spoilt by the last 100 pages which I haven't read—his books have always come to a bad end hitherto. I'm also reading the proofs of de la Mare's Midget book, which is very curious and beautiful—but I haven't got far enough yet to have an opinion about it.

I haven't any commissions for Paris unless it were autographs of Anatole France and Marcel Proust!! My latest acquisitions are Conrad, Chesterton, and the President Elect.

I send you Ivor's love by anticipation, I will give him yours tomorrow when we are meeting at luncheon with Margot and going to the 1st night of Maugham's play which is said to be brilliant.

This isn't much of a *sac d'anecdotes*, but I've just thought of one. Anne Asquith dined lately at the Embassy[2] at the next table to the Lionel Tennysons'[3] who were *en tête à tête*. Their bill was £15, and Lionel suggested double or quits to the headwaiter Luigi, who closed with the suggestion. L. T. lost, so the dinner for 2 cost him £30.

[1] Ivor Novello: 1893-1951. Actor—wrote many popular songs including "Keep the home fires burning".

[2] Embassy Club in Bond Street.

[3] Lionel Tennyson: 1889-1951: Eldest son of 2nd Baron Tennyson whom he succeeded in 1928. m. 1918 Clare, only daughter of 1st Baron Glenconner.

MONTAGU PORCH[1] TO M. B. L.

St Cyprians House,
Coomassie
Gold Coast
December 10th, 1921

Dear Mrs Belloc Lowndes,

Please don't think too badly of me for not thanking you sooner for your very kind words of sympathy. I returned to London in August so dazed with grief and despair I was quite unable to see any of my friends or answer their letters. You will understand, I know.

I adored my wife—we were supremely happy and hoped for many happy years together. With Her all the joy has gone out of my life—my only happiness is now in memories. I often think of happy evenings at Westbourne Street when you came to help us with Her play.

Thank goodness I have work to turn to—I have nothing else to live for now. The business I established early in the year—London & Coomassie Trading Co. is doing very well.

I shall come back to London one day and will see you—I hope.

KATHERINE MANSFIELD[2] TO M. B. L.

Switzerland,
February 1922

I have such a romantic vision in my mind of your house in Barton Street. Thank Heaven for dreams. I have been there on a warm spring afternoon, and there has been a room with open windows where you have sat talking, wearing the same embroidered jacket . . . . Outside one was *conscious* of trees—of their green gold light . . . But it's all far away from my cursed Swiss balcony where I'm lying lapping up the yellows of eggs and taking my temperature in the eye of Solemn Immensities—mobled Kings.

Illness is a great deal more mysterious than doctors imagine. I simply can't afford to die with a very half-and-half little book and one bad one and a few stories to my name. In spite of everything, in spite of all one knows and has felt—one has this longing to *praise life*, to sing one's minute song of praise.

[1] Montagu Porch: 3rd husband of Lady Randolph Churchill who had died in June 1921.

[2] Katherine Mansfield: 1888-1923. m. 1913 Middleton Murry. Novelist and noted writer of short stories.

Will one ever be able to say how marvellously beautiful it all is? I long, above everything, to write about *family love*—the love between growing children—and the love of a mother for her son, and the father's feeling. But warm, vivid, intimate—not "made up", not self-conscious ... Goodbye, I hope you are happy—I hope you are well?

DIARY

March 22nd, 1922

Asquith and Margot gave their last dinner party at the Cavendish Square house on Friday. Margot wrote round to many old friends explaining that she could not have them to dinner as the table only held sixteen, and she had to have all the family and their wives, but imploring them (the old friends) to come in about 10 o'clock. They all turned up, several at some inconvenience to themselves, but found no sign of her at all—she was playing bridge in an inner chamber! At last, about a quarter to eleven Cis Asquith[1] went in and begged her to come along, which she reluctantly did.

She is a queer mixture of selfishness, and humility, for she said to Cis, "They are quite happy so long as they have you all to talk to!" And she seemed really to believe it. She is worried about her book, and apparently it is not now coming out until later.

They have not yet sold the house, for which they are asking £30,000 there being a ground rent of £400 a year. Their new home is a beautiful old house just opposite the George Protheros'. The dining room will only hold ten, and the house is on a tiny scale compared to the one they are leaving. I think she will feel Bedford Square a long way off, though people are moving to that district, the latest being Lady Diana Manners[2] (Cooper) who is just moving into Gower Street. She is becoming British editress of *Femina*, I should prefer, if I were she, doing anything else, as it is a most thankless and wearing job, starting a new paper—for that's what it comes to.

The King and Queen have been giving a series of small afternoon parties, which have aroused more criticism than pleasure. It has been quite impossible for them to ask a hundredth part of the people who think themselves entitled to such an invitation, so they have just picked

[1] Cyril Asquith: 4th son of H. H. Asquith by his first wife.
[2] Lady Diana Manners: youngest daughter of 8th Duke of Rutland. m. Alfred Duff Cooper 1919, cr. 1st Viscount Norwich 1952.

them as if out of a lucky bag—to the indignation of those left *in* the bag! Lloyd George has thrown in his lot definitely with the Conservatives, amid the jeers of everybody: in fact he now, as someone said to me bitterly the other day, "aspires to be head of the British Junker party!"

LADY LAVERY[1] TO M. B. L.

> *Westerdunes,*
> *North Berwick*
> *September 14th, 1922*

Darling Marie,

It was like you to write to me so sweetly. It has been terribly tragic, particularly as we were there at the time of both deaths!

Michael Collins I saw the very last hour when he started for Cork on that Sunday early morning. He came back two days later dead on the same ship which had carried him living and so vigorously confident in his "Star".

Some time I will tell you all about it. Never was there more strange and romantic and fatal a story. It could only take place in Ireland.

I have been very sick in soul and body since, but this sane, healthy, normal place and the great content of Alice[2] and John with this sporting life here makes me less miserable, and the soft, strong air is a great healer. I dread going back to London, but I look forward to seeing you in October.

We *may* go to America—much to my disgust—but John has hundreds of portraits offered and gold is much needed in the Lavery chests just now.

DIARY

> *March 9th, 1923*

I have had large sales in cheap editions. Thus *The Lodger* sold something like half a million at sixpence in the Reader's Library. My early books were all published in America, and years after *Barbara Rebell* had been brought out there by Scribner, Americans would speak to me with real affection for the book and tell me they constantly re-read it. I have

---

[1] Lady Lavery: died 1935. d. of Edward Jenner Martyn of Chicago. m. Sir John Lavery, painter. She was a noted beauty and was much loved by both men and women. Her profile was taken for the Colleen on the Irish Free State coins and banknotes.

[2] Alice Trudeau: Lady Lavery's daughter by her first marriage.

always believed that had I continued to write the kind of books that I began writing, and which I naturally preferred writing, I should probably have made, for me, a very much greater and better reputation than that which has fallen to my lot.

On the other hand the fact, of which I was long ignorant, that I possess hidden away what is called a "plot mind" became of very great importance to me as a writer. A plot mind, is curiously rare, and does secure for its owner a kind of immortality. By that I mean that long after the writer is dead, the books go on being reprinted. Wilkie Collins is an example of this. Another is Dumas *père* who in his day was regarded by the French critics very much as were in my day the author of *The Mystery of the Hansom Cab*, and so on.

The story of *The Lodger* is curious and may be worth putting down if only because it may encourage some fellow author long after I am dead. *The Lodger* was written by me as a short story after I heard a man telling a woman at a dinner party that his mother had had a butler and a cook who married and kept lodgers. They were convinced that Jack the Ripper[1] had spent a night under their roof. When W. L. Courtney, the then literary editor of *The Daily Telegraph*, in order to please a close friend of mine, commissioned a novel from me (I then never having written a novel for serial publication) I remembered *The Lodger*. I sent him the story and he agreed that it should be expanded. This was a piece of great good fortune for me, and would certainly not have been the case among any subsequent editors of my work.

As soon as the serial began appearing—It was I believe the first serial story published by *The Daily Telegraph*—I began receiving letters from all parts of the world, from people who kept lodgings or had kept lodgings. I also received two postcards of praise from two very different people, the one being Lord Russell[2] and my old friend Robert Sherard, who had writen interesting and revealing books concerning Oscar Wilde, including a severe and justified indictment of the *Life* by Frank Harris.

When *The Lodger* was published, I did not receive a single favourable review. When it came to sending a quotation for an advertisement for the American edition, I was not able to find even one sentence of tepid approval.

---

[1] Jack the Ripper: Notorious murderer of women of the street, in East London in the 1880's. It was never discovered who he was.

[2] Lord Russell: 2nd Earl. Elder brother of Bertrand Russell.

Then, to my surprise, when *The Lodger* had been out two or three years reviewers began to rebuke me for not writing another *Lodger*, and reviews of the type of 'Mrs Belloc Lowndes' new book is a disappointment' appeared.

At this time the young Ernest Hemingway[1] was in Paris and years later in A Moveable Feast[2] *he wrote that Gertrude Stein[3] had said to him:*

"If you don't want to read what is bad, and want to read something that will hold your interest and is marvellous in its own way, you should read Marie Belloc Lowndes. . . .

"Miss Stein loaned me *THE LODGER*, that marvellous story of Jack the Ripper, and another book about murder at a place outside Paris which could only be Enghien-les-Bains.[4] They were both splendid after-work books, the people credible and the action and the terror never false. They were perfect for reading after you had worked, and I read all the Mrs Belloc Lowndes that there was. But there was only so much and none as good as the first two and I never found anything as good for that empty time of day or night until the first fine Simenon[5] books came out."

DIARY

September 30th, 1923

I heard yesterday, that Lord Robert Cecil[6] went so much too far in his pronouncements on Italy that Baldwin[7] sent for him to Aix and gave him a very severe reprimand. My informant added that Baldwin, unlike Lloyd George, is always ready to say exactly what he thinks to any Member of the Cabinet, but that he always so far studies their feelings as to do it in private, his motto being "No caning in public".

[1] Ernest Hemingway: 1899-1961. U.S. novelist.
[2] *A Moveable Feast*: Pubs. 1964.
[3] Gertrude Stein: 1874-1946. American writer and art collector who entertained contemporary authors and painters in her Paris house throughout the twenties and thirties.
[4] This refers to *The Chink in the Armour*.
[5] Simenon: Creator of Inspector Maigret.
[6] Lord Robert Cecil: 1864-1958. 3rd son of 3rd Marquis of Salisbury. Cr. 1st Viscount of Chelwood 1923. Lord Privy Seal 1923-24.
[7] Stanley Baldwin: 1867-1947. Prime Minister 1923 and First Lord of the Treasury 1923-24.

I was also given an amusing account of the book which E. V. Lucas[1] is going to do on the Queen's Doll's House[2]. It is written very wittily and makes an allusion to each of the little books. He says in his contribution that no doll is ever found on a dust-heap, that no doll is ever thrown away. It was wondered if the Queen would like the last words of E. V.'s tiny book, which run as follows: "When a good doll dies it goes to Windsor".

I had a most curious talk with Dennis Eadie.[3] He said that public taste altered as to plays ever few years; that he has lately read Harwood's[4] last play and that it had become old-fashioned. We agreed that trying to be clever is a fatal flaw in some modern dramatists. They all try to imitate Bernard Shaw. He said he had just been shown a play by Barker[5] and that he had not been able to make head or tail of it. He spoke with great dislike of Arnold Bennett: said he had "gone off", declared that in his opinion no manager would ever produce Bennett's *Don Juan* which has just appeared in a limited edition.

M. B. L. TO MISS ELIZABETH HALDANE

9 *Barton Street,*
Westminster S.W.
February 1st, 1924

Dearest E.,

Now with regard to G. E.[6] I do not myself in the least believe she had a child, and *if* she had it was certainly not by Chapman.[7] But I am bound

[1] Edward Verrall Lucas: 1868-1938. Writer and essayist.

[2] The Queen's Doll's House was a present to Queen Mary and was shown for various charities. It is now at Windsor Castle and can be seen by the public. It was designed by Sir Edwin Lutyens and all the furniture and fittings were made by noted craftsmen. M. B. L. wrote a short story for the library of the Doll's House, as did other well-known writers of that time. Each story was especially written by a calligraphic expert on tiny sheets of paper which were then beautifully bound in leather.

[3] Dennis Eadie: 1875-1928. Actor-manager. Managed Royalty Theatre with J. E. Vedrenne for many years. Played in *Milestones* 1912.

[4] H. M. Harwood: d. 1959. Manager of Ambassadors Theatre. Playright. m. F. Tennyson Jesse, novelist and special correspondent during the First War.

[5] Harley Granville-Barker: 1877-1946. Playright. Author of *The Voysey Inheritance* 1905.

[6] George Eliot: whose life Miss Haldane was writing.

[7] John Chapman: 1821-1894. Noted Victorian publisher.

to say that I know my mother has always held the secret view that she had a passionate, illicit love affair before she ever came to London, with that very attractive man, I think a Doctor Something, with whom and with whose wife she was intimate as a girl. I am quite sure that if she *had* had a child she would have told my mother and Madame Bodichon. They were her beloved, intimate friends, whom she told of her intended union with Lewes. She asked my mother to walk round Hyde Park with her, and in the course of that walk she told her what she meant to do. My mother reminded her that she, Marian, had not liked Lewes at all when she had first met him, and she told her the infinitely more serious fact that Mrs Gaskell knew a girl whom he had seduced, but that made no difference. She had quite made up her mind.

I lately was lent a most interesting collection of unpublished letters written by Chapman to the woman he really loved during those years when they were all mixed up together. There are practically no allusions of any interest to G. E. Not only had he a wife, whom he liked on and off, but he was having a passionate love affair with another woman, who was really attractive, and who adored him.

For one thing, G. E. left a good deal of money, and she left it all, I believe, to Lewes's children; certainly not to any mysterious individual who might have been her child.

The longer I live the more I feel how little one really knows of one's friends' lives, especially in that all-important matter of sex, and if that is true now, when people are so unconventional and speak so freely to those they care for, think what it must have been in a day when reticence was the absolute rule.

DIARY

January 10th, 1925

Much is left out that should have been put into official biographies, the biographer feeling he must keep a nervous eye cocked on certain members of the family of the man whose life he is writing. I have always felt exceedingly sorry that no official biography of Lord Northcliffe[1] has yet been written by some intelligent and honest man who knew him, and who would have been able to describe both his extraordinary character and astonishing career from an objective point of view.

[1] Lord Northcliffe: 1865-1922. Newspaper owner. Founder of the *Daily Mail*. Reginald Pound wrote a biography of him many years later.

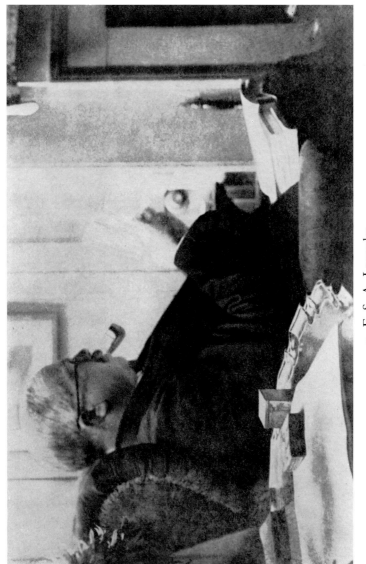

2. F. S. A. Lowndes

3b. His mother, Madame Belloc

3a. Hilaire Belloc by Daphne Pollen
by courtesy of the National Portrait Gallery

My first meeting with Alfred Harmsworth as he then was, took place not long after I had settled down to work in London.

We met in Oxford, where at the time Sir Alfred Harmsworth and his beautiful young wife were spending a few days. We all three lunched with Mrs Baird, whose daughter Dolly[1] was about to make her amazing success as *Trilby* in the play taken from du Maurier's book. I vividly remember that first meeting, tho' something over twenty years went by before I came to know in a real sense the man who had by then become Lord Northcliffe. Even then, our friendship was owing to the fact that Lady Northcliffe[2], hearing from a mutual friend that I was very tired and required a holiday, suggested that I should stay with them in the South of France at the villa they had taken for some weeks close to Monte Carlo.

That journey to France remains very present in my memory. I had been countless times in my life to France and several times to the Riviera, but this expedition was quite unlike any other I had ever taken. From the moment I reached Victoria station I felt I was being treated like a Royal personage, but with none of the disadvantages which must attend the journeys of Royal personages. Every conceivable arrangement had been made for my comfort and convenience by my future hosts, and I particularly remember my pleasure at seeing that placed on the seat next to me in the reserved carriage in which I travelled, was a copy of every paper published that morning in London. I was also handed a most kindly worded note from Lord Northcliffe. It is before me now, and concludes: "I have now to answer two thousand letters, telegrams and cables from all over the world. But I wish to tell you that your letter gave me much pleasure, and I look forward to your visit to Roquebrune".

At that time, and indeed till his death, Northcliffe was regarded with affection and gratitude by the French people and no country ever had a better friend. So my journey was something of a triumphal progress.

I had been sent from Paris by the famous Blue Train and I found the whole party, which included, in addition to my host and hostess, the well-known surgeon Sir Frederick Treves[3] about to start on a picnic.

[1] Dolly Baird: Created title role in *Trilby* in 1895. m. H. B. Irving, the actor-manager, in the following year.

[2] Lady Northcliffe: d. of Robert Milner of Kidlington and St Vincent, West Indies. m. Alfred Harmsworth, later Viscount Northcliffe, in 1888.

[3] Sir Frederick Treves: 1853-1923. Eminent anatomist and surgeon at the London Hospital. Operated on King Edward VII for appendicitis 1902.

There was some discussion as to whether I was to accompany the party to the picnic or to stay at home and rest. Lady Northcliffe suggested I should stay quiet after the long journey, but her husband was determined I should accompany the party, and I did so.

During the simple picnic lunch which took place in a lovely grove of olive trees on the side of a hill near Mentone, Sir Frederick Treves observed that all men and women who had to do much brainwork ought to take a small daily dose of bromide. After we had finished luncheon, Lord Northcliffe decreed that the whole party should drive into the town of Mentone in order to visit every chemist's shop and buy up their stock of bromide. Although I did not tell him so, I had a preparation of bromide with me, for I had taken it for many years.

What I most enjoyed during this visit were my drives with my host to Monte Ajel. There, while he played golf on what I consider is one of the most beautifully situated golf courses in the world, I wrote either letters or articles in the club house. This pleased him, as he disliked to see anyone idle.

One of the things that then struck me concerning Lord Northcliffe was his insatiable interest concerning the nature and character and the way of life of everyone with whom he was brought in contact. I suppose he was used to being told what the person who talked to him thought he would like to hear.

At that time, when I had wakened, I always began writing after I had made myself a cup of tea, and lifted the light cardboard desk I always had with me on to my bed. Then and for a long time after, whenever I was engaged in writing a novel, I would start as early as five o'clock in the morning.

On the first evening, Lord Northcliffe had cross-examined me as to my methods of work, and I had naturally told him the simple truth. However, he evidently doubted what I had said, for I was amazed the next morning, between five and six to hear a stifled knock and to see my bedroom door slowly open and my host look in, and when he saw that I was sitting up writing, he darted across to the wash-hand stand. There, in a serried row were the medicine bottles I took about with me, and as I was expecting to stay in France a month, there were naturally a good many. Lord Northcliffe was profoundly shocked at the sight, and told me triumphantly that neither he nor his wife ever took any form of drug, forgetting the bromide advised by Sir Frederick Treves. He was also distressed at what he regarded as my overweight. He told me that he and his wife weighed each other constantly.

During that strange visit, I formed the impression that I must be one of the very few human beings who ever stood up to my host. I only once saw what may be called the ugly side of his character, and it occurred during this visit to Roquebrune. Some change was being made in the typography of the *Times*. A matter of great interest to myself and my husband, and in one of his daily letters—for we wrote to each other every day when we were apart—he had spoken of it and told me of the change that was going to be made. At that time, Lord Northcliffe was intensely interested in everything that concerned the *Times* and when we were alone together he talked of nothing else. I observed just before we went into dinner that that date would be marked with a white stone in the history of the *Times* as this change of type was going to take place. Lord Northcliffe turned on me furiously and said that it was monstrous indeed that one of his guests, and a woman, too, should have given away a secret that had been guarded with such jealous care. Lady Northcliffe tried to calm him, and at last she succeeded. Before we went to bed, he apologised to me for the way he had spoken, while repeating what a terrible thing I had done, and how deeply I had wounded him.

Both his conduct and his words were the more surprising to me in that, apart from him and myself, no one in the party took the slightest interest in this question.

Perhaps what most impressed me during my long talks with this extraordinary man during our drives to Mont Ajel, was how completely he was absorbed, not only in his own newspapers, but in all the leading newspapers of the world. Thus he told me curious facts concerning the great French newspapers, and I was astonished to learn from him that *Le Petit Parisien* had in France a larger circulation than the *Daily Mail*. In fact, I wonder to this day whether that could have been true.

He also told me something else which, though I am sure he believed in himself, I still wonder whether that too was the truth. This was, that in every capital in the world, he had a number of agents who told him everything that was going on there. These, as he was careful to inform me, were not the correspondents of his newspapers. They were private individuals with whom he had come into contact by chance. One such, a lady who lived in Paris, he said he would introduce to me, and I have always regretted that I did not remind him of this promise, for I should have been curious to make her acquaintance.

October 12th, 1925

A very small gathering at the Thirty. There was an interesting account by Lady Clifford[1] of her life in Ceylon. When she went round all the public institutions of the town it was arranged, without her being told, that the asylums should be left out and the lunatics wrote her a very touching letter which was far more sensibly worded than some of those she received from other institutions. She therefore went to see them and though she thought it would be very painful she found it less painful than visiting an European asylum, for the natives, when taken with melancholia, behave exactly as they do at normal times, that is, sit and stare at the ground.

M. B. L. TO HER DAUGHTER ELIZABETH

The Wharf,
Sutton Courteney
August 21st, 1926

We are going to Stanway for lunch. A great pleasure for me. Barrie[2] takes it, as I think you know, each August and with Cynthia Asquith[3] as hostess, entertains there. *Nine* are going from here I believe. I am having my luggage with me as I fancy Margot wants me to avoid Lord Reading who is arriving for the weekend today. Puffin[4] must have sung your praises very vigorously as last night Elizabeth Bibesco expressed an eager wish to know you.

I like Puffin more and more but I don't think he is really happy. His sister is radiant. How strange with her only child so far from well. I look at her in amazement. When I remember how unhappy she was as a girl, how wretched I've seen her look in this very house and how completely

[1] Lady Clifford: wife of Sir Hugh Clifford G.B.E., Governor of Ceylon 1925-27. Novelist and dramatist. Wrote as Mrs de la Pasture. Mother of E. M. Delafield, the novelist.

[2] J. M. Barrie: O.M. 1860-1937. Playright and novelist.

[3] Lady Cynthia Asquith: Author. d. of 11th Earl of Wemyss and March. m. 1910 Hon. Herbert Asquith, 2nd s. of 1st Earl of Oxford and Asquith. Her *Diaries* appeared in 1968.

[4] Hon. Anthony Asquith: 1902-1969. Film producer. Only son of Earl of Oxford and Asquith by his second wife, Margot Tennant.

happy she looks now, I am astounded at the strangeness of human nature. She is bringing out a volume of verse and a short novel later on.

The kind of brilliance, utter lack of morality and easy-goingness of the Asquith family as a whole, spoils the men who frequent this circle for any other kind of life. Everything seems "flat" and "stupid" after the Asquiths, They have one horror, i.e. "a bore".

As to "first love", "last love", it seems to me to depend entirely upon the enduring quality of the love. I suppose I was your father's "first love" and I hope to be his "last love". I think, with the exceptions that prove the rule, that any good-tempered, intelligent woman can keep any man who has once loved her, I mean "fallen in love" with her, once they are married. Man and woman—as to sex—are quite different, it is bosh to say they are not.

CHAPTER VI

1927-1930

This period of M. B. L.'s life was so filled with the writing of her books, that after the year 1928, with its vivid political sidelights, there comes a long gap before she resumed her Diaries. In 1930, Elizabeth, the elder daughter of Mrs Belloc Lowndes and F. S. A. Lowndes, married the 3rd Earl of Iddesleigh, and they settled in Romney Street, Westminster, not far from Barton Street.

M. B. L. TO MISS ELIZABETH HALDANE

Trent,
New Barnet
December 29th, 1927

The great excitement here is the engagement of Evan Morgan and Lois Sturt—I am very glad. I think Magdalens often make excellent wives. They are *known* to do so in the humbler world. I have known several. This is a delightful house to stay in. Philip Sassoon is such a very *kind* creature—People come and go to meals, Eshers, Lee of Farnham, and so on, in spite of really dangerous snow. One man yesterday took 3 hours coming 20 miles.

A big party will spend New Year's Day, arriving tomorrow, and including Hugh Cecil and I suppose the Winstons. A good deal of talk about the Prayer Book. I think there is *no doubt* that the country, as a whole, is *passionately* against it. Philip had 100 letters against it, from his Constituents, to 1 for it! He did not vote, belonging to the Jewish faith, but he came into my bedroom and *talked* about it for an hour yesterday! I go back Monday. Freddie and I spent a Darby and Joan Christmas, then I came here 26th.

The girls are having a marvellous time[1] and will, I suppose, be back by Jan. 10th or so—as their money is running out. I do miss them very much—But I am thankful they are not coming back in these awful gales.

I am working hard at my new *Daily Mail* serial,[2] which to my grief will be started before it is finished—a very nerve-wracking thing to me. But I get my quiet hours of work here—while my fellow guests play Ping-Pong, Bridge and Tennis (covered court, of course).

I feel sorry, very sorry, for poor Sir Edmund Gosse. I fear he is very ill. But oh! I saw him rebuking a poor girl for calling him *Mr* Gosse— He said "You are making a mistake, I am not Mr Gosse". She was very upset—thinking she had spoken to the wrong person.

---

[1] M. B. L.'s daughters were in Rome.   [2] *The Story of Ivy.* Pubs. 1928.

February 20th, 1928

Lord Oxford's death recalls to me my last stay at the Wharf, when I had several long and interesting talks with him.

Haldane was undoubtedly Asquith's most intimate man friend. He had many close women friends, but I never heard him speak of any other man as being really close to him and this, to me, made their final break the more melancholy.

They became friends at the time when R. B. as many people called him, had already become a popular figure in London society, and I believe that he first met Margot Tennant through Haldane.

I have always felt an interest in Haldane's strange and sad love-affair. Owing to his political and personal intimacy with the then Ronald Munro-Ferguson,[1] he saw a good deal of the latter's sister Val. She kept house for her brother in London and was known to a large circle as an exceptionally brilliant and clever young woman. Haldane, so his mother told me, loved her from their first meeting. He asked her many times to marry him, but she was exceedingly happy in the life she was then leading, and she always refused him. But they did become close friends; when her brother married Lady Helen Blackwood[2] both he and his wife begged her to remain with them. She did so, but found after a while the plan did not work smoothly and the next time that Haldane asked her to marry him, she said yes.

At the time, Haldane was making a very large income at the Bar. He also had inherited money from his father. Long afterwards, Val's mother told me that she had been astonished at the amount of the settlement he was prepared to make on his wife. All went well, and I have read a letter written by Val Munro-Ferguson to Richard's mother. In it were the following sentences: "We have been to see a house in Charles Street which we think will suit us. There is a pleasant room which we hope will be yours when you give us the pleasure of staying with us in London".

Within a few days, the writer of this letter sent a short note to Richard Haldane, breaking off their engagement. His sister happened to be in London at the time. I was walking across Parliament Square and I met

---

[1] Ronald Munro-Ferguson: 1860-1934. Created Viscount Novar 1920 at the close of his Governor-Generalship of Australia.

[2] Lady Helen Blackwood: d. of 1st Marquess of Dufferin and Ava.

them both. I vividly remember the strange look on his face, and its pallor. He was always pale, but on that day he looked as if he were a dead man. He went on into the House of Commons, and his sister Elizabeth, drew me aside and told me that his engagement had been broken off.

Miss Munro-Ferguson entirely refused to see him alone as he begged her to do, but they met once in the presence of her sister-in-law, Lady Helen. Val handed him the jewels he had given her, as well as her engagement ring. His hands were trembling, and he dropped everything: they all went down on their hands and knees to find the jewels, especially the ring, which had rolled right away. But this did not ease the tension, till Val burst into tears and turned her head away. In answer to his questions, she simply shook her head. That was the last time they met till some years after when they happened to be together on a public platform in Scotland.

The break created an extraordinary sensation, both in Society and in the political world. I asked Lord Oxford as to whether he had any theory. He told me that he believed there must have been some secret reason quite unconnected with Haldane for Miss Munro-Ferguson's strange and cruel action. He had seen them together many times, and felt certain she had become exceedingly fond of Haldane. He told me of a small dinner given by Haldane to four friends, his future wife being the only woman there. She sat next to Henry Asquith (as he then was) and talked with eager amusement and interest of the domestic and household side of married life. He particularly remembered a discussion they had as to the number of knives and forks required in such a household as theirs was going to be. She also spoke of their honeymoon and said she was looking forward to the quietitude and peace they would both enjoy and she mentioned the books she meant to read aloud to her husband.

On one occasion at The Wharf, Margot poured out a stream of recollections, opinions, likes and dislikes about Curzon,[1] to Sir Horace Rumbold[2] and myself. She said that Curzon as a young man, was extraordinarily self-confident. This even when he was a boy at Eton, where

[1] Marquess Curzon of Kedleston: 1859-1925, cr. 1921. Viceroy of India. 1898-1904 and 1904-05. Secretary of State for Foreign Affairs 1919-24.
[2] Rt. Hon. Sir Horace Rumbold: 1869-1941. 9th Bart. Diplomat, British Ambassador at Berlin 1928-33. Signed the Lausanne Treaty on behalf of the British Empire 1923.

Asquith examined him, and was more struck by his self-confidence than anything else.

When grown up he became very popular at Glen. He was even then extremely careful with regard to money and on one occasion Sir Charles Tennant[1] paid for him to go and have a cure in Switzerland. One day when Curzon was in Central Asia, he telegraphed to Margot, "Please call on Mrs Leiter[2] and her daughters at Douglas's Hotel. Make them known to all your nicest friends. They are very great friends of mine."

After driving with her father to the City, Margot went off to the hotel, and was struck dumb by the great beauty of Mary Leiter, then eighteen and wearing at that first meeting, a black lace frock with a large picture hat trimmed with roses. There was a great ball being given that night by the Duchess of Devonshire. Margot so arranged it, that Mary Leiter should go with her. She made a prodigious sensation and Margot introduced her to "all the nice people" she knew.

The Leiters were at Glen when George Curzon telegraphed to Mary proposing marriage. She accepted him at once. According to Margot, this marriage had a very bad effect on his character, as his Mary was even more worldly than he was. He was a good husband to both his wives, tho' the only woman who ever really loved him was Pearl Mary Craigie[3] and it was widely rumoured that she would have married him had he asked her to do so when he was a widower. I do not believe this as she was a devout Roman Catholic and her husband was still alive.

As to the Indian quarrel with Kitchener, Margot said that Curzon was passionately devoted from boyhood to St John Brodrick, Lord Midleton.[4] He was his greatest friend and they wrote to each other once a week. He broke with Brodrick over India and used to cut him dead at dinner parties and when they met by chance; and that though the man was trustee to his marriage settlement.

With regard to Indian matters, the mistake, according to the Asquiths, was Curzon being given a second term of office as Viceroy. The first

[1] Sir Charles Tennant: 1823-1906. 1st Bart. Father of Margot Oxford. Glen was their country house in Peeblesshire.

[2] Mrs Leiter: wife of Levi Zeigler Leiter of Washington D.C., U.S.A. Their three daughters married Lord Curzon, the 19th Earl of Suffolk and Berkshire and Col. Colin Campbell of the Central India Horse.

[3] Pearl Mary Craigie: 1867-1906. American novelist. Wrote under pen-name of John Oliver Hobbes.

[4] Lord Midleton: 1856-1942. 1st Earl. Secretary of State for War 1900-03. Secretary of State for India 1903-05.

thing he said when he came back and met Margot was, "Are you a Curzonite or a Midletonite?" She answered at once, "I am a Midletonite", which upset him very much, but he never actually quarrelled with her.

His second wife, as Mrs Duggan[1] came to The Wharf to ask Asquith's advice as to whether she should marry Curzon. Asquith advised against it, but within a month they were engaged. The bitterest disappointment of his life was not having a son.

We all agreed that Lord Ronaldshay[2] is a very odd choice to make for Curzon's biographer. Apparently Curzon left word that all his early letters to Margot were to be printed in his *Life*. She naturally refused to give them up.

Both Margot and later, Lord Oxford agreed that one of Curzon's most unfortunate peculiarities was his rudeness to those whom he considered his social inferiors. Margot also said that he need not have died when he did, but he was insolent to his doctors and refused to follow their advice.

Apparently at the Foreign Office, only Nicolson[3] got on with him. Lord Oxford said that when the Labour Government came in, all the Foreign Office people said, "What a comfort it is to have to deal again with a gentleman," meaning Ramsay MacDonald[4].

What struck me most during this last visit was the extraordinary brilliance of Asquith's intellect. It formed a sad contrast to his physical state, although he was walking about without the aid of a stick. His memory could only be described as prodigious, and he had every sort of out of the way knowledge concerning political, social and religious history. I felt he did not like, or really understand either America or the Americans. In fact he was extremely insular from every point of view.

He always accepts and repeats without question, anything which is disparaging either to France or Italy. He has a slight bias towards Germany because of Margot and Elizabeth Bibesco's curious affection for anything German, an affection and admiration the more odd, because they really, one feels, know nothing about the country. One may almost say that both mother and daughter adore Germany because

---

[1] Mrs Duggan: d. of J. Munroe Hinds of Alabama, U.S.A. and widow of Alfred Duggan of Buenos Aires, m. Lord Curzon 1917.

[2] Lord Ronaldshay: eldest son of 1st Marquess of Zetland.

[3] Hon. Harold Nicolson. Wrote of Lord Curzon in *Some People* 1927.

[4] Ramsay MacDonald: 1866-1937. M.P. Prime Minister, First Lord of the Treasury and Secretary of State for Foreign Affairs, Jan-Nov. 1924.

of the German governess who was so long with them, and who is supposed to have saved Elizabeth's life when she was terribly ill many years ago in Switzerland, and who stayed with them for a considerable time after the War started.

In fact, as Lord Grey told me himself, it fell to him to tell the woman that, under all the circumstances, it was not fitting that she should go on belonging to the household of the then Prime Minister of England. At one moment, Margot said bitterly to me, "It didn't matter what I did during the War, because everybody believed that I was a spy". She explained she had written a letter to the *Times* at the moment of the Leverton Harris[1] row, and that when Leverton Harris was dying, he remembered this letter and instructed his wife to send her two beautiful pieces of china in memory of the help she had given them.

Margot was working at her novel.[2] She told me that she had had an offer of ten thousand pounds from Ernest Hodder Williams, who was willing to buy the book blind. What she ought to do is to have it looked over by someone who could advise her how to make the book into a novel. It is now like a section of her Memoirs told over again, and not told so well.

I was moved by a quotation that Lord Oxford wrote out for me. I believe it was written by his daughter, Violet.

"Life is so short and death so certain, and when death comes, the silence and separation are so complete, that one can never make too much of the ties and affections and relationships which bind us to the living." V.

Marie Belloc Lowndes was intensely interested in the Dilke case. She wrote the following account of a conversation she had had concerning this mystery.

When staying at Cloan with the Haldanes I received from my friend Mrs St John Hankin a pamphlet setting forth the complete innocence of Sir Charles Dilke. It consisted of what was described as a verbatim report of certain passages in the case, and showed that Mrs Crawford[3] was undoubtedly a most untruthful woman.

[1] Mrs Leverton Harris: sent parcels to German prisoners-of-war in England and was much censured for doing so.

[2] This was *Octavia*. Pubs. 1928.

[3] Mrs Nia Crawford: was respondent in the divorce case brought by her husband citing Sir Charles Dilke, which resulted in his parliamentary eclipse.

Reading this pamphlet shook me very much, and one day when I was alone with Haldane and Asquith (he and Margot being in the party) I said I would like to ask them a question.

I then produced the Dilke pamphlet and said that I wished to know their opinion—did they think there was any possibility he could have been innocent, because if so, how terrible to think his career should have been ruined by the machinations of a remarkably wicked woman. They both at once assured me that they had not the slightest doubt of his guilt. Mr Asquith said, "I am going to telegraph to London for something that I think will make an impression on you".

Two days later he showed me a verbatim account of the case. He then asked to see my pamphlet and he showed me that everything that could be said against Dilke had been left out of the passages and, moreover, certain things had been added which made for his innocence, or perhaps more for Nia Crawford's extreme unreliability.

Sir Charles and Lady Dilke had a delightful house on the Thames, and there entertained a great many of the younger M.P.'s. Dilke was always listened to with attention and sympathy in the House. His industry was prodigious and he had a wonderful knowledge of Britain's Colonial Empire, and everything connected with it. One of the few persons in society who never gave him up was Lady St Helier.[1] She and her husband—the latter the President of the Divorce Court—evidently believed him to be innocent. But even she never asked him to anything but a select little gathering consisting mostly of men.

Another well-known person who believed he was innocent was Mr Labouchère,[2] as at the time of the trial it had been rumoured that Dilke had had affairs with various members of Nia's family, and as he had admitted under cross-examination that he had been the lover of her mother many years before, Labouchere singularly observed: "I have no doubt that the wolf got into the fold, but I feel convinced he didn't get hold of this little lamb!"

There is no doubt that at the trial there was a good deal of extremely hard swearing on all sides—probably more on the part of certain witnesses who appeared against Sir Charles Dilke than those who appeared on his side. Everything on earth was done by him and his advisers to

---

[1] Lady St Helier: d. of Keith William Stewart-Mackenzie of Seaforth, m. 1881 the 1st Baron St Helier. President of Probate, Divorce and Admiralty Division of the High Court.

[2] Henry Labouchère: 1831-1912. M.P. Founder and Editor of *Truth*.

discredit Mrs Crawford. I feel certain that some day if a great novelist of the stature of Thackeray got hold of the story, a very wonderful novel might be made out of it, or a play.[1]

DIARY

March 17*th,* 1928

I saw Edmund Gosse and he recalled to me that in his early youth he had read my mother's narrative poem *Gabriel* written in honour of Shelley. He then wrote to Mrs Besant a letter about the poem which touched my mother when Mrs Besant sent it to her.

EDMUND GOSSE TO MRS BESANT

29 *Delamere Terrace,*
Westbourne Square W.
July 17*th,* 1894

Was the lady whom I met in your drawing-room Madame Belloc, who used to be Bessie Parkes? If not, please just tear this up. But if it was, do tell her from me that her *Gabriel* has always been a delight to me, and that ever since I was a schoolboy I have known and loved her lyric about Robin Hood—

"And ever to poets who walk in the gloaming
"His horn is still heard in the prime of the year", etc.

You see I remember the lines still.

It is very touching to meet in the flesh the people one used to wonder about when one was in one's teens. I used to write vile poetry in imitation of Bessie Parkes!

M. B. L. TO HER DAUGHTER ELIZABETH

9 *Barton Street,*
Westminster S.W.
June 10*th,* 1928

I had a most interesting talk with Mrs Hardy.[2] She was 40 years younger than T. H. Her account of the *tortures* she has gone through

---

[1] A novel was based on the case, *The Tangled Web,* by Betty Askwith, who has also written *Lady Dilke, A Biography.* A play on the case was produced in London.

[2] Mrs Thomas Hardy: b. Florence Emily Dugdale. m. 1914 as his second wife Thomas Hardy O.M., who had died on January 11th of this year.

4a. Charles

4b. Susan

4c. Elizabeth

4d. Sister John Mary,
M. B. L.'s eldest
grandchild

5b. Margot Asquith
dressed as an Indian rajah

5a. Lord and Lady Northcliffe
by courtesy of Sir Geoffrey Harmsworth, Bt., F.S.A.

and is going through, from the Inland Revenue authorities made me—literally—quiver with horror. They valued a deal writing table which had cost 30/- at £130 because T. H. had written *The Dynasts* at it. They took his 3 only good years and multiplied them by 7 hence the £90,000. She had to pay, as a *first* cheque, £18,000 *at once*. Had the money not been there they would have forced a sale of some of his copyrights. She is coming to London for a bit, is very forlorn. I said I hoped she would come to supper with us.

MRS THOMAS HARDY TO M. B. L.

Max Gate,
Dorchester
September 8th, 1928

I am so pleased that you think my husband's work is appreciated by young writers, for that means so much. T. E. Lawrence suggested that I should let Max Gate to some broken-down poet. But it really seems a part of my husband. His cat is lying within a few inches of my pen as I write, as he always does. In some ways it seems my duty to remain here and cherish everything that belonged to him.

DIARY

October 21st, 1928

I was delighted to receive among my Press Cuttings this poem from a woman's magazine.

Facts about Fiction

("Love stories are popular because most people have been in love, or would like to have been in love, or will be in love."

—Mrs Belloc Lowndes).

You throngs who lap up serials
In which the Sheik abounds,
Your secret is revealed my gals,
By Mrs Belloc Lowndes.
You'll *be* in love, you'll *be* in love,
You long to be that She, in love,
With whom in fiction you adore
Some swarthy brute wipes up the floor
On insufficient grounds.

But why—the question just occurs—
Still more than Love in books
Do you like tales of Murderers,
And Torturers and Crooks?
Are *you* a Crook? Were *you* a Crook?
Or will you be, '*mong us*, a Crook?
If Mrs Lowndes has found the crux,
Why then, my Wallace[1]-loving ducks,
It's time we took our hooks!

TOMFOOL.

MRS HAMLYN[2] TO M. B. L.

28 Sussex Square,
London W.2
March 21st, 1930

My dear Mrs Lowndes,
I am simply furious at hearing from quite a roundabout source that one of your girls is engaged to Lord Iddesleigh. I don't even know whether it is Susan or Elizabeth. To think I heard this great and exciting news not from the Lowndes family, but through a Northcote relation. It is really a *delightful* marriage—as though I have not seen the present Iddesleigh since he was a little boy at Clovelly—running about with long fair curls, still I have heard from many of his relations how clever and nice he is and I have never yet seen a Northcote that was not a Dear. His grandparents were my Mother's great friends—and were so good to us when we were left orphans before we grew up. I feel whichever it is, Susan or Elizabeth that they almost belong to Devonshire already. Lady Margaret Shelley, his Aunt, and my oldest and most faithful friend, is coming to luncheon here next Thursday 27th at 1.30. Do tell the Bride elect that I beg her to come that day too—and to bring Lord Iddesleigh with her if he is about.
I shall only be here till April 7th. Dear Mrs Lowndes. You and her

---

[1] Edgar Wallace: 1875-1932. Author of a vast number of thrillers including *Sanders of the River, The Ringer, The Terror* and several successful plays.
[2] Mrs Hamlyn: the well-known owner of Clovelly, the unique village in North Devon.

Father will I know, be sad at parting with one of the precious girls—
but you always realized they could not always be with you—and will
want them to be happy.

Ever your affectionate
Christine Hamlyn

P.S. Your letter has just come. All is forgiven.

CHAPTER VII

1932-1936

The decade of the thirties was a time of intense work for M. B. L. In one month she had stories published in each of the glossy magazines on the bookstalls and she started to sell the serial rights of her novels in the United States. But even when she was working as hard as this, Marie remained absorbed in public events, and in the lives of those around her.

Every year she went to New York to see her editors and publishers, and there she made a large number of American friends.

DIARY

September 30th, 1932

Last night I dined with Lord and Lady Hutchison.[1] Field-Marshal Sir William Robertson[2] and Lady Robertson were there. He has greatly altered since I saw him in Cologne after the War. Last year it was thought he was dying, but he has now lost two stone in weight, and he looks perfectly well. He spoke with slight bitterness about the fact that he had been given ten thousand pounds grant as against the hundred thousand given to Beatty and Haig. He told us that the Treasury officials had made a great fuss, and had not wanted to hand over the money, but to invest it and give him the dividends. His solicitor was so indignant that he offered to fight the Treasury for nothing. He said: "Field-Marshal, the country has given you this money without any conditions. You must get it and do exactly as you like."

Both he and my host were very amusing about big game shooting in India. Tigers are driven up, so as to be easily shot. One of the men told a story about Lord Lloyd.[3] There was some difficulty in getting a tiger, but at last one was seen behind a screen of leaves, and at the psychological moment Lord Lloyd shot the beast. Then to the embarrassment of his host, an Indian Rajah, he asked to see it. "Good God"! he cried, "this tiger has been dead a week!"

Another story was told about Lord Irwin[4] who, having got a tiger,

[1] Lord Hutchison of Montrose: 1873-1950. Director of Organisation at the War Office 1917-19. Paymaster-General 1935-38.

[2] Sir William Robertson: 1860-1933. Rose to Field-Marshal from the ranks. Chief of Imperial General Staff 1915-18. Commander-in-Chief British Army on the Rhine 1919-20.

[3] Lord Lloyd: 1879-1941. High Commissioner for Egypt and the Sudan 1925-29. Founded the British Council.

[4] Lord Irwin: Viceroy of India 1926-31. Succeeded his father as 3rd Viscount Halifax 1934. Earl 1944.

turned to his Indian host and said, "I would like my A.D.C. to have the next". His host said is was not possible, as if it was done Lord Irwin would have to change places with his A.D.C. This Lord Irwin at once did, but the A.D.C. got no tiger and afterwards the Rajah observed to someone, "I was not going to lose one of my beautiful tigers to an A.D.C."

When Freddie came in last night he told me a most curious piece of news. When all the mystery was going on about Gandhi's flight, they sat up at the India Office on Sunday very late discussing what should be done. At last they found a formula which was to be cabled to India, but the question then arose as to how this important secret document was to be typed. One of the men said he knew a place in Jermyn Street which was open all night. He was sent off there, but it was shut owing to it being Sunday. He then remembered the *Times* office where it was typed.

DIARY

October 1st, 1932

I heard that when King Edward was staying with the Arthur Sassoons[1] at Brighton at the time when there was the question of creating an enormous number of new peers, Mr Asquith was coming to see the King privately about it. Mrs Sassoon suggested that he should ask Mr Asquith to stay to lunch. "Certainly not," said the King.

This made her feel uncomfortable and inhospitable, but after a short interview with the King, Mr Asquith was bidden 'good-bye' and went off to make his way to London by train. Then Mr and Mrs Sassoon and the King and Mrs Keppel[2] all went for a walk on the front. After a while they changed places. Mr Sassoon chatted to the King and the two ladies walked behind. Mrs Sassoon asked Mrs Keppel what had happened. She said, "It's quite all right, they're not going to make the new peers". This being so, Mrs Sassoon felt that Mr Asquith might have been asked to lunch after all.

Apropos of Mr Asquith, there was a good deal of talk concerning those passages of his life which appeared in the *Times*. His son, who has

[1] Arthur Sassoon: 1840-1912. s. of David Sassoon, founder of the dynasty. m. Louise Perugia, elder sister of Marie de Rothschild.

[2] Mrs Keppel: d. of Admiral Sir W. Edmonstone. Bt. and wife of Lt.-Col. Hon. George Keppel, s. of 7th Earl of Albermarle.

written his father's life, was only fifteen months old when his mother died, so could only know by hearsay anything of his parents' married life.

To my mind, infinitely the best account of Asquith written by anybody since his death is that contained in a volume called *Portraits* by Desmond MacCarthy. It is an admirable and most living picture.

In some ways Asquith is deeply reserved. I believe he destroyed all his first wife's letters to him, and all his letters to her. In fact it is clear that he wished no real record of his first married life to survive.

DIARY

October 3rd, 1932

Staying with Mr and Mrs Walter Runciman[1] at Doxford, Lord Grey asked me over to see him at Fallodon. It was strange going to the house which I had known, filled with so vivid and brilliant a personality as that of his wife, Pamela. He took me into a small study, and for the first time during the many years I have known him he talked to me of his first wife, and showed me her portrait. He then took me out of doors and showed me the two gardens he had made, one in memory of Dorothy, the other of Pamela. I said that there had never been to my mind a good picture of Pamela since the *Three Graces* by Sargent. He asked me if I would like to see the one in his bedroom, so we went upstairs and I was much touched to see how everything there spoke of her. On what had been her dressing table there was a large photograph of her and in other parts of the room there were photographs taken at all times of her life from early childhood. They had become closer and closer during their comparatively short married life. I think he was aware that I knew she had not wished to marry a second time. She would have liked to have gone on with the friendship which for so long had meant so much to her. I told him of the last words she had said to me three days before her death. We spoke of the coming winter, and she said to me "I feel it will be my pleasure and my happiness to spend the winter at Fallodon[2] rather than at Wilsford[3]".

[1] Walter Runciman: 1870-1949. President of the Board of Trade 1931-37 when he was created 1st Viscount Runciman of Doxford.

[2] Fallodon—Lord Grey's house in Northumberland.

[3] Wilsford—Lady Grey's house in Wiltshire.

J. C. O'G. ANDERSON[1] TO M. B. L.

Pakhoi
January 23rd, 1934

Thank you for your kind letter. Yes, Stella was quite happy about her writing, was sure of herself there, and had no thought of not being sufficiently appreciated. Her only real grievance was her health, which made so many things that she wanted to do an exhausting effort. But she could never resist making the effort. I expect she was a remarkable writer, but I am certain she was a remarkable woman. Such wonderful courage and honesty. Did you know that she was a direct descendant of Pepys' sister Pauline (poor Pale)? She left her diary—kept for over 30 years—to Cambridge, to be read in 50 years from now. I think she counted on her diary enormously, as a friend and as a way to a little fame. Thank you for asking me to go and see you. I will, if I go home.

FROM OSBERT SITWELL[2] TO M. B. L.

Hotel Royal,
Bride-les-Bains
August 15th, 1934

Edith and I motored here via Beauvais and Avallon and Mantua. At Beauvais we found a nice selection of those literary bores—the sort whom you avoid for years but persist in bouncing out at you, when you least expect them, from behind Gothic screen or Attic pillars. However we settled them with a glass each of the strongest Marc-de-Bourgoyne and left them to their own devices of "Do you *really* think Mr T. S. Eliot means it?" and "Do tell me, is James Joyce *nice*?"

As for this place, it is too horrible; an alpine valley crammed with monsters so obese that they seem to have fallen like H. G.'s Martians, from another planet. They make me feel thin: for which I like them. But they are so cross, from starvation, and have nothing to do but teach their children—for once obedient—to jump and skip in a variety of ways over my head. The favourite time for this is 6 o'clock of a morning.

[1] J. C. O'G Anderson: husband of Stella Benson the novelist, who had just died, author of *I Pose* 1915 etc. She was a niece of Mary Cholmondely. He was in the Chinese Customs Service.

[2] Sir Osbert Sitwell: 1892-1969. 5th Bart. Poet. Essayist. Novelist. He and his brother Sacheverell and sister Edith revitalised poetry in England in the 1920's.

January 10th, 1935

I have been intensely interested in Mr Carter's book.[1] As a young woman I had heard of Mr Wise as a famous collector of books and autographs, and I admired his edition of Robert Browning's letters—my mother possessed a long letter written by Browning to her in which he gave an amusing account of having met Carlyle, and of the talk he had with him, and I knew Mr Wise would be interested to see it. I therefore decided I would go and see him, the more so that I felt considerable curiosity concerning his collection, especially as regarded letters and poems written by Dante Gabriel Rossetti, which I knew to be in his possession.

I therefore wrote to him, without mentioning the Browning letter, and asked if I might call on him. He assented, and I went and spent an interesting afternoon in the large room he had built to contain his treasures. Among many other remarkable objects I especially noticed a small glass box, containing a dark, curling lock of hair. This was inscribed "This lock of Elizabeth Barrett Browning's hair was held by Robert Browning in his hand while he was dying".

As my mother had known the Brownings and had an especial feeling of admiration for Mrs Browning, I felt much moved when I saw this relic.

Though he was most courteous to me, I did not altogether like Mr Wise, and I did not, after all, show him the letter from Browning. At the time when I saw him, he was greatly esteemed as a collector and had been given Degrees by many of the great Universities both English and American.

Then my friend, Lady Ritchie[2] gave me the great pleasure of taking me to call on Robert Browning's daughter-in-law. Mrs Pen Browning gave us a strange account of what occurred when Mr Wise, who was aware that she possessed everything connected with the Robert Brownings, sought her out, where she lived in the depths of the country. He pointed out how important it would be for posterity that a man like himself, who had arranged to leave his collection to the nation, should be entrusted with these relics. Mrs Browning was an American, old-fashioned, and shy, and I should think absolutely unsuspicious by

---

[1] *An Enquiry into the Nature of Certain Nineteenth Century Pamphlets*: by John Carter and Graham Pollard. Pubs. 1934.

[2] Lady Ritchie: d. of W. M. Thackeray, widow of Sir Richmond Ritchie.

nature. Mr Wise so worked on her feelings that, in the end, she did give him almost everything she possessed connected with Robert and Elizabeth Browning. Later on, during a stay in London, she wrote to Mr Wise and asked if she could come and see his collection of autographs and books. He agreed and she therefore travelled to his house in Hampstead.

Mr Wise went out of his library for a few moments and while he was absent she suddenly noticed with astonishment the small glass case in which was a lock of hair, while under it was the inscription I had seen.

As soon as Mr Wise came back into the room, she exclaimed, "Someone has taken you in, Mr Wise. I was with my father-in-law when he died, and he was not holding a lock of his wife's hair in his hand. In fact, I much doubt if the lock of hair you have in that case was ever on his wife's head." Mr Wise looked at her, smiled, and exclaimed, "If he was not holding a lock of her hair in his hand, he ought to have done so!"

M. B. L. TO HER DAUGHTER E. I.

Cumberland Lodge,
Windsor
May 6th, 1935

I sat next Mr Baldwin last night and he asked after you affectionately. Is it not *extraordinary* he must have the same kind of literary *mind* I have (and that my mother had!) for to my amazement he reeled off exactly the same books I put first in my broadcast. Beginning with the Strafford ghost in *Inglesant*[1]—going on to *A Beleaguered City*.[2] Both passage and books no one has ever mentioned to me since Granny used to talk about them when I was a girl. It was the same with other books. Our minds, about literature, are twin minds.

M. B. L. TO HER DAUGHTER E. I.

Port Lympne,[3]
Hythe, Kent
August 10th, 1935

I already feel much better for the one day lying out in the air. Also the divine beauty of the place, inside and out, so enchants me.

[1] *John Inglesant*: by J. H. Shorthouse. Pubs. 1881.
[2] *A Beleaguered City*: by Margaret Oliphant. Pubs. 1880.
[3] Port Lympne: Sir Philip Sassoon's house in Kent.

A very good party—Anthony Edens, Lord Hugh Cecil, the Hardinges, Lady Desborough, Osbert Sitwell—and—Rex Whistler[1]. He asked at once after you and the children. He, of course, is rather "odd man out", though he is so quiet and unassuming that everyone likes him.

I hear Margot, said the other day, to Algernon Cecil[2] "All the Cecils are shy (seizing him). Not you darling!"

The tale goes that Sibyl Colefax[3] has sold her house to Mrs Simpson. It is under five minutes from Buckingham Palace, if you may pass the lights as all Royalties do! Their chauffeur gives a curious squeak, and they rush through. It *is* true that Sibyl made a great mystery to me as to *who* she had sold the house to. It is for 60 years! I wonder will the affair last as long as *that*!

DIARY

October 20th, 1935

Thirty Club yesterday. We were thirteen. I sat between Marie de Rothschild and old Lady Leconfield[4]. Others there were Gertrude Tuckwell[5] and Julia Maguire[6]. There was a great deal of talk about Geneva, most of them being very bitter against Mussolini. I told Marie of the Dutchman who had said to me that Eden was playing Hitler's Game. One of them said, which interested me deeply, that John Morley had always been against the League of Nations and had said it would lead to grave international complications. As to the General Election they were divided. Helen Maclagan[7] being violently against its being held so soon.

[1] Rex Whistler: 1905-1944. Painter killed during landings in France 1944. Joined Welsh Guards 1939.

[2] Algernon Cecil: s. of Lord Eustace Cecil. Writer, essayist. An old friend of M. B. L.

[3] Sibyl Colefax: wife of Sir Arthur Colefax K.C., K.B.E. A noted hostess at Argyll House in the Kings Road and then in Lord North Street.

[4] Lady Leconfield: widow of the 2nd Baron. She was 89 at this time.

[5] Miss Gertrude Tuckwell: niece of Lady Dilke. Edited the *Life of Sir Charles Dilke*.

[6] Hon. Mrs Maguire: d. of Viscount Peel and w. of James Rochfort Maguire C.B.E., M.P. She was descended from Sir Robert Peel.

[7] Helen Maclagan: wife of Sir Eric Maclagan, Director of the Victoria and Albert Museum. d. of Hon. Frederick Lascelles.

Julia said she had been to see her man of business in the City and he had told her he had just done a big deal with Italy. Someone said they hoped he had got his money. She said he had been paid, and she asked us to guess what form the payment took. Of course none of us could do so. She said he had been paid with an enormous quantity of the very finest wine, the whole of which had been taken up at once by West End wine merchants, so the man had done a good deal. I had heard that they were paying Germany with fruit.

In the afternoon I called on Sarah Bailey. We had a curious talk on Spiritualism. She mentioned her sister-in-law Mrs Alfred Lyttelton[1] and agreed that she believes she has direct communication with her husband. I did not repeat to her what someone said to me the other day: that Alfred Lyttelton would be far too busy in heaven talking to Laura, to have any time to spare for D. D. Mrs Bailey told me that John Morley, when asked his opinion on Lloyd George had answered at once, "As for friendship—Brutus. As to truth—Ananias".

DIARY

October 22nd, 1935

I have read Curtis Brown's[2] book *Contacts*. I was deeply interested in his account of Shaw. Every word he said was true as to Shaw's odd ways with regard to contracts. Philip Sassoon asked Shaw's advice about his contract with Heinemann—Shaw wrote him a long amusing letter and also pulled the contract to pieces.

I was, however, surprised to note that Curtis Brown claims to have made the arrangements concerning Mr Asquith's War book. He may have done this with regard to foreign American rights, etc. He did not do so with regard to the English rights, for I heard at the time from the man concerned, that a representative of the publishers went down to see the Asquiths about something concerning one of Margot's books.

After they had had their talk, the publisher put down on the table a cheque for two thousand pounds made out to Asquith. Asquith took it up and said, "What's this?" The man said, "This is a fifth part of what we are willing to pay if you write your War memoirs". It was well-

[1] Mrs Lyttelton (D. D.): d. of A. Balfour and widow of Rt. Hon. Alfred Lyttelton whose first wife, Laura, was a sister of Margot Oxford.

[2] Curtis Brown: Managing Director Curtis Brown Ltd. The largest literary agency in the world.

known that Asquith had said he would never write his Memoirs in any shape or form.

Asquith walked across to the window—a French window leading into a garden at the other end of which stood the large barn where Margot worked. He waited there for an appreciable time, then he turned round and said "I'll do it". Taking up the cheque he observed "This bait has caught the fish".

He had never kept a diary, and it was his custom to destroy all the letters he received. He was, however, a great letter-writer. There were at least ten women to whom he wrote quite often. When faced with the necessity of writing the book, he wrote to all these ladies and asked them to return his letters. They all refused, with the exception of Mrs Harrisson. She at once did what he asked, and that is the explanation of his having left her £2,000. But for her he could never have written the book.

It was with great regret that I read Asquith's letters to Mrs Harrisson[1] when she decided to publish them. My regret was owing to the fact that they gave an entirely false impression of the writer. Asquith had an enormous following among Nonconformists. They regarded him as a stern man of God, a Cromwell, who by some freak of circumstance had married Margot Tennant of whom they knew very little, and of the little they knew they disapproved. To all these people, the publication of what appeared to be a series of love letters came as a fearful shock. To the people who knew Asquith, the letters meant less than nothing because they were all well aware that all through his life—even before his first wife's death, he had always had these affectionate friendships with women.

After the Harrisson letters came out, Margot was terribly distressed at the effect they produced. I had a talk with her about it and I entirely agreed with her that there were several women who could have produced letters of exactly the same kind, many of these ladies being well-known women who certainly were not in love with Asquith nor he with them. He always began a letter to any woman who could in any way be described as attractive with 'darling' or 'dearest'. In a way this was strange, because he did not fling about those terms in everyday life.

One woman known to me still has an Italian marriage-chest full of letters from him. She is a highly intelligent woman; the letters to her are

[1] *H. H. A. Letters of the Earl of Oxford and Asquith to a friend.* 2 vols. Pubs. 1933 and 1934. Edited by Desmond MacCarthy.

really worth printing for he wrote with great freedom on all political and literary subjects.

When Mrs Harrisson lent Asquith the letters for the purpose of his memoirs, after making notes, he began tearing them up. Margot stopped him, exclaiming: "Don't do that! She probably values your letters very much". If this story is true, how very much she must have regretted having stopped him in his work of destruction. The person to get all the criticism was the editor Desmond MacCarthy. I do not feel he was to blame, owing to the simple fact that he was so close a friend both of Asquith and of Margot that what amazed and shocked those who did not know them, made no impression on MacCarthy at all.

DIARY

October 24th, 1935

I met a diplomat who is an intimate friend of the parents[1] of the Duchess of Kent. He gave me an account of how the engagement came about. He said that they received a telegram saying that Prince George[2] was coming over to Paris for a few days and would be so pleased if he might stay with them. They were somewhat surprised and, according to my informant, had no idea of why he was coming, except that the British Princes do fly about the Continent more than is generally known. Thus the Prince of Wales last year constantly went over to Le Touquet for lunch and even for dinner, the fact not being recorded in any paper.

The visit of Prince George went off in a quite ordinary way until the last evening, when the young people stayed behind after the others had gone up to bed. An hour later they went up to her sister's bedroom door, knocked, and told her they were engaged.

It is true that none of his circle in England had the slightest suspicion of what was going to happen. I know this because at the time I was at Lympne where some of his friends also happened to be staying. They were astounded at the news and not, I think, over-pleased. None of them had ever heard of Princess Marina with the exception of one lady who had met her when she was in England staying with some member of the Royal family. She told us the following story:

There is a fortune-teller in Regent Street, whose name and address

[1] Prince and Princess Nicolas of Greece.
[2] Prince George, Duke of Kent, 4th son of King George V. m. 1934 Princess Marina of Greece.

she gave us, to whom she took Prince George some months before his engagement. The woman told him, to his great annoyance and surprise "You are not going to marry the English lady whom you like. You will marry a foreigner." The woman had no idea who he was. He protested loudly that nothing would induce him to marry a foreigner. The girl he was in love with, and who would not have him, was the daughter of a well-known peer. That part of the story at any rate is true.

DIARY

October 28th, 1935

Major Yeats-Brown[1] is going to spend the weekend with me at Cumberland Lodge. He rang me up to ask if he could drive me down. He said that Italy has now 300 bombers and that anything like Military Sanctions, even of the mildest kind, would mean these planes being used against British possessions in the Mediterranean. He believes this has had a certain effect on the hot-heads in the Government.

M. B. L. TO MRS KING PATTERSON[2]

9 *Barton Street,*
*Westminster S. W.*1
October 30th, 1935

I am fond of my brother's book *Hills and the Sea*,[3] but I prefer another book of his which is comparatively little known called *The Eye Witness*[4]. I am sending it to you. The idea, as you will see, is to describe certain historical events through the eyes of an eye-witness. The execution of Charles I, and the trial of Marie Antoinette are the two I like best.

[1] Major Francis Yeats-Brown: 1886-1944. D.F.C.: Indian Army. Served France with 5th Lancers and Mesopotamia with Royal Flying Corps, in First World War. Prisoner in Turkey 1915. Escaped 1918. Assistant Editor of the *Spectator* 1925-28. Author of *Bengal Lancer*. Pubs. 1930. *Golden Horn*. Pubs. 1932, etc.

[2] Mrs King Patterson: wife of proprietor of *New York Daily News* which published several of M. B. L.'s novels as serials as well as her short stories. She became an intimate friend.

[3] *Hills and the Sea*: by Hilaire Belloc. Pubs. 1906.

[4] *The Eye Witness*: by Hilaire Belloc. Pubs. 1908.

November 1st, 1935

While I was staying away last weekend I heard a most interesting account of haemophilia, the disease which almost certainly came into the Royal Family through the Prince Consort. There was a discussion as to whether Queen Victoria brought it in. It is an extraordinary fact that, of Queen Victoria's nine children, only one had this disease, her youngest son. His daughter, a beautiful, healthy woman, transmitted it to her son. None of Princess Alice's children had the disease, yet her daughter, the Empress of Russia, transmitted it to her son.

My hostess said that when dining at Windsor the day that Lord Trematon[1] had an accident in France, his wound was so small that only two stitches had to be put in. The Queen said very sadly: "If the stitches burst he will die".

I remember as a small child being much impressed by hearing that when the Duke of Albany married and went to live at Claremont, stone and marble floors were put whenever possible where he was likely to spend his life, as he so constantly bled. The reason then believed was that he had a skin less than other people, but he was simply suffering from this terrible disease.

December 3rd, 1935

I lunched at 44, Bedford Square with Margot Oxford. There was a German Count, an American journalist, John Gunther[2] and his wife, and Peter Lubbock. Margot talked all the time, and as always her conversation was brilliant and interesting.

She talked a good deal about Kitchener, but I wondered if she were not mixing him up with someone else. For I remember during the War being told that he never spoke to her if he could help it, because he had a great fear of having anything he said repeated. She began by telling us that he had been asked to go and join the French Army in '70, but as a matter of fact he ran away from, I think, Woolwich and joined the Army on his own, being almost cashiered in consequence.

[1] Lord Trematon: son of the Earl of Athlone and H.R.H. Princess Alice, d. of the 1st Duke of Albany. Lord Trematon died after a road accident.

[2] John Gunther: News Correspondent in London and elsewhere. Author of *Inside Europe* pubs. 1936, etc.

She then went on to divorce, which she would like to see made easier. I observed that the peculiar anomaly of our present law was in a great measure owing to the efforts which were made by Gladstone. He was then a young Member of Parliament, but already very influential, having fought passionately against any divorce law being passed, he did everything in his power to make it difficult and disagreeable for couples to get a divorce. Margot contradicted me and said the divorce law was far older than Gladstone. She always sees him in her own mind as a devoted admirer of her own.

She thought of Mark Twain observing that there was no one left alive in England who had known him. It is not too much to say that, of the people present, only two are now too young to have known him. She sat next to Mark Twain at dinner as a young woman, but when he said to her: "Though my name is Clemens, you probably know me as Mark Twain," she had no idea who he was, and had never read a line of his books.

DIARY

December 17th, 1935

Last night I had a talk with a very interesting man. His name is Ronald Armstrong, and he is British Consul at Geneva, married to a most attractive Dutchwoman. His position at Geneva gives him a unique opportunity of meeting not only all the League of Nations people, but all those who go there in order to be interested or amused.

During the last few weeks his job has been a very anxious one. For no day goes by without the most terrible anonymous letters arriving threatening the lives of one or other of the people of the League. Mostly just now Anthony Eden[1]. He pulled out of his pocket one such letter. It was written in French and was signed 'a Swiss who hates War'. It began: 'Not only your days, but your hours, are numbered'. And then it went on to pour abuse, couched in very plain language, on the British People and on Anthony Eden himself.

He and I agreed that it was probably written by an Italian. It gave me the feeling that Eden must be an extremely brave man, for apparently he takes no notice of these terrible threats. I then reminded Mr Armstrong

[1] Anthony Eden: 1st Earl of Avon. Prime Minister 1955-57. Before becoming Secretary of State for Foreign Affairs 1935-38, he was Minister without Portfolio for League of Nations Affairs 1935.

of the fate which befell the Empress of Austria at Geneva where she was murdered by an Italian. It is a fact that any man who does not mind losing his own life can always murder another. It was more difficult when famous people drove about in high carriages, though even then determined murderers generally succeeded. Carnot was murdered in Lyons when driving in a high vehicle.

Mr Armstrong is naturally heart and soul with the League. He assured me that Sir Samuel Hoare[1] would resign and that Eden might well be made Secretary of State for Foreign Affairs. I told him in my view, that would never happen. He said what I thought not true, that Baldwin backs Eden. A thing he told me which did surprise me was that from the very first it was his own impression that Eden and Hoare did not like one another.

DIARY

December 19th, 1935

Wickham Steed came in to see me and talked with great excitement of what has happened over the offer of peace terms to Italy and Abyssinia. He said it was the greatest betrayal of history and put it all down to Laval[2]. He did tell me a curious fact, which is that when he wrote a letter to the *Times* in the middle of October, he received a note from Sir Samuel Hoare assuring him that there was not a word of truth in the rumour, but once the Election was over the Government meant to do everything they could to stop the Abyssinian war, without referring the matter to the League.

I told him that I had met Sir Samuel Hoare at various times and saw him at intervals at a friend's house, and that he seemed to me the last man in the world to engage in a deep plot. I feel sure there is something more behind the whole matter than anything to do with Laval. It appears to me plain that the Cabinet are irritated that France does not go further, and I cannot conceive why they should have given in to any plan of Laval's unless they had a very much stronger reason to do so than has yet come out.

[1] Sir Samuel Hoare: Cr. Viscount Templewood 1944. Secetary of State for Foreign Affairs 1935.

[2] Pierre Laval: French Foreign Minister who with Sir Samuel Hoare arranged the secret terms of the Hoare-Laval Pact over Italy and Abyssinia, which brought about Sir Samuel Hoare's resignation.

I did not like to tell him what I believe to be the truth. This is that Italy has been quietly massing troops along the edge of British Somaliland. There are very few English troops there, and it would be quite easy were oil sanctions imposed, for Italy to seize this British Colony. It would be extremely difficult to dislodge them as well, of course, as starting a war.

It is my impression that this determined effort to stop the Italian Abyssinian war is owing to something of that kind, as also to the troubles in Egypt. No doubt Laval is delighted but nothing would make me believe that the British Cabinet would give in to Laval's wish, threats, or promises, were it not that some important British interests were involved.

DIARY

January 25th, 1936

So little did even those who ought to have known expect that the King[1] was going to die last week that a small luncheon party which was going to be given by Julia Maguire for the Baldwins was not put off till the afternoon of the King's death. Then, and not till then, did Mr Baldwin himself telephone to Julia to say he feared the news had suddenly become very much worse.

On the Saturday I lunched with Margot Asquith, there was a great doctor there and he said he had been assistant to the specialist who had pulled the King through his last illness in 1928/29 and that the King's recovery then had been in the nature of a miracle. He declared that not a single doctor thought he could possibly survive. That being so he seemed to think it very probable that the King would pull through this time and in any case he was convinced that the illness would drag on for some time.

My younger daughter managed to get through Downing Street and so had a very good view of the procession as it came down Whitehall from the station on its way to Westminster Hall for the Lying in State. She told me that she had never seen anyone look so ill or as unhappy as the Prince of Wales looked that day. He was evidently going through the most fearful mental and physical anguish. And I heard from someone else that in Trafalgar Square they were afraid he would not be able to go on to the very end.

[1] King George V died at Sandringham on January 20th.

137

My son-in-law[1] described the marvellous scene in Westminster Hall when all the Lords and Commons received the coffin. The three Royal Duchesses came separately and joined the Queen. They were all wearing continental mourning, swathed from head to foot in black.

At seven the same evening my son-in-law telephoned and said that if Susan and I could come at once he could take us into Westminster Hall. So we hurried along to the Peers' entrance and walked through till we came out at the top of the steps leading into Westminster Hall. It was a most wonderful sight and we stayed long enough to see the changing of the various Guards, including the Gentlemen-at-Arms. There was more colour than had been the case with the Lying-in-State of Edward VII, which I remembered vividly.

M. B. L. TO HER DAUGHTER E. I.

Ritz Tower,
Park Avenue, NY
April 18th, 1936

.... Yesterday I had a real thrill. I had tea with J. P. Morgan.[2] A huge mountain of a man. Five detectives lounging outside his plain substantial house. They all took a dreadful interest in me, though I drove up in an ordinary car. His pictures gave me exquisite pleasure. There was no one there but Mildred Buxton[3]. Apart from the pictures, it might have been the *very* Victorian drawing room of a big Manchester manufacturer, who wouldn't allow his wife to have in a modern decorator.

I have had the Edmund Pearsons[4] to dinner, and they are taking me to the play. All New York is horrified over the murder of a woman writer, Mrs Titterton[5] strangled on Good Friday. She was about thirty and happily married. I say to the reporters it is like a lunatic's murder. Oh, dear how I long to be home again!

[1] 3rd Earl of Iddesleigh: 1901-1970.
[2] John Pierpont Morgan: 1867-1943. Head of J. P. Morgan and Co.
[3] Mildred Buxton: widow of Earl Buxton and daughter of Hugh Colin Smith, Governor of the Bank of England.
[4] Edmund Lester Pearson: 1880-1937. Editor of publications at the New York Public Library. Noted criminologist.
[5] Mrs Lewis H. Titterton: w. of an executive in the National Broadcasting Co. A paroled convict, John Fiorenza, confessed to the crime and was convicted and executed.

CHAPTER VIII

THE ABDICATION

Marie Belloc Lowndes' account of the experience of the Abdication, shows her own very individual theories on the whole episode. For contrary to what many believed at the time, the affair is now seen as only an episode, dramatic and startling though it was to those who lived through it, and not as a major upheaval in the history of Britain.

DIARY

January 20th, 1937

I remember the first time I heard of Mrs Simpson. It must have been about three years ago. I was acquainted with some pleasant Americans named Paul and Lily Bonner[1]. She was the daughter of a lady who had been kind to me in New York, and whose husband had built up an immense fortune in some business. Mr Bonner had a fine taste in pictures. They had taken a house in Chelsea, where there was a big studio and there they gave amusing cocktail parties.

An American friend of Mrs Bonner having accepted an invitation, telephoned the next morning to explain that she had not been able to come because a Russian Grand Duke had called on her and she had not liked to bring him on, as he would probably have known nobody at the party. Mrs Bonner's reply was, "At any rate I think he would have known the Prince of Wales. He was at my party." I said to my friend who told me this tale, "But how did the Bonner's get to know the Prince of Wales? He lives in such a curiously restricted circle."

"But don't you know that the Prince is now devoted to an American couple called Simpson? He goes with them everywhere, and they know the Bonner's."

From then on, I heard more and more about the Prince's growing infatuation for Mrs Simpson. How gradually he was dropping his English friends, and being surrounded more and more by Americans. The next thing I heard was that when King George and Queen Mary were shown the final list of invitations to a State Ball, and that the Prince had put in the Simpsons' name among the list of those he wished included, the King had drawn a line through the name. The Prince hearing of this went to his parents and said that if he were not allowed to invite these friends of his, he would not go to the ball. He pointed out that the Simpsons were remarkably nice Americans, that it was

[1] Mr and Mrs Paul Bonner: friends of Alexander Woollcott.

important England and America should be on cordial terms, and that he himself had been most kindly entertained in the States.

His parents gave way, and the Simpsons duly came to the ball. There had already been enough talk to arouse among the guests a great deal of curiosity concerning Mrs Simpson and several of my friends gave me a satirical account of the lady and how she had worn a very showy, red dress.

The gossip increased in volume. The Simpsons were said to take their Royal friend to all kinds of night-clubs night after night. And then to my astonishment someone told me that my old friend Sibyl Colefax often entertained the Prince of Wales and the Simpsons at dinner and supper.

The next time I found myself alone with her I said, "I hear that you are now on very affectionate terms with the Prince of Wales". She got very red, and said "I know him through my friends the Simpsons. I have known Mrs Simpson for many years." I was again greatly surprised, as I had never seen either Mr or Mrs Simpson in her house.

She then suddenly exclaimed "Of course I know, Marie, that people are speaking in a very horrid way of the poor Prince and Mrs Simpson. It's awfully unfair, and pure jealousy on the part of the women he has liked in the past, and who all of them made him dreadfully unhappy. Not one of them was even ordinarily faithful to him. Almost all of them had lovers and of course that made him feel wretched. Mrs Simpson is quite a different sort of woman. She doesn't pose as being young and in fact must be nearly forty. She is clever and intelligent and is interested in everything that interests the Prince, including gardening."

I then said "But how about Mr Simpson? What is he like?" She then used an Americanism: "Ah! That's not so good! I don't know much about Mr Simpson. He is said to be part English, part American and part French. Still, there's no harm in him, and the Prince of Wales has become very fond of him too. In fact, he keeps a special brand of cigars for Ernest Simpson, and I have often seen him hold out a cigar and say, 'Here is your cigar, Ernest." That evening I told my husband this story. He laughed, and said that he had often heard of the price of shame, but that he had never heard of its taking the form of a cigar.

With the one exception of Lady Colefax, a long time went by before I met anyone else who knew the Simpsons, though it became widely known that they spent a great deal of time at Fort Belvedere, the Prince's country house.

I was often at Cumberland Lodge in Windsor Great Park on visits to Lord and Lady FitzAlan[1] during the Simpson friendship. In that neighbourhood there was naturally a good deal of conversation concerning the Prince's American circle of friends, but neither my host or hostess, though they naturally knew him well, and were personal friends of King George and Queen Mary, ever saw or met any members of the Fort Belvedere Circle.

During the next visit I paid to America I learned that my friend Alexander Woollcott[2] when passing through London a short time before, had been asked by Mrs Simpson to meet the Prince of Wales at dinner. He gave me an amusing account of the party, where among the other guests was Margot Oxford. "She talked so much that I felt I wanted to strangle her," he said. I asked him whether he thought the Prince of Wales was really in love with Mrs Simpson. He said, "Yes, she has him like *that*".

After I came home I went to stay for a week at Trent Park with Sir Philip Sassoon, as I always do each New Year. The day I arrived we were all sitting in the drawing-room, when at about six o'clock "Mr and Mrs Simpson" were announced.

Most of the people in the house-party did not know them and we all felt a very real sense of thrill, of interest and of curiosity. I was at once impressed by Mrs Simpson's perfect figure. She was of medium height, and beautifully dressed in the French way, that is, very unobtrusively. I did not think her in the least pretty. She was very much made up with what I would call a Red Indian colouring, that is, yellow and brick-red. Her hair appeared at night very dark, and was cut much shorter than was just then the fashion among Englishwomen. She had an intelligent but in no sense a remarkable face.

While the Simpsons were being shown their rooms, some discussion followed as to whether Mrs Simpson would be put next to her host. It was finally decided that she would be treated just like an ordinary guest. She was, therefore, put in the middle of the table some way from her host, while Philip had at either side the Duchess of Rutland[3] and some other woman whose rank entitled her to be next to him. There

---

[1] Lord FitzAlan: 1855-1947. 1st Viscount. Viceroy of Ireland 1921-22. m. d. of 7th Earl of Abingdon.

[2] Alexander Woollcott: 1887-1943. Noted American wit, journalist and broadcaster.

[3] Duchess of Rutland: d. of Francis John Tennant m. 1916 9th Duke who died 1940.

had been a discussion as to who should sit next to Mr Simpson, and I asked if I might do so, as I felt so interested in them both. This aroused some amusement, as no other woman wished to sit next to him. I had heard very varying accounts of this gentleman, one greatly to his credit, from the man who had been his Colonel in the 1914 War, and I was curious to make his acquaintance.

Mrs Simpson was just opposite me, and Mr Simpson and I talked practically without interruption throughout the whole of the dinner. She was wearing a plain dress, high at the throat, but with bare arms. She wore a very great deal of jewellery, which I thought must be what is called "dressmaker's" jewels, so large were the emeralds in her bracelets and so striking and peculiar a necklace. She did not talk much during dinner and showed nothing of the wit and brilliance with which she was credited.

Mr Simpson talked without stopping, and gave me a long account of his life. He reminded me of a good many American businessmen I had met, and that although he was technically an Englishman, having, I believe, become naturalized to fight in the War. He asked me almost at once where I would send an American girl child to be educated in Europe. I asked if she were Protestant, and being told that she was, I said that I personally would select a good Swiss school. He then told me that he had in mind his own daughter, whom I gathered was about eight years old. I felt much surprised and I suppose glanced at Mrs Simpson. He hastened to tell me that the child was not the present Mrs Simpson's; that she was a child of a former wife of his. He appeared devoted to the little girl and said he had been back to America especially to see her the summer before.

This explained to me his absence, which had caused comment, from a party given by the Prince of Wales on a yacht. The yacht had cruised in the Mediterrenean, and there had been a good deal of gossip concerning the way the party went on, spending a great deal of time on shore, bathing and basking in the sun, winding up each day in places which were not considered to be suitable resorts for the future King of England and his friends.

Mr Simpson then said that he understood I was a writer, and added that he was very fond of reading, but had practically no time to indulge his favourite pursuit. In fact, he said, it took him many months to read one book. He explained that this was owing to the fact that his wife and her friends were very fond of going out at night—that they went from night-club to night-club—he ran off the names of half-a-dozen—

and that when they finally got home in the morning, he was so tired that he could read only a few lines of the book in hand.

He went on, "I have to get up early, too, for I take the Tube to the City at nine o'clock every morning". I said I wondered he didn't go by car, as it would be so much less tiring than travelling in the rush hour. He then observed rather sharply that he and Mrs Simpson were not at all well-off, and so did not own a car. He added after a moment's hesitation that friends were very kind in lending them cars, but that he wouldn't care to have a friend lend him a car to go to the City every morning.

A quiet evening followed. Mrs Simpson was taken off to a distant sofa by one of the ladies present and as I go to bed fairly early, I did not talk to her at all. On the other hand I was impressed by the fact that she seemed to feel anxious concerning her husband's position among all these well-known English people. Twice she said to her host: "I think Ernest would like to meet——" The first time this happened it was quite obvious that—— did not wish to meet Ernest, and I could not help feeling rather sorry for her.

Some time went by, and then she said " I think my husband would like to meet Lord——" Lord—— proved more amenable and they were introduced, but I felt that the unfortunate Mr Simpson was regarded with a considerable measure of contempt by all the men there. He was obviously regarded as *un mari complaisant*. That, I am convinced he was not.

I generally had a bedroom on the ground floor at Trent, and the next morning while writing as always in bed, I saw through the window, the whole party go off to play golf. Mrs Simpson was as beautifully and suitably dressed in the morning as she had been during the afternoon and evening before. The two went off before lunch, a car being sent for them to stay with Sir Robert[1] and Lady Vansittart.

At lunch the whole party made fun of me because I had got on so well with Mr Simpson, and they told me that I was the only person to whom the Simpsons had sent messages of farewell. They were amazed to learn from me that Simpson had a child. Two or three of them who knew him did not believe it.

Several of my fellow-guests asked me what I thought of her. I said what had struck me most were her perfect clothes and that I had been

[1] Sir Robert Vansittart: 1881-1957. Diplomat. Permanent Under-Secretary of State for Foreign Affairs 1930-38. Chief Diplomatic Adviser to Foreign Secretary 1938-41. 1st Baron 1941.

surprised, considering that she dressed so simply, to see that she wore such a mass of dressmakers' jewels. At that they all screamed with laughter, explaining that all the jewels were real, that the then Prince of Wales had given her fifty thousand pounds' worth at Christmas, following it up with sixty thousand pounds' worth of jewels a week later at the New Year. They explained that his latest gift was a marvellous necklace which he had bought from a Paris jeweller. They were also amused and incredulous when I told them that in my opinion Mrs Simpson was very fond of Mr Simpson and anxious to make it plain that she was a good, thoughtful and affectionate wife.

During that winter, the talk about the Prince and Mrs Simpson increased considerably. Indeed, it recalled to me what went on at Versailles during the reign of Louis XIV when hundreds of letters were written day by day about them all, as is happening now.

The death of King George took place rather unexpectedly at Sandringham, and within a day or two I was told, that the new King had insisted on flying to London the day following his father's death, the real reason being that Mr and Mrs Simpson were on the point of starting for America.

My view then, and it has not changed, was that Mrs Simpson, supposing that everything would be so altered that her royal friendship would come to an end, felt that the most dignified thing would be for her to leave England for a while. Long after I learnt that the new King had arranged to meet her at the Ritz. She was ten minutes late and Lord Charles Montagu[1] whom I met shortly after saw him stamping up and down the long corridor, looking angry and anxious till she came in and joined him.

Mr and Mrs Simpson lived in a comparatively small apartment in a block of flats near the Marble Arch, and there the King spent much of his time when in London. It was told how he would come down into the street with Mrs Simpson's little dogs; how, when the lift was engaged he would sit down in the porter's chair and read a paper. In fact, he behaved exactly as does any ordinary young man who is infatuated with a married woman, and who has enough money and leisure to spend with her every moment she is willing to give him. He often dined with her there to meet her friends, foreigners included. He was very angry when one of her guests published an article in a New York weekly—*Dining with the King*.

---

[1] Lord Charles Montagu: s. of 7th Duke of Manchester.

Little by little the two began to 'shed' Mr Simpson. He was less and less with them, and people of a certain type began giving dinner parties and evening parties 'to have the honour of meeting His Majesty the King', and of course Mrs Simpson. This was specially the case with some women who were American by birth, but married to Englishmen. The most prominent of these ladies was Lady Cunard[1]. She constantly entertained Mrs Simpson, both with the King and without him.

The King's invitations, however informal, were regarded as Commands, and of course accepted. Mrs Simpson now spent every weekend at Fort Belvedere, though there were always others there too. The King sometimes asked the younger members of the Government and their wives to lunch or dinner at the Fort, and stories of the extraordinary informality which prevailed were told.

According to my own view, but many people did not agree with me, and thought me very simple and charitable to hold such an idea, the King and Mrs Simpson had not lived together as man and wife during their 'friendship', when the Simpsons were apparently on the best of terms. Again and again during those two or three years people who knew Wallis Simpson very well, said to me, "She is delighted and flattered by the Prince of Wales' devotion, but she is in love with her husband".

Then came the exciting and terrible incident when a half-crazy Irishman threw a pistol at the King as he was riding with the Duke of York behind him, in Constitution Hill. The then King is an extremely brave man, and though he believed the unloaded pistol which had struck the hoof of his horse was a bomb, he remained quite still, and I heard at the time that he said to his brother, "We have sixty seconds to live".

When he arrived at St James' Palace, Mr and Mrs Simpson were there. They were naturally full of excitement and horror, and what the French so well call *emotionné*. Then they all three for the *first time*, spoke openly together of the peculiar situation in which they found themselves. As a result the King made a strong appeal to Mr Simpson to allow Mrs Simpson to have what was called "an arranged divorce". He said "I cannot live without Wallis". Mr Simpson agreed, and small wonder, for the unfortunate man by this time must have felt his position quite unendurable, both among his own friends and the public at large.

[1] Lady Cunard: widow of Sir Bache Cunard, 3rd Bart. d. of E. F. Burke of New York. Well-known London hostess, mother of Nancy Cunard.

The next thing was that Mr Simpson left the flat where he and his wife had lived together and went to live in a Club. Then came the news that the King had taken a villa in the South of France. But the French authorities felt nervous because of the situation in Spain, and a yacht was substituted for the house. Several people whose names were mentioned as among the intended guests were not, in the end, asked. The yachting party was a small one.

After they came back, it became known that the King was going to spend a short time at Balmoral. The composition of the house-party was curious. In addition to his brother, the Duke of York, and his Duchess, were the Duke and Duchess of Rutland, the Duke and Duchess of Buccleuch[1] and Lord and Lady Rosebery[2]. After two or three days the King explained that it was impossible for him to open a hospital of which he had laid the first stone as Prince of Wales. He was said to have had a chill, and the Duke and Duchess of York took his place. In actual fact he motored sixty miles to Aberdeen, to meet Mrs Simpson who had travelled up from London through the night.

The train was late, and he had to wait some time in the station. Though he wore motoring goggles, which he apparently thought would conceal his identity, of course everyone there recognised him, except one policeman, who 'told him off' for leaving his car in the wrong part of the station yard. He took this good-humouredly and moved his car.

In the castle Mrs Simpson was given the rooms which had been in turn inhabited by Queen Victoria, Queen Alexandra and Queen Mary, from there she used to issue forth late each morning, in shorts. She and the King, both wearing shorts, would go about the village of Crathie, exciting horror and disapproval by their appearance. Soon her friends, Mr and Mrs Herman Rogers[3] arrived. The King evidently liked them very much, for when later on the question arose as to where he should go when he left England—to the Duke of Westminster's country house in France or to the Austrian Rothschilds, he decided on Austria because the Rogers were about to pay a visit to the Baron and Baroness.

[1] Duke of Buccleuch: 8th Duke, m. 1921. Vreda Esther Mary, d. of Major W. F. Lascelles and Lady Sybil Lascelles.

[2] Lord and Lady Rosebery: 6th Earl, m. 1924 Eva, Lady Belper d. of 2nd Baron Aberdare.

[3] Mr Herman Rogers: 1891-1957. Major in First War. m. Katherine Moore, former wife of Ernest A. Bigelow Jr.

That he did not do so, was owing to the fact that Mr and Mrs Rogers were then sheltering Mrs Simpson after her flight to France.

There was considerable speculation as to whether Mrs Simpson was to be present at the Coronation. It was said that the King wished her to occupy a pew which would have been erected for her sole occupation, and some wit said it should be called "the loose box". There is no doubt that Edward VIII intended Mrs Simpson to become in the full sense of the term, his Consort. An American friend of mine had seen a letter by her to a lady in New York, who had been kind to her in her youth, and in the letter she said: "Strange as it may seem, I am going to be Queen of England". But no one that I met at the time connected the Simpson's divorce with any thought of *marriage* on the part of the King. What many believed, even those who were closest to him, was that Mrs Simpson was going to become his *maîtresse en titre*. That at last the mask was being thrown off.

However, among those convinced that Mrs Simpson would become Queen of England was Lady Colefax. She was a very near neighbour of mine in London. I met her one day in the street, and I said, "Is it true that you believe Mrs Simpson is going to be Queen of England?" She looked mysterious, but at last said that, yes, she did believe it. I observed "I am sure you are wrong; the British people would not stand for it. If the King chose to marry a girl of any class she would be accepted, but not an American woman who has two husbands living."

The Cabinet was much perturbed over the coming divorce, but no enquiries were made, and those most perturbed did not even take the trouble to find out *when* the divorce was to take place, and still less, *where*. The case would have normally come on at the London Law Courts in March as the Simpsons lived in London.

That the divorce should take place at Ipswich seems to have been due to the very foolish advice given by Mrs Simpson's lawyer. These country divorces were an innovation, and were allowed only to save expense to poor petitioners. Certain people in society discovered that such cases were not reported in the London papers, and so arranged to be divorced in an Assize Court. This was regarded as an abuse, and a vigorous effort had been made to make it impossible for Londoners to take advantage of this plan. So true was this that I was told by some-one who had been there that the Judge was astonished when the Simpson case came up, and said "But surely this is wrong?"

Then the Chief Constable of the County whispered to him that the lady was an American, that she and her husband were friends of the

King, and that this was being done to avoid unpleasant publicity. As a matter of fact, it enormously increased the publicity, though there is little doubt that both the King and Mrs Simpson believed the proceedings would be unreported.

Immediately after the Simpson divorce had taken place I went to America arriving there on October 27th. There were an unusual number of reporters to meet the boat at New York, and eight of these gentlemen came up to me and asked simultaneously: "What do you think of your new American Queen?" At first I could not imagine what they meant. In fact I thought they were talking of a big literary prize which had been awarded to an American woman. I said, "I have no idea what you mean or whom you mean". Whereupon they all exclaimed, "Then you have never heard of Mrs Simpson?" I said yes, that I had heard of Mrs Simpson, but being a writer I knew very little about the Royal Circle. Much the same thing was said by the other English people on board.

On my reaching the house where I was going to stay during my visit to America, a member of my hostess' family came into my bedroom and showed me the *New York American* of the day before, that is, of October 26th.

Across the top of the paper ran the words "King Edward VIII will marry Mrs Wallis Simpson on June 8th". There followed a high-flown announcement, some eight hundred words in length, explaining that the King had a pure, noble and beautiful love for this American lady, and that they would be married just after the Coronation. I was in America for three weeks and every day thare was an article concerning this supposed forthcoming royal marriage in the *New York American*. I soon learnt from some of my journalist friends that the first announcement (that of October 26th) had been dictated, word for word, by Mr Randolph Hearst[1] from his castle in Wales. I was further told that he had never personally dictated any article from Europe before.

Everyone I met spoke to me of the matter. All the other papers naturally "got busy" and, for the whole time I was in New York, very little else was published of any importance in any paper.

Meanwhile, not a word was published in any English newspaper. Also, the big English newsagents had met together and decided not to sell any American paper with anything in it about the supposed coming marriage. On the other hand, those papers that were sent, by post to

[1] William Randolph Hearst: 1863-1951. Editor and proprietor of *New York American*, and a large number of other American newspapers.

subscribers in England were not tampered with. Any foreign paper sold at news-stands had the passages concerning the King and Mrs Simpson either blacked out or cut out.

Those closest to the King and Mrs Simpson never believed for a single moment that there was any idea of marriage. Indeed, to two people I know, Mrs Simpson positively denied that there was any thought of it, and showed indignation and confusion when it was suggested to her. Yet someone must have been supplying Randolph Hearst with material for the extraordinary articles which were coming out every day in the *New York American*. I received this paper and many others from the States during this crisis, sent me by an old friend. Queen Mary's lady in-waiting asked me one day if I would give her a certain copy of this paper for the Queen.

When I got back from America I saw Lady Colefax who was very interesting and told me all her views, and curious views they were, though not lacking in sense. According to her, Mrs Simpson had been advised immediately the divorce was through, to take refuge in a convent until the decree should be absolute. I laughed, but she went on "A convent can be quite a nice place—you have to come in rather early at night—that's the only thing against it, but the nuns are kind and you can see anyone you like in the daytime".

M. B. L. TO MRS KING PATTERSON

9 Barton Street,
*S.W.*1
November 26th, 1936

Poor Queen Mary is in anguish. She can neither sleep nor eat. Being deeply religious she does not believe a divorced person can make a *real* Christian marriage. She and the Holy Father see eye to eye about that!

All classes now know about the affair, and Mrs S. receives by every post frightful letters from religious lunatics threatening to kill her. She is being closely guarded, and goes practically nowhere. Of course she does not realise that apart from a certain smart, rich set, divorce is practically unknown in England. It is increasing but not enough to count among ordinary people.

I saw yesterday one of Queen Mary's favourite ladies-in-waiting, who is with her every day. She looked *years* older since I last saw her, six weeks ago.

The bitterest feeling is in Scotland, where the fact Mrs S. was at Balmoral, Queen Victoria's cherished home, so enrages them, that a number of Scotch peers and peeresses don't mean to attend the Coronation. They say in Scotland that if the King marries Mrs S. it will simply be "an open adulterous connection".

I myself am astonished at the strength of the feeling. It is amazing!

DIARY

January 28th, 1937

A good many people believe that the King did a very noble action in not doing what Winston Churchill would have liked him to do, namely, remain quite silent till after the divorce decree was made absolute. I feel convinced it was by Mrs Simpson's wish that the King told his Prime Minister of what he meant to do at the first possible moment.

On the first day that the friendship of the King and the lady became known, officially to the British people, Mrs Simpson received a large number of threatening letters. The King asked the Chief of the London Police whether she could be efficiently guarded. The answer was that no one could prevent vitriol being thrown at any person, unless he was confined to the house, and never saw anyone. As it was, two well-dressed women had obtained access to Mrs Simpson by pretending they were personal friends, and then had violently abused her.

She grew terribly alarmed, and when all the windows of the house next to her home were broken in error, she took refuge at Claridge's. It was after this refusal of the Police to protect her that Mrs Simpson expressed a wish to leave England—her reason being that she wanted to stay with friends who had asked her to visit them in the South of France. The King asked first one and then another of his gentlemen to escort her, but with one exception they all made a good excuse. The exception was Lord Brownlow[1]. He and his wife had taken a villa not far from where Mrs Simpson had been living in the South of France the previous winter, and they were good friends. Lord Brownlow, who at the time was a Lord in Waiting to the new King, consented to accompany her during her long motor drive through France, and when they reached the villa for which she was bound, he was photo-

[1] Lord Brownlow: 6th Baron. Served First War in Grenadier Guards. m. Katherine, d. of Sir David Kinloch, 11th Bart.

graphed with her and her host and hostess. This picture appeared in certain London papers.

I have always felt considerable interest in the part an unfortunate Frenchman named Bedaux played in the Duke of Windsor's and Mrs Simpson's life. Bedaux's parents belonged to the humblest class of Paris worker but they must have been clever, determined people, for they saved enough to go to America when their son was three years old. After he grew up, he was doing the hardest, most ill-paid work in New York—that of a labourer. But he had such money sense, that in thirty years he became a millionaire, so he must have had an astonishing business ability. He invented a system, hated by workers, but much approved of by some employers, by which production in factories was greatly speeded up.

I do not know how he came in contact with Mrs Simpson, but he did, and ultimately through her, with Edward VIII. At one stage he must have formed a business friendship with certain leading German-Americans—a strange thing for a Frenchman to do. But whatever the reason, he did persuade the Duke of Windsor and Mrs Simpson to pay a visit to Hitler. This Bedaux was extremely anxious that the Duke of Windsor, accompanied by the Duchess, should go to America and make a tour of certain big American business plants, in which the system of organized work invented by Bedaux was in being. Then, to his anger and surprise Bedaux was told that his return to the States would not be welcome to American industry and the visit was cancelled.

The Duke of Windsor's friendship with this man did him great harm in America and considerable harm in France where, however, Bedaux and his pro-German activities were known only to a comparatively small circle. So little was known about him that, though I read newspapers of every type, and also receive several American papers, I have only once seen an account of Bedaux which I thought authentic. It was published just after his suicide, in one of the great New York dailies, and was studiously moderate in tone. He must have been a singular human being. He worshipped the Duke of Windsor whom he always addressed as 'Sire'. The old French mode of addressing a sovereign.

I shall always believe that had Mrs Simpson stayed in England instead of going to France, it is probable that Edward VIII would never have abdicated. It is a very different thing to advise a man over the telephone to do this or that, and to beg him to do what you wish to be done when you are actually with him. There seems little doubt

153

that Mrs Simpson was kept in complete ignorance of what was really going on during those crucial ten days, for I have heard that the news of the Abdication came on her as a terrible shock and made her very angry. She is said to have rung up the King and cried "Call out the soldiers!"

I also believe that had Mrs Simpson had one sensible, intelligent friend of either sex who knew something of the world or of human nature, she and the King might actually have carried through their scheme of marriage. Had she, for instance, been content to wait her turn for a quiet divorce in London, while nothing could have prevented the American Press making the most of it, there would have been no crowds, no local gossip, no scandal such as was caused by the case being heard at Ipswich.

If she had then lived in retirement, even close to London, for the six months, seeing only a few people and giving out that it was her intention in time to return to America—and had the King meanwhile contented himself with not seeing her under his own roof—there would have been very little talk. Of course the King would have had to force himself to be courteous to the Archbishop of Canterbury, and the more old-fashioned of his parents' friends, with regard to the Coronation Ceremony. Then, had he been crowned and so became 'the Lord's Anointed', when the divorce decree was made absolute, he could have married her and Mrs Simpson would then have become Queen of England, and I cannot believe, great as would have been the shock and anger of the British, that there would have been any serious effort made to compel him to abdicate. At every point of the story the two behaved with extraordinary folly and lack of ordinary good sense.

I spent this New Year at Trent. Among the guests was Winston Churchill. On the last day of the week the party had become much smaller. We were all going away on Monday. Churchill said to Philip that he would like to sit next to me at dinner, as he had not yet done so. After a little while I said to him, "We have heard everything you had to say concerning the King and all that has happened; but you have never once mentioned the person who seems to me to be all-important in the matter". He exclaimed: "Who do you mean?" I replied "I mean Mrs Simpson". He answered: "That——." I said "Yes, that——. You have never mentioned her yet. Surely she is playing a great part in this melancholy business." He turned on me and observed in a scoffing tone, "I suppose you know very little of the King and his ways?"

As a matter of fact, I knew a great deal, partly owing to my friendship with one of the ladies with whom the King had believed himself to be in love. Also because I was on terms of friendship with one of the King's gentlemen. However, I remained silent. He went on, "If you knew much about the King, you would know that women play only a transient part in his life. He falls constantly in and out of love. His present attachment will follow the course of all the others."

During the fearful and what may even be called terrible weeks which preceded the Abdication, Churchill was passionately anxious that Edward VIII should remain King. He was constantly at Belvedere, and I remember someone telling me that Winston had said in a despairing tone: "There is about him an eel-like quality. He slips through one's fingers. In the morning he makes up his mind to stay: by the evening he had decided to go and give up everything."

Churchill undoubtedly did his very best to persuade the King to 'stick it out'. At the time there were people who meanly said that this advice was owing to the fact that because the then King's character was weak and irresolute, if he remained on the throne, Churchill would be the 'power behind it' and really rule the country. This I regard as a wicked libel. Churchill had a great sense of the value of continuity in history and he believed that the Abdication would shake the country to its foundation.

CHAPTER IX

1937-1939

In the two years that led up to the Second War, Marie Belloc Lowndes was much occupied with family matters. Her husband retired from the Staff of The Times *after being in Printing House Square for over forty years. The last twenty years had been happy ones, for Lord Northcliffe, seeing his ability, had asked Freddie Lowndes to reorganise and direct the Obituary Department of the paper.*

F. S. A. L. had a very wide, usually unspoken, knowledge of affairs and of the men and women in whom The Times *readers would be interested. So he was able to make the Obituary columns of real worth. He knew who would be the fittest person to write an obituary either for 'stock' or in time for the next day's edition, and in this work, M. B. L. with her own interest in literature and politics, was of the greatest help to him.*

At the end of 1938, their younger daughter, Susan, married Luiz Marques, a Portuguese writer and Foreign Correspondent, and went to live in Lisbon, where M. B. L. visited her the following spring.

DIARY

January 2nd, 1937

Elizabeth and I saw *The Boy David* and admired it very much. I think few people realise that Sir James Barrie began as a playright with a number of failures. But he was a man of iron will and determination, and at last he made a success of *Walker, London* which was a rather thin, but an amusing little comedy, laid on a house boat. It certainly showed no promise of such plays as *Dear Brutus, Quality Street* or *The Admirable Crichton.* I myself always suspect that he deliberately made up his mind to get into the theatre by writing something which he knew the managers of that time would take—hence *Walker, London.*

I met Cannan about that time, and I well remember my surprise when he came up to me, and with great emotion, said that Mary Ansell[1] had lived the life of a captive bird in a gilded cage when she was married to Barrie, and that he thanked God that his was the hand that had opened the door of the cage.

The divorce made a great sensation, and undoubtedly caused Barrie the most acute anguish. He always had a morbid dread of publicity and I was told he wrote to a great many important people, among them Arthur Balfour, imploring them to use their influence to prevent the

[1] Mary Ansell: Barrie's actress wife who ran away from him with Gilbert Cannan, the playright.

divorce case being reported in the papers. Very short reports were published, though the then new picture papers, did feature it.

Mary Barrie married Gilbert Cannan immediately the decree was made absolute, and for a while they lived in a tiny house off Camden Hill. It was really like a cottage, and when I went to see her there she seemed radiantly happy, and so did he. He must have had private means, or may have come into money, for they then moved to a much bigger house in St Leonard's Terrace. I think it was there that things began to go wrong. It may have been something to do with his mental state, for he afterwards became insane. Be that as it may, he made her extremely unhappy. In the end he left her, and for a while she was in frightful difficulty about money. Then some legal friend approached Barrie, and suggested that he should give her an allowance, which he did.

Many years after she had parted from Cannan she made a move to resume friendly relations with Barrie, and when I stayed with Lord and Lady Northcliffe at Roquebrune after the War, when I met her in the Casino at Monte Carlo she said to me: "J. M. B. has been writing me a warning letter about this place. He says he has read a book of yours called *The Lonely House*[1] which shows the danger of lodging with foreigners in Monte Carlo."

I saw Barrie lately at a party given by Cynthia Asquith at which were the Duke and Duchess of York and a small number of writers. I had a talk with him, and he enquired after my work.

Cynthia Asquith has been his secretary for many years. It would be impossible to describe all she does for him, especially in guarding him from the many bores and tiresome people who are determined to make his acquaintance. They come from all over the world, and almost always it falls to her lot to deal with them in a way that will not anger them, or destroy their admiration for Barrie. He is devoted to her sons—in fact he has an adoration for all children, as long as they are children.

M. B. L. TO MRS THOMAS HARDY

9 Barton Street,
*S.W.*1
June 21st, 1937

Dearest Mrs Hardy,

I have thought of you so often during these sad days. I think you were, in a way, the closest to Barrie's[2] heart. Yet what a singular and

---

[1] *The Lonely House.* Pubs. 1920.
[2] Sir James Barrie had died on June 19th, 1937.

enigmatic human being! I knew him before his marriage. And saw him, often at very long intervals, during the years that have elapsed between then and now. Our early acquaintance, and I fancy he remembered that fact every time we did meet, was because I was very intimate with a young woman, now long dead, who was Mary Ansell's beloved friend. As of course you know, all that about her nursing Barrie is rubbish. She refused to marry him many times. Then he fell ill at Kirriemuir, and his mother telegraphed to Mary who came and they were married on what was supposed to be his death bed. He told all this to Mrs Oliphant who told me and my mother, just after she had seen him. Fondest love, from Marie Belloc Lowndes.

M. B. L. TO HER DAUGHTER E. I.

Port Lympne,
Hythe, Kent
Easter Monday, 1938

The Hythe Catholic Church, which is built most oddly above the priest's house, was so full that it made me feel faint. Then we sat out all afternoon.

Hannah[1] gave me by far the best, most interesting and I felt true account of the Duke of Windsor anyone has ever given me. At one time—over years—she saw him constantly. Once he dined with her and her husband 16 nights running. She is attached to him, says he is unselfish, *always* puts the woman whom at the moment he loves, on a pinnacle. She thinks him faithful by nature. Of late years he was bitterly enraged that Hannah would never receive Mrs Simpson. This was the more unpleasant as she used to meet them out. And always the Prince, King or Mrs S. made determined efforts to force her to do so. The very last time the King and Mrs S. dined out together was at Park Lane[2] (to see film of his tour in Wales). Hannah, of course, was there and Mrs S. was really rude to her, speaking coldly of Hannah's friendship with the Duchess of York.

Now Philip is uneasily debating if he ought to see the Windsors in Paris. (Most people who knew him as King do so), and the present King accepts the fact.

[1] Hannah Ezra: cousin of Sir Philip Sassoon from whom she inherited Port Lympne and Trent Park. m. David Gubbay, Chairman of David Sassoon and Sons.
[2] Sir Philip Sassoon's house in London.

Hannah said she had hundreds of the Duke of Windsor's letters written during his tours, and that they are very good letters. Now she is really intimate with the Duke of Kent. Sees a great deal of him. Antique and curio hunting. The Duchess of Kent is said to be quite uninterested in that sort of thing. Her whole soul is entirely absorbed in her mother, sisters, brothers-in-law, and her husband whom she adores, and in her children.

What an extraordinary life Hannah has had. She is extremely clever, prudent and I feel, completely cynical, as well she may be.

CHARLES MORGAN[1] TO M. B. L.

16 Campden Hill Square,
London W.8
September 2nd, 1938

I am so very grateful to you for such charming fellow guests and for so brilliant a hostess—and, if one may be materialistic, such miraculous fish. It was very kind of you to ask me.

I think you and your Susan ought to be painted together. There was a moment when she, seated in a chair higher than yours, was looking down at you while you talked. If ever my daughter listens to me with such an expression on her face I shall feel that life hasn't been wasted. Alive, tender, amused—and with the repose of a drawing by Holbein.

I am very alarmed by the European development. I distrust the Germans as profoundly as any Frenchman and I am passionately Francophil, but if the French *neither* march *nor* negotiate then I think they are wrong. Either one says: "The Germans mean war in their own time and no treaty with them is of value"—in which case, the right thing to do is to fight now, before they are ready. Or one says: "On paper, Hitler's proposals are valuable. Let us investigate"—in which case one makes a last attempt at settlement. But to sulk on legal grounds is madness. Either fight now or negotiate now. The alternative is war at the discretion of Berlin.

---

[1] Charles Morgan: 1894-1958. Novelist. Dramatic critic of *The Times* 1926-39. His *Portrait in a Mirror* won the Femina-Vie Heureuse Prize 1930, *The Fountain*, the Hawthornden Prize in 1933 and *The Voyage*, the James Tait Black Memorial Book Prize in 1940.

September 19th, 1938

I heard some talk concerning the House of Commons. One of the Prime Minister's friends, who had been in politics many years, says that the worst of Chamberlain[1] is that he is a business man and he knows that employees can be browbeaten: he regards the MP's as his employees.

Susan and I heard over the wireless on September 15th that Chamberlain was flying to Germany. From the moment I heard the news, I felt full of dismay and fear. I had made up my mind that Germany did not intend to go to war for the sake of the Sudeten Germans and I believed what I think will turn out to be true, that the visit of Chamberlain will hearten not only him but the German people and make them think what is certainly not true, that England would be behind them and not behind the Czechs; whatever be the truth, the feeling has altered a great deal in the last two days, and I hear that not only was the Cabinet violently divided all through, but that the French Ministers, who came over, told Chamberlain that if the Czechs were given up to their fate, it would probably mean the fall of the French Government, for there, as is of course natural, the feeling against Hitler is intensely bitter and that quite apart from any question of the Czechs.

It has been a tactical error on the Prime Minister's part not to make any effort to get in touch with Prague. Meanwhile Lord Runciman undoubtedly is convinced that the Czechs will fight. If they do, it will be extremely difficult for France to keep out.

Charles showed me today a most interesting letter from Lily's[2] uncle[3] written from Luxemburg. He said that last Wednesday things looked very bad but that Chamberlain's coup might stop war at the expense, as he put it very plainly, of honour.

Meanwhile the papers entirely back the Prime Minister. The one which is most independent and has the most news is the *Daily Telegraph*. The *Times* is induced to print on its leader page a letter from Lord Allen of Hurtwood[4] with the absurd heading *Justice with Security*.

[1] Rt. Hon. Neville Chamberlain: 1869-1940. Prime Minister and First Lord of the Treasury 1937-40.

[2] Lily Belloc Lowndes: M. B. L.'s daughter-in-law, née Pescatore.

[3] M. Auguste Dutreux.

[4] Lord Allen of Hurtwood: 1889-1939. Chairman Independent Labour Party 1922-26. Member of Executive League of Nations Union.

It would be more true to call it *Injustice with Insecurity*. What strikes me is that Russia, bound to play a considerable part whatever happens, is scarcely mentioned. What Moscow does is at any rate all important from the French point of view.

I have just read the fourth volume of Reginald Esher's[1] *Journals and Letters*. To me, the most interesting passages of this fourth volume are the allusions to the then Prince of Wales. He was evidently really fond of the youth. These references include a remarkable letter to the Prince written in 1916 to try to console him for the decision Kitchener had taken, that it was not right that he should go to the Front. Esher ended his letter saying that if the Empire was to hold together, the Prince would provide a rallying point that no one else could provide and that therefore he must sacrifice for England his inclinations and his secret wishes. He gives a curious glimpse of the Prince in a letter written in 1928 when he and Lady Esher lunched with him— "Just a little round table wheeled up to the fire in his sitting room". He adds: "Who would credit such a proceeding by the light of the Prince Consort! This boy is a Stuart, not a Brunswick."

I was particularly struck by his account of the Empress Eugenie, as I am making a study of her life with a view to a novel.[2] As a schoolboy, he was at the last ball given by the Empress: she wore no jewels. He says the Emperor was half stupefied with morphia. That I daresay was true enough, though I have never seen it mentioned in any account of Napoleon III. There was no doubt that he was in constant acute suffering. Lord Esher saw her after the last war lunching at the Savoy with some French people. He says that the beautiful lines of her head and shoulders were still discernible.

To me it was a curious fact that he picked out as being among the greatest men during the war, Edward Grey, Robertson and Kitchener; and amongst the French, two soldiers, Foch and Gouraud and one politician, Millerand. Yet after Kitchener's death, he wrote a little book[3] about him which made Kitchener's friends very angry. The day it came out I was present at a lunch where Sir George Arthur[4] was a fellow-

---

[1] Lord Esher: 1852-1930. 2nd Viscount. Governor and Constable of Windsor Castle. Joint editor of *Queen Victoria's Letters*.

[2] *She Dwelt With Beauty*. Pubs. posthumously 1949.

[3] *The Tragedy of Lord Kitchener*. Pubs. 1921.

[4] Sir George Arthur: 1860-1946. 3rd Baronet. Private Secretary to Lord Kitchener 1914-16 and author of *The Life of Lord Kitchener of Khartoum*. Pubs. 1920.

guest. He was so enraged that he couldn't speak about it and it certainly was a most cruel little book. So cruel that it is astonishing to read the letters he wrote to Kitchener and which are printed in this fourth volume.

DIARY

September 29th, 1938

The crisis is not over, as so many people seem to think, but it certainly is suspended and I should be much surprised if it comes to war now. I still entirely believe that Hitler was bluffing and—I think it will come out in time—that if only he had been told quite plainly that the three great countries were going to war if he attacked the Czechs, he would have drawn back exactly as he did in May. Though there can be no doubt Chamberlain meant it for the best, I am convinced that had he not flown to Germany, but contented himself with simply sending a threat from London he would actually have done better for the whole world than he has done now, for it is plain that whatever happens, the Czechs will be to a great extent sacrificed.

All the main roads out of London are an astonishing sight jammed with cars, and the scenes at the railway stations are also extraordinary: as a man said to me, "Just like an August Bank Holiday!"

The Westminster boys were all sent home yesterday. I hear that the Dulwich boys have also gone—each parent paying £3 so that proper army huts might be built on the Kent-Sussex border. This flight from London is a great misfortune for tradespeople and indeed anyone connected with trade in any way. Large numbers of people have given their servants a week's notice and a week's money, so London is full of servants with no jobs.

Yesterday a great rush for provisions began. One lady I heard of has her house quite full of tinned foods of every kind. The only thing I bought was my special brand of China tea: I have got 14 lbs which will last me for a year. I also got last week rather more methylated, rice and matches than usual, but nothing out of the way.

I was guided by my experience in the last year. The fact that I had a gross of matches in the early August of 1914 was of the greatest value. It is one of the things—strange to say—in which there quickly becomes a shortage. I also found then the great value of rice when cooked and mixed with fried onions and a little butter: it really makes a meal for anyone. I ran out of methylated in the last war and had great trouble making my early morning tea before my work—in fact, I was forced to use the Tommy Cookers and the stuff people used for heating their hair tongs, both expensive and unpleasant to use.

I have committed one act of great extravagance: I have bought a new wireless for Wimbledon[1]. For many years I have had an ordinary battery model, given me by a dear friend. It cost £30 but is hopelessly out of date, a great worry and perpetually having to be mended. I said to myself it would be a frightful thing for me should war come, to be out at Wimbledon with no wireless, so yesterday I telephoned a man I know who is in a big radio concern.

He brought me out the best new Ecko model[2] and fixed it up for me with an aerial. I decided to do so when I realized that if war should come any money I get from America would be enormously more in pounds than in dollars. The day before yesterday I should have made 4/- on every pound.

DIARY

October 7th, 1938

I am reading the memoirs of Lord Ernle.[3] I knew him very well for nearly thirty years and paid him and his wife Barbara some delightful visits at Oakley House, Bedford. In those days he was still Rowland Prothero. He was a singular man, with a very fine delicate taste in Art and Literature. He had passionately loved his first wife, the mother of his son and daughter. He once spoke to me with the deepest feeling about her. She was a good deal older than himself, and he said that when people asked his advice concerning such a marriage, he always strongly advised it. In some ways he was very reserved. All he says about his first wife in his book is: "Our marriage brought me 7½ years of perfect happiness. I will not speak of it further."

His second wife was a brilliant, clever, generous-hearted woman. She had kept house for her uncle—Charles Hamley—who was the author

---

[1] M. B. L. and her husband had a weekend cottage on Wimbledon Common.

[2] This radio went on working perfectly until 1960 when it was given in part exchange for a new one.

[3] Lord Ernle: 1851-1937. m. 1891, Mary Beatrice, d. of John Bailward of Horsington Manor, Somerset. She died 1899. He married secondly in 1902, Barbara, d. of Lt.-Col. Charles Ogilvy Hamley.

of a book famous in its day *The Battle of Dorking* which showed what would happen to England, unprepared as she was then, if there was an Anglo-German war. He also wrote a book, which I believe still holds its place called *The Operations of War*.

His book, which is rather oddly called *Whippingham to Westminster* —suffers from being far too discreet. He devotes a little paragraph to the Empress Frederick but no one would guess from the book that she wrote to him every week, and he to her. I suppose he got to know her very well on the Isle of Wight. His father was Rector of Whippingham, so that when the Royal Family was at Osborne, the children of the two families were a great deal together.

He helped me considerably, in an anonymous life I wrote of the Empress Frederick. He made suggestions, and he read the proofs. The history of that book is curious. When I thought of writing it, I suggested the subject to Mr Murray and to Messrs Longmans. They both said that all interest in her had died.

It was finally taken by Nisbet, of which the Managing Director was a friend of mine, Bertram Christian. He gave me an advance of £200. The book made £500 for me and over £100 in America. It was re-published during the war under the title *The Kaiser's Mother*. The best chapter was written by my husband and dealt with the Schleswig-Holstein question. There was a great deal of curiosity about the book, especially among the Royal Family. I was sorry that Princess Christian was deeply hurt because I said, what was true, that the Empress' favourite sister had been Princess Alice and not herself. I heard that King Edward often gave copies to his friends.

I was once staying at Oakley House when Mr Prothero took me over to see the Dowager Lady Ampthill[1] who had been an intimate friend of the Crown Princess during the years Lord Ampthill was Ambassador to Berlin.

She told me that Queen Victoria and the Princess Christian had both been intensely anxious to know whether the Empress Frederick had contracted—after her husband's death—a secret marriage with Count Seckendorff and though both separately asked Lady Ampthill what she thought, she prudently answered that she had no theories on the subject! It was widely believed in Germany.

Seckendorff was one year younger than the Empress and had been

[1] Dowager Lady Ampthill: widow of the 1st Baron and d. of 4th Earl of Clarendon.

made her page when she came to Germany as a bride of 17. He devoted his whole life to her and never left her, except on one occasion when she begged her eldest brother as a personal favour to herself to ask him to go with him to India. This the then Prince of Wales did. He outlived the Empress, but fortunately for himself, died before the Great War. He was always trying to make Germany and England friends. A most touching and delightful account of him appeared in the *Spectator* at the time of his death; possibly written by Lord Ernle.

I was interested in what Lord Ernle said concerning Edward Grey. Lord Ernle had entered the House of Commons in the June of 1914 and so was present at the famous scene on Monday, August 3rd, when Grey made his great speech. In this book is the best account of what then happened as I remember having it described to me. He says that the speech bore no trace of preparation and as a matter of fact, Grey had not prepared it. He also says it was transparently truthful—a plain unvarnished statement of facts as Grey knew them.

When he next saw Pamela Glenconner that same day, Grey told her that for the first and only time in his life since his wife Dorothy's death, he felt her presence during his speech. It was as though she stood by his side. Pamela told me this and I was very much impressed, for Grey was the most truthful man I have ever known.

DIARY

February 28th, 1939

I sat next to George Peel[1] at luncheon. George Peel, as always, was most interesting. He has an unrivalled knowledge of France and of French politics, and he has lately been to Paris. He was very much impressed by the determination of the whole Nation not to give in to any threat. In fact he seemed to think that the Italian Government would be careful, in view of this strong feeling, not to do anything which might provoke war.

I said that I felt sure Mussolini would provoke a conflict if he were sure of the support of Germany. But from what I heard, Germany has no intention of fighting Italy's battles. Bogie Harris was amusing and malicious; he did not seem in the least alarmed and does not believe in the coming war.

[1] Hon. George Peel 1868-1956. Son of 1st Viscount Peel. Was M.P. (Lib.) for Spalding Div. of Lincolnshire. Governor of London School of Economics.

March 1st, 1939

Violet Carruthers came to lunch. I spoke to her of my fear of the coming visit of the King and Queen to America. She said she had written to John Buchan—Lord Tweedsmuir[1]—and that he had told her that it was all newspaper talk and didn't really matter.

At the Wiseman Dining Society[2], I sat next the lecturer Shane Leslie[3]. He gave a most brilliant address on Mrs Fitzherbert. He threw some light on her early life—that is to say, after her first marriage. He said her first husband was a very old man. Her second husband died of consumption very soon after the marriage. One curious story he told us was that when she fled to France to escape the attentions of the then Prince of Wales, the Prince wrote her letters of such enormous length that one of them had taken Shane Leslie himself two hours to read.

I myself heard years ago that she had had three children; that each of them was taken away from her within one week of birth and sent to America. It was said that there was one boy and two girls, and that there are descendants of these children in America.

An American friend has sent me a cutting by Charles Morgan. It gives a sad picture of England at the present time and especially of what happened at the moment when it was expected that there would be a second crisis. The theatres were practically empty for a week and several intended to close, but the week after, business picked up. I rang him up and he said he had been to the Admiralty—as he is in the Naval Reserve, and it is his opinion that they were expecting some kind of crisis.

What is of great importance and I can say it reassured me very much with regard to my coming visit to America is the fact that Goering, his wife and baby are going to Italy for five weeks. During those five weeks Mussolini will not be able to do anything, partly because it would undoubtedly be a very serious thing for Germany were Goering to be as far away as Italy at a time of crisis.

[1] Lord Tweedsmuir: 1875-1940. Then Governor-General of Canada.
[2] Wiseman Dining Society. A Catholic Dining Society, founded in 1922 by Mrs Belloc Lowndes, Mrs Wilfred Ward and Dame Una Pope-Hennessy. It then met at Claridges, and still holds dinners during the winter months.
[3] Sir Shane Leslie: Author and journalist. Cousin of Winston Churchill. Wrote *Life of Mrs Fitzherbert* 1939.

The death of Lord Colebrooke[1] is a great distress to me. I liked him very much and always enjoyed meeting him. He was a shrewd, kindly, highly intelligent man of the world, and though he must have been discreet (for everyone about the Court has to be discreet) he never gave me the impression that he was keeping anything back. He had a considerable sense of humour. I am also very fond of his daughter, Lady Victor Paget, who has some of his qualities.

DIARY

March 3rd, 1939

I am much impressed by the way Lord Castlerosse's[2] illness is being kept from the people who would naturally be interested in his personality; there has not been a single word about it in any newspaper. His mother is in great anguish and distress. I felt touched, for she asked me for the address of a certain person who is very holy, in order that she might ask this person to pray for her son. It would be difficult to find two human beings more unlike their child than Lord and Lady Kenmare[3]. She has a miniature in her drawing room of Lord Castlerosse as a child of two which is in a way very like him now—a fat, determined, not very pleasant child. His death would be a real loss to the *Sunday Express*—not so great a loss as it would have been some years ago.

I was once in a country house where they were compelled to take every Sunday twelve copies of that paper, as all the ladies wished to read Lord Castlerosse's column *The Londoner's Log.* I think of late he has lost some of his popularity for he was more in the world then, than he is now. Also, his matrimonial affairs interested a considerable number of people. I believe he and his wife are now divorced. His mother naturally always hoped that he would marry a Catholic girl. He could do this, for he was not married in a sacramental sense the first time.

[1] Lord Colebrooke: 1861-1939. 1st Baron 1906. Permanent Lord-in-Waiting to King George V 1924-36 then Master of the Robes to King Edward VIII 1936.

[2] Viscount Castlerosse: 1891-1943. e.s. of 5th Earl of Kenmare. Journalist and columnist.

[3] Lord and Lady Kenmare: 5th Earl, m. 1887 Hon. Elizabeth Baring, d. of 1st Baron Revelstoke.

During the last month, I have been trying to help Hester Fuller[1] (Thackeray's grand-daughter) to write an account of the one woman Thackeray deeply loved during his life. I have always felt greatly interested in the personality of Jane Brookfield. I already knew a certain amount about her, because my mother used to talk to me a good deal of Thackeray. Like most of the people who knew him, she did not like Mrs Brookfield. It became very clear to me as I read the letters, published and unpublished, written by Mrs Brookfield to her husband, to Thackeray, and to her friends, that she had only a slight affection for him.

When she first knew him, he was quite unimportant. Then gradually, as Thackeray became better and better known, and those about him recognised him as a great writer, Mrs Brookfield's attitude to him changed. She began to realise that the man whom she had really bewitched was well worth cultivating, and little by little led him to believe that she returned his feelings.

I think what has impressed me most in my life of observation of human beings is the lies that are told with reference to the relations of men and women. In some ways the Victorians were more honest than are their descendants. But even they would often write—especially if they disliked the man or woman—in a way that conveyed an entirely wrong impression.

M. B. L. TO HER DAUGHTER S. L. M. IN LISBON

Cunard White Star,
H.M.S. Queen Mary
March 22nd, 1939

..... I feel *very* uneasy with regard to public state of things—and I bitterly regret I did not turn back (as I was *strongly* tempted to do) at Southampton.

Apart from what, at times, has been acute anxiety, I have had a *far* pleasanter voyage than usual, with Jimmie Smith[2], Freddie Lonsdale[3],

[1] Hester Fuller: d. of Sir Richmond and Lady Ritchie. m. Richard Fuller of U.S.A.

[2] Hon. James Smith: 2nd son of 2nd Viscount Hambledon. Was a Director of W. H. Smith and Son.

[3] Freddie Lonsdale: 1881-1953. Well-known light comedy playwright.

and Sir William Wiseman[1] on board. The latter a big international banker, who refuses to think there is *any* cause for anxiety.

What alarms me is the condition of Germany. After all one can't eat munitions. Italy, also, is thought to be in a desperate state as to lack of money to buy necessities. Both these countries have everything to gain by War, and nothing, or very little, to lose. It is *that* which frightens me. On the other hand, the more Germany grabs in the way of alien peoples, the worse will be her condition when she gets any reverse, for they, naturally will stab her in the back.

Jimmie Smith is also very anxious but (like me with Daddy) he has arranged with his brother Lord Hambleden, to send him a cable or better still, *telephone*, if things get really serious.

Poor Chamberlain! Even *I* can find it in my heart to feel sorry for him *now*.

M. B. L. TO HER DAUGHTER E. I.

Ritz Tower,
New York[2]
April 2nd, 1939

I hope the boy is better. Uncle Hilary had all those sort of ailments as a child, he was frightfully delicate. Yet he grew up into an exceptionally healthy young man, till he had pneumonia at the age of about thirty-five, he never even had colds. And he got over that terrible illness amazingly well, reckless as he has always been over his health.

Everyone talks of War. The News theatres are full of pictures showing British babies in gas masks.

Yesterday everyone was dithering with fear over Hitler's speech. I stuck to my view he would back down. Oh, what a sad thing to think of all the torture and misery for thousands of human beings which could have been saved if the P.M. could have been induced (great efforts were made) to say the same thing even as late as two months ago.

I have nearly finished the story for Mary King[3]. I have begun at six every morning to get it done. It is called *It is Happening Now* and

---

[1] Sir William Wiseman: 10th baronet. Chief Adviser on American Affairs to British Delegation, Paris, 1918-19. Member of the banking firm of Kuhn, Loeb and Co, New York.

[2] M. B. L.'s last visit to the States.   [3] Mary King Patterson.

describes the black-out and the rehearsal of a raid in a Dorset town, with a fussy Mayor and a scene at Kingston Lacy. It is sentimental and leads to reunion of a man and woman who had had a child.

I try not to get tired, but it is difficult. *People* are so tiring. But on the whole one does get to bed early as almost everyone dines at 7.30 often at 7.00, in my kind of set. Yesterday I dined with a millionaire and was asked for 7.30, we sat down at 8.45. The active fear of War means that no-one, however rich, is buying anything not regarded as essential.

Darling, I so long to see you all again. I am counting the days. But I am very, very glad I came. It has certainly been more than worth while, but if I ever come again I will have a car.

I could not help laughing when someone telephoned just now and said joyfully "England has given Hitler an unpleasant weekend".

CHAPTER X

1939

*The last half of 1939 saw the declaration of war and in this chapter
there start the excerpts from a series of letters which Marie Belloc
Lowndes wrote to her younger daughter, who was living in Lisbon. They
are vivid, tender and filled with news which must often have surprised the
Censors.*

*Freddie and Marie decided to give up their Westminster house in which
they had lived for thirty years and move to a weekend cottage they had had
for some time in the Crooked Billet, off Wimbledon Common.*

*Their son and son-in-law joined the Army and their elder daughter
moved temporarily from London to a house in Essex.*

DIARY

June 1st, 1939

I lunched at Margot's and sat next to Jacques Cartier, the great
jeweller. He is an agreeable man, speaks perfect English, and his wife,
with whom I made friends some years ago, comes of a great banking
family: I thought her one of the nicest women I ever met. They have a
large family of children.

We began talking about the Duchess of Windsor. I said that I
supposed he knew her very well. He said though he did know her, he
had not come across her often, and that she had a great many fine jewels,
including an engagement ring given to her by King Edward VIII—
which is one of the great emeralds of the world and belonged to the
Grand Mogul. In those days it was as large as a bird's egg, and in connection with this he told me the following story:

Cartier's heard that certain people in Baghdad were anxious to sell
their jewels but that it would take some time as they were not allowed
to do so, and it would all have to be done secretly. Cartier's sent out one
of their most trusted emissaries. After he had been there for some time
he telegraphed home for a very large sum of money: they were taken
aback but thought that he must be on the point of procuring an enormous number of precious stones. They sent him the money and awaited
his return with great excitement. When he arrived they were surprised
to see that he had with him only a little bag, and to their increasing
dismay, out of it he brought this immense emerald.

Their dismay increased for, as they pointed out to him, there was no
one in the world—now that the old Russia had been destroyed—who
would give a large enough price for it to make a profit. He then suggested

that it should be cut in half and re-polished. This was accordingly done, making the two most splendid emeralds in the world. One was bought in due course by an American millionaire—the other by the King.

He also told me that the Stock Exchange is the great jeweller's barometer. When business is going well, men pour into his shop to buy jewels, for wives, sweethearts or—sometimes—women friends.

Late that afternoon I went to Bognor where I heard some amusing talk concerning Windsor and the present Court. The King constantly talks of his brother: it is as if he can't think of anything else; he seems haunted by him. Although the Duke of Windsor longs to come back to live in England, he will never do so, as long as no concessions are made with regard to him over income tax and supertax: his eighty thousand a year would be cut by more than half.

M. B. L. TO HER DAUGHTER S. L. M. IN LISBON

9 Barton Street,
*S.W.*1
June 25th, 1939

I fear war is coming and I believe it will be in September. I mean by that Hitler will 'take a chance' at Danzig, hoping Chamberlain will again give in. Then there will be war. I can't understand how anyone can doubt it considering the way Hitler and his gangsters are going on now. It is known here that Ribbentrop (who was right last September) is more convinced than ever that England is bluffing. And *he* has Hitler's ear. I know a great deal I don't care to write. I am thinking of having Dr P's portrait[1] at Wimbledon, though a far safer place would be Daisy's cottage,[2] but it is *so* precious and valuable that I fear to send it far. By the way, I don't believe in the heavy bombing of London, though the Government do. But they are generally wrong. I feel sure the Germans will concentrate, rightly, on munitions and Air Fields. They would be idiots not to. And they can't replace their war material, as can England and France. They will have to keep their bombs for use, not for causing terror.

[1] Portrait of Dr Joseph Priestley by Gilbert Stuart, painted in America.
[2] Miss Daisy Hersee living in Slindon, Sussex. For many years housekeeper to M. B. L.'s mother.

M. B. L. TO HER DAUGHTER E. I.

28 *Crooked Billet,*
*Wimbledon Common SW.*1
September 4th, 1939[1]

The P.M. was kept in wicked ignorance of the rising tide of anger and of shame in every class. When he sensed the temper of the House of Commons he turned so pale that the people near him thought he was going to faint, they meant to wait till Tuesday, by which time Poland might have been over-run and all the wobbly countries would have turned to Germany. However, as Daddy says, Chamberlain is a "House of Commons man" and he didn't lose a minute. I think Sir Nevile Henderson[2] was the villain of the piece. He honestly believed in the Hitler regime. The Russo-German pact hit him like a bomb.

There was a raid warning at 11.30, it was thought quite real but it may have been a rehearsal. I don't believe myself that Hitler will bomb London after his promise to Roosevelt.

M. B. L. TO HER DAUGHTER S. L. M.

28 *Crooked Billet, S.W.*19
September 16th, 1939

I myself believe that the War will not be a long one. But I must admit that few people agree with me. You will have already heard about Harry and Charles. They are both joining up. Charles hopes very much to be with Colonel Richard Crosse, his old Colonel—in fact, he has gone to see him today. I'll try and send you the first Boulestin book[3] which was published in 1924, and is by far the best and most straightforward. *Good* cooking, is always *simple* cooking. I am distressed at the elaborate and very silly recipes advised in the War Catering Columns of the popular papers.

You must think of us, Darling, as very well, and everything going well. It is not too much to say that both England and France are magnificent. In between my work I am trying to keep a diary.

[1] War was declared on September 3rd, 1939.

[2] Rt. Hon. Sir Nevile Henderson K.C.M.G. 1882-1942. British Ambassador in Berlin since 1937.

[3] *Simple French Cooking for English Homes*: by Marcel Boulestin, the well-known restaurateur and music critic.

October 3rd, 1939

I dined with Lady Hall. There was only one other woman and a most interesting man from Scotland Yard. I said to him that I believed it true that a German went all through the last war in the British Censors' Office, sending most valuable information to Germany. He looked rather taken aback, but did not deny it. I remember reading the book written by the man, translated into English. Oddly enough, I recently found a reference to the man in question and the writer said he particularly remembered this very able censor, who was a man with a beard, and more intelligent than any of the others, so that when any of the humbler censors were in any difficulty they always went to him! He learned with great astonishment that he was a German spy, and got away after the War was over.

We had some talk about the state of Germany. He told us that about a year ago he had dined with a man in the German Embassy. Something was said about the morale of the German people and the man replied, 'Whatever they feel, they will stand anything if told to do so, bless their hearts". Therefore, he disagreed with me that there is any hope of a breakup in Germany.

October 5th, 1939

Lunched with Margot Oxford. I was astonished at the size of the party—we were ten in all. We had an extremely simple meal just one dish and some cheese. I was put next to Sir Frederick Leith-Ross[1]. He said he had been to America twice in his life. After a while I asked him if he ever listened in, whereupon he said in an explosive tone: "NEVER". I observed that one learnt a good deal from listening in, owing to the fact that every country now pumps out propaganda night and day. He actually seemed surprised to hear this, although he has some important job at the present time. I told him I thought that even a person like myself could learn a great deal by listening to both the French and English broadcasts from Germany, that in my opinion an extraordinary change had taken place in the last few weeks.

[1] Sir Frederick Leith-Ross: was then Chief Economic Adviser to the Government.

MARIE BELLOC LOWNDES' AUTOGRAPH FAN

Signatures reading clockwise

Edmond Gotz, Doyen de la Comédie Française.
William T. Stead.
Jane Nadine (?)
Blanche Barretta Watson (?). Balfour.
Isabel Somerset.
Francis E. Willard.
J. Reichenberg.
Frank Leslie. Duff Cooper.
? Coquelin Cadet.
Winston S. Churchill.
Emile Zola. Philip Sassoon.
Paul Verlaine. Dr M. Nordan.
Thornton Niven Wilder.
Alphonse Daudet.
Julia A. Daudet.
Jules Cheris. Anita Loos.
Edmond de Goncourt.
Oscar Wilde.
Gyp. Sarah Bernhardt.
Juliette Adam.
H. G. Wells.
Bartholdi. Robert
Bridges. Berners.
Victorien Sardou.
1894 Rejane (Sans-
Géne). Lucy Clifford.
Henry M. Stanley.
Dec. 28th, 1893.
Dorothy Stanley.
Caran d'Ach.
Yvette Guilbert 1896.
Ronald Gower.
John Blackie. W. W. Jacobs.
Edward FitzGerald.
William Watson.
Thomas Hardy. Marcel Prevost.
Robert Sherwood.
W. Holman Hunt. Edward Clodd.
Dan Van Paarl.
Edouard Detaille. Jan Fabricius.
Vernon Lee.
Jules Verne. Anatole France.
André Maurois.
Jules Lamartin. François Coppin.
Mathilde Blind.
H. H. Asquith. Richard le Gallienne.
Burdon Sanderson. Charles Richet.
Oliver Lodge. Pamela Grey of Fallodon.

Among the signatures on the back are those of the three Sitwells
Jules Romains, Albert Einstein and George Moore.

7b. Rex Whistler

7a. Drawing of M. B. L. by Rex Whistler

The early German broadcasts had been very arrogant, and I should think on the whole correct as to the information they gave, naturally full of the glorious exploit of Germany in defeating the Poles, and with a good deal about Russia, even a little about Italy. All that has now changed. They content themselves with vulgar abuse mostly of Churchill, though Chamberlain comes in a good second. They also go back to the atrocities committed by the British a hundred years ago in India, and in other parts of the world.

I did not say so, but I think their cleverest propaganda is that directed to the French. It consists of intelligent abuse of the British, the constant reminder that in the last war the French lost in dead immensely more than the British, which is quite true, making great fun of the small number of British who are in France now, compared to the number of French who have been called up.

I asked Sir Frederick whether he had ever seen Hitler. He answered "Yes," in a somewhat curious voice—that he knew him quite well. I said how was he impressed, whereupon he muttered something about his looking like Charlie Chaplin!

On my other side was Puffin Asquith. He was, as always, extraordinarily nice, but I was surprised to find how very little interest he seemed to take in the war news. He asked why I thought the war would not go on for very long, though I always added the proviso: unless Russia comes in in a real sense, either by giving a tremendous lot of gold and material to Germany, or—which I realise is most unlikely—joining Germany as an ally. I told him that what made me think the war would be short was the fact that ever since the last War I have read a great deal about Germany in both French and English, that I have always taken a keen interest in that country, as must do any intelligent French person. I said they are brave, but extremely hysterical.

The lunch was soon over and all the ladies went into the next room, the library, where Margot spends a great deal of her time. I sat down on the sofa by Miss Campbell, Margot's friend and secretary, a very pleasant and highly intelligent woman. She told me in a low voice that she had seen a director of Shell-Mex. He told her that according to their information, Germany was so terribly short of petrol that it would not be possible for her to stage a big raid on London, until and unless she obtained possession of the oil wells in Roumania. I thought this information worth everything that anyone had said in the dining room, because it is plain that Shell-Mex must have a complete knowledge of the oil situation all over the world.

Up to the time when Hitler began his persecution of the Jews, Margot was what used to be called pro-German, for she was passionately in favour of doing everything possible to restore Germany to her old place in Europe after the First War. The persecution of the Jews, however, completely altered Margot's view of the nation to which she had been so devoted.

A true story is illustrative of how she regarded the First War. She and Mr Asquith, with a couple of friends, were motoring shortly after the end of the War. Mr Asquith began talking of the great commanders who had taken part in the struggle and he observed that if Von Sext had been in Germany he believed that the War would have been lost by the Allies.

"Why wasn't he in Germany?" asked Margot. "Because, my dear, he was in Africa. Don't you remember the great fight that he put up there?"

"But why didn't he go back?" with surprise in her voice, whereupon Mr Asquith looked at her, and after a moment's silence said, "You forget the British Navy".

M. B. L. TO HER DAUGHTER S. L. M.

*28 Crooked Billet, S.W.*19
October 7th, 1939

You will be amused to hear that Randolph Churchill[1] met Pamela Digby in a blackout. She was with a lot of people and they were all in the street together. He and she made friends, and he did not *see* her for about an hour! This was only three weeks ago! They were actually engaged *one week*. All this is true, told me by Eddie[2] (who sent you his love).

The Ivy[3] is fairly full at lunch-time but very few at night. I am not at all afraid of the black-out. I always have a taxi, and make it go *very slowly*. Phyllis de Janzé[4] taking Venetia Montagu[5] to dinner with Lady

---

[1] Randolph Churchill: 1911-1968. Son of Sir Winston and Lady Churchill. He married Hon. Pamela Digby, d. of 11th Baron Digby this same year 1939.

[2] Edward Marsh.

[3] Ivy Restaurant in West Street, St Martin's Lane, M. B. L. had an account there for many years.

[4] Phyllis de Janzé: an old friend of M. B. L., d. of Capt. Arthur Boyd and Lady Lilian Boyd.

[5] Hon. Venetia Montagu: sister of 5th Lord Stanley of Alderley and widow of the Rt. Hon. Edwin Montagu P.C.

Cunard, smashed her little car into a refuge, and had concussion. But they are going to have a little more light now. Daphne Bankes[1] is driving an ambulance at night.

I sat next H. G. Wells at lunch on Tuesday, He said that like me, he did not think the war would be long. He is *very* shrewd. I have known him about 40 years!

M. B. L. TO HER DAUGHTER S. L. M.

9 *Barton Street,*
*Westminster, S.W.*1
October 23rd, 1939

The removal man who came to look at the furniture was very nice, and over a good glass of neat whisky he became jovial and told me some interesting things about the art of moving and storing furniture. How lucky it is that you and I and Elizabeth are all interested in everything! I tritely add that it makes life so much more thrilling.

It seems so strange to leave this house, where I used to see Charles off to the Front in '16, '17 and '18 and where I wrote *The Lodger,* and from where you and Elizabeth were married. It will have more ghosts now—*my* ghost certainly.

DIARY

November 14*th,* 1939

Long before I had any idea what the initials stood for I read a most remarkable and brilliant account of an early flight over Constantinople in *The Spectator*. It was signed Y. B. and it lingered in my mind for two reasons. It was the first account of an aeroplane flight I had ever read, and secondly because it was such a remarkable piece of writing.

I cannot remember where I met Francis Yeats-Brown, but I do recall that when he mentioned *The Spectator* I said at once, "Did you write that wonderful article?" He said, "I did." He then asked if he could come and see me, and we became friends. As I came to know Yeats-Brown really well I discovered with astonishment that he not only was an exponent of Yoga but that he constantly practised it, and I once saw him sit on the floor and do strange exercises. The best description of

---

[1] Daphne Bankes: sister of Ralph Bankes of Kingston Lacy and Corfe Castle and of Mrs Norman Hall.

him ever written was that which described him as a "pig-sticking Cavalry officer and a mystic hungry for the wisdom of the East".

Strange to say, in spite of his having a great deal of charm in appearance and manner of speech, he was not a success as a lecturer. He was naturally keen to write another book. I advised him to stick to India, the more so that *Bengal Lancer* was not a long book, and he had a great deal more material, but he was apparently anxious to write a War book, for in the First War he had taken part in the campaign which had included the siege of Kut. He wished to call the book *Many Confinements* but finally settled on *Golden Horn* which I thought an excellent title.

DIARY

December 7th, 1939

When I used to stay at Wilsford, near Salisbury, I constantly saw Sir Oliver Lodge[1]. Lord Glenconner had lent him a charming old house and he had also built on top of it a splendid room where Sir Oliver was able to work in peace and carry on his scientific experiments. It was within a short walk of the Glenconners'.

His personality did not appeal to me, but I greatly honoured him for his open and constant avowal of his belief in life after death, and in Spiritualism. I suspect he felt a hearty contempt for the ignoble attacks made on him by many of his fellow scientists who thought that his mind must have given way for him to have accepted such beliefs.

He was once at Glen when I was staying there, and we had a long walk together, when I had the only real talk I ever had with him. In a sense he was preaching to the converted, for I have always believed that communication with the dead is possible. He told me on that occasion he had never accepted 'spirit photographs' because they could be so easily faked.

I became very fond of Lady Lodge who for many years entirely disagreed with her husband. But in the end she became convinced, and through a curious circumstance, which she told me.

She had known a man in her youth of whom she had never spoken to her husband or to her children. And although they had been very attached to one another, she had not seen him for years, and indeed she had no idea that he was dead. One day she received a message from him recalling their early friendship. From then she became a believer in

[1] Sir Oliver Lodge: 1851-1940. Scientist. Physicist. Pioneer in Wireless Telegraphy. m. 1877 Mary Fanny Alexander.

communication with the dead. She was a small, delicate, fragile looking woman, who before her marriage had been a painter. She had a large family of six sons and six daughters. After Lady Lodge's death in 1929 her husband believed he was constantly in touch with her.

Sir Oliver had a most delightful brother, a distinguished professor in Edinburgh. He came and spent an evening at Wilsford and tried to explain the Einstein Theory to the young people. I had the good fortune to be present, and he did it so admirably that I understood something of what he was driving at—as my mother would have said.

It is a curious fact that after the death of Lord Glenconner, his widow at once made an effort to get in touch with him, but failed. But in time he 'came through' in the Lodge's house and gave an account of how he was greeted on the other side by many friends who had long been dead. But most important of all, he had seen their son, Bim, who was killed in the First War.

Lord Glenconner was for many years quite out of sympathy with his wife's interest and belief in Spiritualism. But there came a day when he suddenly changed—I don't know the reason. I knew him very well, but I learned this fact in a strange way. I was acquainted with Sybil, Lady Brassey[1], and going to see her one day she told me that she had just had a visit from Eddie Glenconner, that they were very old friends, and had known each other as children. She said to me, "I'd no idea that he had become a Spiritualist".

He did however testify publicly to his belief at a great Spiritualist meeting. I regard this as having been very brave for he was extremely reserved. The speech he then made was printed and his widow sent me a copy of it after his death.

Some time later Lady Glenconner arranged for a seance in the drawing-room at Wilsford. It was in order to carry through what are called 'book tests'. Lord Glenconner had one great hobby and interest in life, and this was forestry. When I stayed at Glen I used to go for walks with him, during which he used to talk of very little else. Among the terms employed in forestry are some that are very peculiar—at least to my thinking. When these 'book tests' were being carried out at this seance, in every case the page and line indicated by the medium had something to do with trees, or with forestry. In two cases the peculiar terms used in forestry were printed on the page in question. This made a great impression on me.

[1] Sybil, Lady Brassey: widow of 1st Earl Brassey.

CHAPTER XI

1940

In March, Marie's husband died suddenly, after only a few days' illness. The shock was very great and she alludes to her sense of loss and desolation in her letters.

The people of Britain were slowly getting adjusted to total war and it is an interesting fact that there were many fewer rumours flying around than in the 1914-18 war.

When the bombing began, M. B. L.'s elder daughter and her family moved to Shropshire to Brand Hall near Market Drayton, after being for a brief time in Essex and at Esher where her husband was stationed. Marie Belloc Lowndes stayed for long periods with her daughter and grandchildren, returning to the Crooked Billet at times, and also staying with various friends at their country houses—Renishaw, the home of Sir Osbert Sitwell, and Mells with Mrs Raymond Asquith among others.

DIARY

January 4th, 1940

I dined last night with Sir Edgar[1] and Lady Bonham-Carter. There were five men all engaged in war work—no women except her and me. Sir Edgar's brother is Governor of Gibraltar. There was the Warden of New College—Fisher,[2] the great education man; Christopher Hobhouse[3] and Leigh Ashton[4] who runs the financial side of the Ministry of Information.

They talked very freely and Fisher told me a most interesting story which he had had from Arthur Lee[5] (of Fareham). Some years before the last war when this happened, Lee had been appointed Civil Lord of the Admiralty. He had been staying in Berlin with the Ambassador and was travelling in a first class carriage when the train—an express—drew up at a small station where a number of German officers were standing about.

One of them—an Admiral—came into his carriage, and at once

[1] Sir Edgar Bonham-Carter: 1870-1956. K.C.M.G. Barrister. Judicial Adviser Mesopotamia 1919-21. m. Charlotte, d. of Col. William Lewis Kinloch Ogilvy C.B.

[2] Rt. Hon. H. A. L. Fisher O.M.: 1865-1940. Warden of New College since 1925. Trustee of British Museum.

[3] Christopher Hobhouse: author of *Fox*. Killed by a bomb in August 1940.

[4] Sir Leigh Ashton: Director of Victoria and Albert Museum 1945-55.

[5] Viscount Lee of Fareham: 1868-1947. Presented Chequers to the nation as a country house for the Prime Minister.

opened out a big sea map. Lee felt uncomfortable and rather ostentatiously waved the *Times* which he had been reading, before him. But the Admiral was completely absorbed in his job of looking at the map. He spread it out and immediately Lee saw that mines being laid at sea were marked here, there and everywhere. He had a good look at the map while the officer was examining it.

He then went straight back to Berlin and gave all the information he had obtained to the Naval Attaché there, who knew absolutely nothing of this plan. The map was actually marked in German "In case of War with England".

I asked Sir Edgar, whom I know to be a very clever man, if he had any views as to when the war would end. He said he had been so wrong other times that he was afraid to say anything. He and his wife were in Czechoslovakia last summer. He was having a cure for arthritis. At that time he approved of the Munich settlement because he believed Hitler would keep his word. But he now thinks it was a great mistake, and that the Czechs would have fought bravely. No one there was at all willing to give any theories as to the course of the war. But they all believed that if Germany and Russia obtained any serious success, America will certainly come in. They all want America to be a benevolent neutral and not join in, because of the fact that if she came in she would want to have a big hand in the arrangement of the peace.

My remembrance of the last War makes me realize with what extraordinary frankness people do talk in Government and allied circles. The nearer they are to the centre, the more indiscreet they are apt to be. Unhappily for me I had to leave at a quarter to ten, as I didn't feel I could keep Bliss[1] out longer, and I must confess that I've never been out in so black a night.

There was some talk about Charles Morgan, not a single man there liking any of his books unlike Charlotte[2] and me. They all knew however that he was in the Admiralty (this is supposed to be a deadly secret) and exactly the kind of work he is doing.

DIARY

January 5th, 1940

I have just been talking to Jimmie Smith over the telephone. He is now in the Anti-Aircraft stationed at Sevenoaks, but will come up one

[1] Bliss. Driver of the car which M. B. L. used to hire as she and her husband gave up their car and chauffeur at the beginning of the war.

[2] See footnote 1 on p. 189.

day fairly soon and give me dinner and take me to a play. He gave me a very funny account of the unfortunate young officer who is being so much talked about at the moment, as much sympathy is felt for his very nice parents over his terrible motor smash, although it was not put in the papers, this young man got very drunk one night and was caught in the street by a special constable. He was being marched off to Vine Street when he knocked his captor down. The man had on spectacles which fell off, whereupon the young man danced upon them, smashing them to pieces. At Vine Street the magistrate was so angry that he remanded him in prison for a week.

He then received through his commanding officer an invitation from the King to shoot at Windsor, and as the King must be obeyed, the young man was let out of prison to go and shoot, his commanding officer having charge of him and giving his word he would not escape. Then he was marched back to prison.

M. B. L. TO HER DAUGHTER S. L. M.

*28 Crooked Billet, S.W.*19
January 8th, 1940

You will have been thrilled to see your old friend Hore-Belisha[1] has got the sack. All sorts of rumours are flying about, probably all false. I shall know the truth after I have been to lunch at the Thirty Club. I do believe it is true that till last Thursday morning, he hadn't the slightest idea that he was going to be dismissed. Both Daddy and I have the feeling that he is lending himself too much to newspaper publicity. Thus, today, every popular paper has pictures of him with his dog in his Wimbledon home.

Unlike most people, I don't consider the Reith[2] appointment a good one. While he was with the BBC he half-despised the Press, a fact of which all Fleet Street is well aware, though they also know the great contribution he made to the high repute in which British Broadcasting is held all over the world. You remember them living opposite to us in Barton Street and their bringing his remarkable mother to see us.

[1] Rt. Hon. Leslie Hore-Belisha: d. 1957. M.P. (L. Nat.) for Devonport. Secretary of State for War since 1937. Cr. Baron 1954.

[2] Sir John Reith: 1st Baron 1940, Director-General of B.B.C. 1926-38. Appointed Minister of Information 1940 and later in the same year Minister of Transport.

January 19*th*, 1940

As was the case last week, almost the whole of the talk at the Thirty Club was about the Hore-Belisha affair. Two of the members believe he will never come back to public life—I mean by that, be asked to join the Cabinet.

What struck me in reading the *Hansard*[1] giving the verbatim account of the debate was that so many of the Members who spoke, while showing perfunctory disdain for the late Minister of War, evidently did not like him personally. I also hear that he was very good indeed the first year when he made many reforms but that lately he has become what was to me described as 'lazy'. He was much less frequently at the War Office, and was rather fond of receiving people in his own house.

I had a talk with a man in the Admiralty about the loss of the *Royal Oak*. He said bitterly that the fault lay with the Treasury officials who, when asked to provide the money to do what was necessary to make Scapa Flow safe, had laughed at the idea that there was any real danger of war. This was apparently in July or early August. The Treasury is the watchdog of the Navy, but it was a very unfortunate thing that the people who really decide what money is to be released for defence, did not believe in the war up till the very last moment.

Meanwhile opinions as to the length of the war are extraordinarily divided. There are still people who believe it will go on as did the last war. But on the whole, the more thoughtful do not believe it will last longer than a year.

I went to an interesting dinner party—all the men were doing Government work and were inclined to be very angry at any public criticism either of the Government or of the department with which they were concerned. The one in the Ministry of Information was particularly bitter—that is the Ministry which comes in for most complaints and cricitism. It has certainly been very badly managed up till now. The most remarkable thing I heard was that the German High Command have managed to get in touch with the French and British High Command. It was said that their proposals were such that they could have been considered, but when they came right down to it, it was clear that Hitler was still in supreme command and that these offers had been made without his knowledge.

[1] M. B. L. was a subscriber to *Hansard* for many years.

The German High Command has always kept itself apart from Hitler. There is no doubt that at one time they were in close touch with the Russian High Command at a time when Hitler and the whole of Germany did nothing but abuse Russia and the Russian system of Government. The fact of this closeness between the Generals became known to Stalin and was the real reason for those terrible 'purges'.

But in war everything seems incalculable. The U-boat menace was regarded as being mastered by every British expert up to the opening of the war. On the other hand even now the German Air Force is regarded as superior to that of the British or the French. And yet these German airmen fly almost every day over a part of Scotland and make endless efforts to get direct hits on British ships but they turn tail and fly off the moment British aircraft go up and chase them.

M. B. L. TO HER DAUGHTER S. L. M.

28 *Crooked Billet, S.W.*19
January 20th, 1940

The great excitement about Hore-Belisha has died down somewhat, but I go on hearing extraordinary stories. Yesterday I had a long talk with General de la Panouse[1]. He was naturally full of it. The Hore-Belisha faction have made one fearful mistake. They have allowed some-body to pay for huge advertisements running on the lines "We want Hore-Belisha." "He must come back. Write to your Member of Parliament".

Only the *Evening Standard* and *Express* printed these absurd ads, but they were offered to every paper. Had they been taken everywhere, the cost would have been in the neighbourhood of £30,000. So someone very rich must be behind it. I think it is probably some woman who admires him.

F. S. A. Lowndes was not well. To his wife's dismay he insisted on going to London to The Times *office. One day in March he came back feeling ill and stayed in bed. He seemed to be recovering, when he died in an instant from a heart attack on March 26th with Marie sitting beside his bed.*

[1] General de la Panouse: sometime Military Attaché to the French Embassy.

28 *Crooked Billet, S.W.*19
Tuesday

My dear Mary,

I know that you will grieve for me—My dear husband died very suddenly, on March 26th. He had been ill under a fortnight and was supposed to be much better. In fact I was taking him to a house the Iddesleighs had just taken near where my son-in-law (now an officer in the Welsh Guards) is stationed. I shall always be very, very glad I was with him, and alone, when he died. We had had a happy talk that morning, for we intended, if the war did not interfere, to spend part of next winter at Lisbon. And he was telling me of the beautiful places he meant to take me to see.

We were very united, and were interested in all the same things. He was a real newspaper man, the *Times* was his life. He was on the staff 46 years, and was doing work for the paper up to the last few days of his life. There was a beautiful Memorial Service with all the *Times* folk there, including the owner, Major John Astor, in St Bride's, the old Fleet Street Church.

SIR FRANK BROWN[1] TO M. B. L.

Annery Bungalow,
Bideford, N. Devon
March 28th, 1940

Dear Mrs Belloc Lowndes,

I had the privilege of working in the closest contact with your husband in connection with the scores of Obituary Notices of men and women connected with India I prepared year by year. They averaged at least six a month—some of them of considerable length; and he would often discuss with me the Indian side of the work of such men as Curzon or Morley. Sometimes the work was done under great pressure when nerves might well be frayed. But never was there an angry or hurtful word from him. The emendations he made on my MSS were invariably an improvement and his wide knowledge of the personalities of the day was ever at command. It was a privilege to be thus closely associated with so great a master of his craft; so warm-hearted a friend, and one who could at all times lighten up the work of the evening with a good

[1] Sir Frank Brown: 1868-1959. On the editorial staff of *The Times*. Correspondent of *Times of India*.

story or an animated share in a discussion of men or events. I have lost in him a cherished friend, and I feel I must send you a line of sympathy upon your so much greater deprivation.

REX WHISTLER TO M. B. L.

27 York Terrace,
Regents Park
March 28th, 1940

Darling Mrs Lowndes,

I have just heard with great pain of your loss.

There is nothing that I can say—or probably anyone else—that could in any way alleviate your great unhappiness, particularly as, with the person you so love, must seem to have gone too all those long loving years of peaceful contentment and delight. It is true, I think, that they only *seem* to have gone, for that lovely store of golden years which you made together—years of life well lived, full of delightful interests shared and lovely pleasant things, is really as much with you now as, say last month—last year—any time, for the triumph and delight of such a thing as you both made of life is a *cumulative* one.

Any one day of it has no more power than another, and yet the *whole* —whether yesterday or thirty years ago—being the Past, cannot be affected by the Present.

But all that of course you know, and the pain in your heart is for the Present and the Future without that companion who made life so agreeable and lovely in the past. But in your unhappiness now I am very sure you are nearer and more in touch than ever I shall be, with the one unfailing source of comfort and strength to the spirit.

I have often thought how curiously short lived and how small is the *quantity* of happiness we are allowed at a time (the *quality* of happiness is of course beyond measure). We seem to pass so rapidly from light into shadow, and when in light again, darkness seems invariably to follow, so *much* too quickly.

And yet I suppose it is really the exquisite *taste and economy* of the Genius who draws our lives which makes life so infinitely lovely and moving, stirring and glorious. It is as though we presumed to stand by the side of a great painter imploring him not to use the dark tones and shadows, but only to put on light and more light. How *can* we know what the great mind has already conceived the finished work to be?

My darling Mrs Lowndes, I feel deeply for you in your grief and for your dear sweet Elizabeth and Susan, and I only hope you will believe this, and not think this foolish 'rigmarole' a duty letter. I keep you always in my heart as a *very dear friend*. On no account think of answering this

Very affectionately always

Rex Whistler

M. B. L. TO HER DAUGHTER E. I.

*28 Crooked Billet, S.W.*19
April 14*th*, 1940

Narvik is most important. More so than they care to say as it will cut off iron ore in any quantity from Germany.

I am working very, very hard, sending a short story to Mary King next week. If she takes it, it is £189 in my pocket. It seems to me that the next four weeks will be crucial. A lot of instructed opinion here think they will go for Paris next. I feel that their bolt is shot, the accounts of the boy prisoners, of the idiotic waste of bombs and ammunition on refugees.

It does prove, I think, that they have become crazy and out of hand. Italy coming in would, no doubt, prolong the war somewhat.

M. B. L. TO HER DAUGHTER S. L. M.

*28 Crooked Billet, S.W.*19
April 16*th*, 1940

Well! I spoke more truly than I knew when I said the war might be intensified. Uncle Hilary wrote me a very kind letter about your father, and *also* rang me up. He had just come back from France. He said he thought all that is now happening would probably shorten the war. That cheered me up.

Charles[1] has just got Embarkation Leave for France and comes home today. I am so very glad Elizabeth is here with Stafford[2]. The child looks very well.

The story is *done* now. I am starting the Empress Eugenie novel tomorrow. I will write soon about my plans as to here. I feel that *if* I

[1] M. B. L.'s son Charles, who was a regular officer in the First War, had joined up again.
[2] Viscount St Cyres: elder son of Lord and Lady Iddesleigh.

196

can get good commission for the first half of my memoirs, it might pay me to stay *here* till they are finished, as *all* the material is here. I feel much better for working again. Flaubert said *"Ecrire est une fonction physique chez Madame Georges Sand"*. And it is the same with me. I am unhappy if not writing.

DIARY

April 30th, 1940

Una[1] said that the general belief in political and War Office circles is that owing to the immense number of men he has under arms, Hitler will have to strike out much like the spokes of a wheel, here there and everywhere, and the hope and belief is that soon he will find it impossible to get all his wars going together, owing to difficulty with regard to food and lines of communication.

I had some talk with Una's husband Richard, as he rang up to speak to her. He told me he thought everything was going well and would go better and better but as everyone knows Trondheim is very important. It will have to be re-taken. Apparently no one realized that Germany had sent her best troops to Norway, obviously well aware that there would be trouble and that they would not have a walk over as they had in Denmark.

ALICE DUER MILLER TO M. B. L.

Neshobe Island Club,
Bomoseen, VT
1940. (No date)

Dear dear Marie,

What a time to live in—when you could have lost your husband, and I not even know it. And now I do not know when it was. Knowing that he liked my books, I was looking forward to his reading a new one I have written in verse called *The White Cliffs*—like *Forsaking All Others* —only about an American girl married in England. I read it to Lynn and Alfred Lunt[2] the other day, and Lynn cried all the time and means

---

[1] Dame Una Pope-Hennessy. D.B.E. Author. Wife of Col. Richard Pope-Hennessy.

[2] Lynn and Alfred Lunt: American married couple who usually acted brilliantly as a team.

O

to read it on the air. I shall send it to you, as soon as it is published—in mid-September.

Echoes of war get to us even on this Island. Laurence Olivier[1] goes every day to a flying field, getting his last necessary hours in the air, and soon can be seen circling over us in an orange plane—very tiny and insecure in appearance, and Vivien Leigh tries to ignore what it means.

Alec is better. The important thing I always want to know about friends of mine who have been through a critical illness is whether their personality has changed—Well, his hasn't. For a time his mental processes were very slightly slowed, but now he is exactly as he always was. His diet has cut his weight down by twenty-five pounds, I should think, and that makes him look younger and better than he has for years. He means, I think, to go back into the play[2]. This I fancy is not a wise decision, but no-one can decide it except Alec, and if he thinks he can do it, he probably can.

Harry, who you may not know, worked so hard for "Fighting Funds for Finland" in the late winter, that he had appendicitis as soon as I had got off to Hollywood, is better than he has been for years. He is building a tiny house for Alison and Denning[3] on a mountain near his place—a mountain in the English meaning of that word. I am so pleased about this.

I can't work much. I have been reading Lord Granville's letters, and they console me somewhat. How similar England's position was in the last days of the Eighteenth Century—at least is seemed so to them then, though Napoleon to us seems very mild. However, Lady Stafford wrote that to make peace with him seemed to her like making peace with the devil. Dear Marie, all my love and sympathy. How wisely Susan chose her new country.

Affectionately
Alice D. M.

DIARY

May 17th, 1940

Among the things I heard yesterday was that some German para-chutists in Holland had in their planes tiny pit ponies who carried

[1] Lord Olivier: Actor-manager.
[2] *The Man Who Came to Dinner*: by George S. Kaufman and Moss Hart. Alexander Woollcott acted a caricature of himself in this play in New York.
[3] Their son and daughter-in-law.

machine guns on their poor little backs. I believe this because the lady who told me had seen the Queen of Holland. She did not tell me so, but I thought it obvious that that was from where this strange information had come. In any case, it is far too odd to have been invented.

I went up from Wimbledon on business connected with the possibilities of a film, but in the end I missed the film agent and spent the afternoon at the London Library working at my *Julie*[1]: then I went to see Phyllis de Janzé. There I found Diana Cooper, Juliet Duff[2], Sylvia Henley[3] and the art expert Tancred Borenius[4]. He has long cherished a hopeless passion for Phyllis; he is a Finn. They had all come in to listen to the wireless—which to my astonishment the Coopers don't possess. They live just opposite, so they are a good deal in and out. It was widely believed in London yesterday that the Germans were going in to Switzerland that afternoon.

None of them believed in the parachutists ever coming here, but several of them did believe that London was in great danger of being bombed. Borenius, who knows Germany well, says that if they ever bomb London it will be at the very end in desperate revenge.

DIARY

May 30th, 1940

What struck me at the Thirty was that each of us—we were five— had a completely different opinion of what would happen. Helen Maclagan expects Germany to attack England within the next week or two. She regards the danger as very serious as well as imminent.

Tiny Huth Jackson[5] does not believe they will ever attack England. That is my view, modified by my being willing to admit that they may

[1] M. B. L. long wished to write a study of Julie de Lespinasse, but she never completed the work.

[2] Lady Juliet Duff: only d. of 4th Earl of Lonsdale and widow of Sir Robert Duff, 2nd Baronet.

[3] Hon. Mrs Henley: d. of 4th Baron Sheffield and widow of Brig.-Gen. the Hon. Anthony Henley. C.M.G., D.S.O. son of 3rd Baron Henley.

[4] Tancred Borenius: 1885-1948. Professor of History of Art, University College, London, 1922. Author of a number of learned works on art.

[5] Mrs Huth Jackson: d. of Rt. Hon. Sir Mountstart Elphinstone Grant-Duff G.C.S.I. m. Rt. Hon. Frederick Huth Jackson 1895.

make a last desperate attempt when they see they have lost the war elsewhere.

May Tennant[1] a highly intelligent woman, seemed to think it possible that if Italy comes in, Germany might choose that moment for an attack on England. But I could see she thought it extremely unlikely.

Gertrude Tuckwell was not, I felt, very strongly interested in the war. She is absorbed in the question of whether what is going on now will be injurious to the future of the factory workers. She spoke with bitterness of the fact that the employers are trying to force the women of a factory to pay a contribution towards the air-raid shelters the Government make them provide.

Helen Maclagan was most indignant and said that the workers ought to pay. I agreed with Gertrude. To my mind the shelters ought to be paid for by the employers, who can take the money out of the large profits that they will not, I hope, be allowed to keep all for themselves.

One of the members made us laugh. She said she had a nephew with her on leave when news came about the King of Belgium. He immediately said: "But this is very serious for me, for I am interested in a girl in Antwerp. I'll have to try to get her out!" His aunt told us that he had a girl in almost all the capitals of Europe, and he would have his work cut out if he tried to get them all out!

Almost everyone I meet believes in Fifth Column activities in this country. No doubt there were a great many spies before the war broke out, but I should think every one of them was known to the police. If the Germans landed in force there would be a number of refugees who would welcome them. What happened in Holland has produced a fearful impression, but people don't seem to realise that the so-called Fifth Column in Holland consisted of Germans who were living there. They were not spies, but they had gone there to avoid the discomforts of living in Germany; but they were Germans, and naturally when the Germans came they did everything to help them.

DIARY

May 31st, 1940

To me it was most interesting to have the opinion of a professional soldier like Richard Pope-Hennessy. He said that during his stay in

[1] Mrs Harold John Tennant C.H., d. of George Whitley Abraham. Mrs Tennant had been Superintending Inspector of Factories and member of several Commissions concerned with women workers.

Berlin after the First War he had been on friendly terms with the German Generals now fighting this war. He spoke of the Commander-in-Chief as being a remarkable man, but remembered the kind of loathing with which he had spoken of Hitler in the old days. Yet now he is Hitler's right hand, and must at any rate pretend to be devoted to him.

He thought their greatest mistake was not to content themselves with taking Holland. Had they done that, and from Holland attacked this country, they might have had a chance of knocking us out. It would have been an unexpected attack for which no preparations had been made.

He considers the invasion of Belgium was foolish, though it is true that owing to the King having appealed to France and England for help, it did throw out the plan made in France. Had the King given in then, Weygand might have stopped the German onrush. But he had to alter all the dispositions which had been worked out by the French General Staff. He believes the Germans may effect a landing here, probably in Scotland.

DIARY

July 30th, 1940

My elder daughter had taken a house in Essex as her husband was stationed at Colchester. Bombing of England had just started and though some fell close by I do not remember it causing us any special anxiety, but we were in the danger zone and my son-in-law decided he would like us to move to a safer part of the country. My daughter and I went to Shropshire to look for a house. She chose that county because Lady Jaqueta Williams[1] lived there: the best and kindest of sisters-in-law to my daughter. We saw a number of houses and then she heard of The Brand four miles from Market Drayton. It stands in a large park, and has great charm. It must have belonged at one time to a member of the Grosvenor family as the Grosvenor coat-of-arms is over the door. It is a roomy house, very suitable for a big family. We have our meals in the hall, out of which opens a pretty double drawing-room.

[1] Lady Jaqueta Williams: J.P., wife of Philip Victor Williams of Hinstock Hall, Market Drayton.

August 21st, 1940

The bombing of Britain has begun in earnest and every night we hear the planes roaring overhead on their way to Liverpool. But there was only one night when I felt really afraid. All the children were there, together with their nurse, the cook and a very young housemaid. My daughter was in Esher with her husband. I was sitting in the drawing room reading just after dinner—it may have been about half past eight. Suddenly I heard a bomb fall. It sounded as if it were just outside the window. As a matter of fact it was a quarter of a mile or more away. I had all the lights put out and we all took refuge in the space under the staircase. What made me uneasy was the knowledge that there was a railway line at the back of the house.

M. B. L. TO MRS KING PATTERSON

Brand Hall,
Market Drayton
Shropshire
August 23rd, 1940

I think I told you that Elizabeth's husband is an Officer in the Welsh Guards, and my son Charles has joined up. He is just being moved—I believe to Wales—unless he goes back to his old Regiment, which he certainly will do should there be an invasion. He was in the Regular Army for eight years, after getting his Military Cross when only eighteen. But his present job is of more interest, especially now as he is Adjutant of the Camp. Of course he is a good bit older than the soldiers serving under him.

I have just seen a copy of one of the leaflets dropped from the skies by Hitler. It is almost as big as *The Daily News* in size, though it only has four pages. It gives the whole of Hitler's speech to the Reichstag, and is headed *A Last Appeal to the British People by Adolf Hitler*. We are astonished to see how large it is, though it is printed on very poor paper. Really it looks like a war paper, for of course all our newspapers have been reduced now, even the *Daily Telegraph* having only six pages. The *Times* alone looks pretty much as it used to do, a fact which would have given my dear husband pleasure.

All the same, I am glad my husband did not live to see what has happened in the last three months. He would have been so well aware of the real anguish the collapse of France caused me at the time, and ever since. I think of it constantly. There are a great many Frenchmen in England, and an ever increasing number. A party flew their own planes over from Africa to England the other day. It has made me all the more wretched, because I had hoped to be in France part of every year from now on.

Elizabeth had four offers from America to take her children. But both she and her husband think that children should stay with their parents, sharing with them whatever dangers there are. I entirely agree with them.

It seems to me that Hitler hopes to bomb and frighten England into giving in. An absurd idea, given the kind of peculiar, stubborn character of the British people. And their absolute confidence in themselves. An old saying: "Say *'blackbird'* and pass it by," might well be their motto. I see it in my cook-housekeeper, who has been with us 6 years. She is hysterical and fussy about little things, but the very serious bombings near my house (where she was quite alone) have not affected her. She only rang up, afterwards, to ask my advice as to whether "next time" she had better "stay under the staircase as before" or go to a shelter outside. I said "the staircase", for one risks splinters, to say nothing of bombs in the open.

I wish you could see 3-year old Hilda's[1] gas mask. It is so cunning! I am going to try and get one to bring to America some day. It is called the Micky Mouse Gas Mask.

DIARY

August 25th, 1940

I have begun writing *I, Too, Have Lived in Arcadia.*[2] Eddie Marsh to whom I spoke of this book objects to the title which he considers too long. However it is the only title which to my mind suits the book. I am writing it because I feel that after my brother's death his life is certain to be written, and I alone know everything about our youth in France, and the history of my French family.

I have been fortunate in receiving an introduction to Messrs Macmillan from my friend Desmond MacCarthy. They will pay me a hundred pounds advance.

[1] Lady Hilda Northcote: younger daughter of Lord and Lady Iddesleigh.
[2] *I, Too, Have Lived in Arcadia.* M. B. L.'s first volume of memoirs about her childhood in France, which had a great success. Pubs. 1941.

The other night the warning went again and bombing, machine-gunning and anti-aircraft firing started. This went on till half-past five the next morning. I stayed in bed but perhaps foolishly left my door open, so my poor Frances[1] came in and out most of the night. She was very brave, but fancied that every burst of fire was a bomb. There were some very big bombs, but the sound was quite different, and each time there followed a fearful, overwhelming crash.

I couldn't sleep after the 'all clear' and felt too tired to go out. There were various warnings during the day. We did hear that the station had been hit, and houses at Putney destroyed, but it was impossible to telephone. I soon heard that there was no invasion, it had been a false alarm. I did some work, but felt very queer. It was so strange not being able to get authentic news of what had happened in London. We did get newspapers, but they of course said nothing.

Then in the afternoon, about half-past six, Frances was in my bedroom when like a flash there came bombs, anti-aircraft firing and guns. The whole house shook violently. I did think a bomb had fallen just outside. We both rushed downstairs and took refuge in the little space under the stairs. It was a violent dogfight in the air going on a few yards to the right of us. Five planes were brought down by the RAF making even more noise than the bombs as they fell. I think the whole thing was over in about ten minutes, but it seemed like an hour. It stopped almost as quickly as it had begun.

Some people nearby told Frances about the planes having fallen and Harry[2] (who came to dinner shortly after) actually saw three German planes shot down. He had got his men into the trenches; he didn't go in one himself. A bomb fell right through the lodge of the house where he is billeted. I didn't think he would come to dinner, but he did and so did Lily.[3]

During the time they were there, though we now and again heard a bomb far away,—probably Putney—there was comparative calm. Lily went off at once because of the two children[4] and her Nannie, but Harry

[1] M. B. L.'s excellent cook-housekeeper at Wimbledon—Frances Baird.
[2] M. B. L.'s son-in-law, Lord Iddesleigh.
[3] Lily Belloc Lowndes: M. B. L.'s daughter-in-law.
[4] Richard and Veronica Belloc Lowndes: M. B. L.'s grandchildren.

stayed on nearly an hour. He told me one of the biggest bombs had fallen about half a mile from Crooked Billet on a by-pass.

I heard that every big London station had been hit except Paddington. Harry had seen a good deal of the damage, and he begged me earnestly to go back to Shropshire. Indeed I felt that he would have liked me to leave next morning at cock-crow.

The next morning early I telephoned to Elizabeth and she said she wanted me to come as soon as possible. Harry had been gone about an hour when the serious business began again, just the same as the night before—in fact, in some ways worse—and waves of raiders came over, an enormous number of bombs of every kind, except incendiary bombs, being dropped. The nearest to us was on a road leading off the Common. Wimbledon Common is now a huge camp. In addition to the factories, the Germans were trying to get the soldiers. Luckily there were none of them under canvas, all being billeted, so at night they cannot be seen.

Naturally I felt the second night much more than the first, partly because of the fight in the air at four-thirty that morning. The raid on the second night lasted longer, the 'all-clear' not being sounded till eight-thirty in the morning. But after it became light the bombing became much less. I had my blind up the whole time and I lay in bed watching the wonderful searchlight effects. The Anti-aircraft fire was quite incessant.

What added to the terrors of the second night was that the electric light failed for about an hour. To my surprise it came on again. I thought they had got Lots Road Power Station. They have been trying to get it all the time, but so far have not succeeded.

There were no warnings yesterday morning before I left. I naturally told Frances she could go home, but she preferred to stick it out as her family live at Gravesend, where things are even worse than at Wimbledon. Also she adores the little house. It is her pride and joy. Everything was exquisitely neat and clean, though she had not been to bed for four nights before I arrived.

Persistent efforts were made to destroy Westminster—the Houses of Parliament, War Office, etc. etc. So far they have entirely failed, but I think they are being specially protected, for when driving through St James' Park, I was struck by the number of balloons in the sky.

Miss Callaghan was caught by a raid on Friday night in Westminster Cathedral and had to stay there in the crypt with about fifty people. She was cheered by the recollection that Susan had been married there! They kept thinking, poor creatures, that the Cathedral was going to fall in upon them. At five o'clock in the morning a priest came down, and said Mass. Masses were said at intervals of half-an-hour until the 'all-clear' when Miss Callaghan crept back to her flat, very much worried that she had not been at her office all night, as she is the Head of the Westminster Health Society.

Wimbledon Common looked most beautiful and peaceful, with no sign of damage. Bliss came for me at twelve noon: at Putney I saw that a large shop was in ruins, and all the way up to London roads were barred off. Instead of going along the Embankment, as we always do, we were diverted up the Cromwell Road, constantly passing roped-off streets.

We went down Marylebone Road and there I saw by far the strangest sight of all, the front of Madame Tussaud's with every window out, but the back was as if a giant knife had cut through the whole of the building. That impressed me more than anything—it was done by one bomb. Every window on each side right up to the Edgware Road was broken. A second bomb had fallen on Baker Street Station, but with no damage that I could see from the outside.

Most impressive, was the absolute emptiness of the streets. There was not a person in sight, and not a car in Oxford Street—all had fled somewhere when a warning was heard. The chauffeur, who up till now has not minded anything, confessed he had been caught in the afternoon raid the day before, going to Camberley. He had seen a bomb burst thirty yards off, and that had shaken his nerve. He suggested that we should go into a garage. I said "No, I have a friend who lives in Orchard Court, a large building close by, we'll go there". We were welcomed most kindly and asked to go to their shelter. That I wouldn't do, as I fear shelters. As the chauffeur wouldn't leave his car, they allowed him to run it in to their own huge garage under the building. By then it was a little after one o'clock. When the 'all-clear' sounded we went off again—to the Times Book Club first, where I got two books, for what I knew would be a long journey. One was an autobiography by Katherine Furse.[1] I was lucky to get some newspapers on my way to the station.

We reached Paddington by twenty minutes to two: there the scene defies description. Thousands of people were sitting outside the station on their luggage waiting for porters. Bliss had brought some people up from Wimbledon for the nine o'clock train and he said it was much worse then. I began to think that I should never get off. But a porter

---

[1] *Hearts and Pomegranates.* Pubs. 1940.

206

who fortunately recognised me as being a good tipper (as also luckily is Elizabeth, with whom I have travelled several times) came up and managed to take my luggage. There was an enormous queue at the Ticket Office, but I got there at last, and the porter got me a seat. When the train came in—very late—it was taken by assault and in the corridors the people stood two deep all the way down.

It was an extraordinary journey, frightfully tiring, but interesting too because they all told their experiences. One man, obviously the owner of a little business, was there with his wife and child. They lived in a huge block of flats in Edgware Road. They saw the bomb fall which killed fifty people in a shelter. It was seeing the dead being carried out which made them decide to leave London. They were especially interesting to me for the man's father had a business in Paris, and he had escaped from there with his wife, who is half French, and the child, partly by car to Bordeaux. So thick was the crowd leaving Paris that they went only fifteen miles in one day.

One woman had come from the Isle of Wight, starting in the night, only to arrive in the middle of the London raid. Another passenger had with her a Siamese cat in a basket. It screamed like a child the whole way. She was the wife of a man high up in the Air Force. A bomb had fallen and destroyed a house next door to where she lived in Chelsea.

Somebody told me then the truth about Saint Paul's and Guildhall. Bombs fell close to both, but though Guildhall has been injured, Saint Paul's was not even touched. Then someone else gave me an astonishing account of the effect of a bomb throwing huge blocks of stone up in the air as though they were cricket balls. He said a great many people were killed by these blocks falling on them. The first bad night people did not go into shelters, they stood outside watching the sky.

At Wellington I changed in to a local train where there was only one passenger in my carriage, a lady, coming to spend two days with her son in the Air Force here. Her husband is a specialist. They live on the Golf Course at Leatherhead. The Clubhouse was destroyed two nights before by a large bomb falling, not on the house, but in front of the house. So great was the explosion that the Clubhouse, though a modern building, had gone completely flat, and it was most astonishing to see the furnishings—heavy leather sofas, etc.—flung in some cases fifty yards off on to the Course. The caretaker, his wife, and child had gone off to a shelter when the warning had sounded. Otherwise they would all have been killed outright.

M. B. L. TO HER DAUGHTER S. L. M.

The Manor House,[1]
Mells, Frome
December 9th, 1940

I have been here since the third and I am having a very nice time. Indeed I feel much better, owing partly no doubt to the delicious cooking, which suits me. It is a full house, Perdita Jolliffe[2] with children, nurse, governess, Helen[3] who does her school inspecting from home; Daphne Pollen[4] who has four children extra to baby just born. *She* lives in the Cottages, but comes in to dinner. We also have officers in to meals. Uncle Hilary was here when I arrived. He is very feeble, which distresses me. He was very affectionate to me, and sends you and Luiz[5] his love. He is rather mournful, as his contract with the *Sunday Times* is ended. He went on to Tetton—Mrs Herbert[6]. I came to Bristol, not a pleasant experience. So I shall go back via Frome, changing at a healthier place. We hear there was a heavy raid on London last night.

M. B. L. TO HER DAUGHTER E. I.

28 *Crooked Billet, S.W.*19
December 15*th,* 1940

I had a most interesting hour with a Frenchman really well informed as to what is happening everywhere and what has happened. He loathes Darlan but regrets all the fuss.

He says it is unfortunate that no-one except the Prime Minister and a handful of men in various walks of life did not and do not now, realise that the whole civilised world believed the British Empire must fall and if it had to be, wished it to happen quickly so that the world could settle down. He said that belief amounting to certainty is and was the key to

[1] M. B. L. was staying with Mrs Raymond Asquith.

[2] Lady Perdita Jolliffe: m. 1931 Hon. W. G. H. Jolliffe who succeeded his father as 4th Baron Hylton 1945. Sister of 2nd Earl of Oxford and Asquith.

[3] Lady Helen Asquith: sister of above.

[4] Hon. Dapne Pollen: d. of 3rd Baron Revelstoke, m. Arthur Pollen, the sculptor.

[5] Luiz Marques: husband of M. B. L.'s younger daughter.

[6] Hon. Mrs Mervyn Herbert: d. of Joseph Willard, U.S. Ambassador at Madrid, widow of Mervyn Herbert, 3rd son of 4th Earl of Carnarvon.

everything. He was intimate with Mr Bullett[1] whom he was often meeting with the Windsors. I asked him about General de Gaulle, of whom I thought he gave a very true description.

I am going to Cumberland Lodge for Christmas and I shall say I *have* to write for three hours each morning—the trouble is I can't very well say that as to Christmas Day or Sunday. It is really true that I must get the book done. Love to dear Harry. *"Quand deux cœurs s'aiment bien, tout le reste n'est rien"*, is a very old French saying.

[1] Mr W. C. Bullett: U.S. Ambassador to France since 1936.

CHAPTER XII

1941-1942

Marie Belloc Lowndes' book on her parents' marriage and her own and her brother's childhood, I, Too, Have lived in Arcadia, *came out at the end of* 1941. *It was written at Brand Hall. To her great joy it was an instantaneous success. Marie's greatest interest while she was staying with her daughter was the meeting and entertaining of members of the Free French Forces who were stationed nearby, for as she said of herself "Je suis toute Française de cœur".*

In 1942 *she returned to London and took another house in Barton Street, on the other side of the street to No.* 9. *Her daughter felt great anxiety because of the rocket bombs and the V2s, but M. B. L. was a courageous woman and the bombing seldom forced her out of London.*

America entered the war and all her dear friends from across the Atlantic went on sending Marie Belloc Lowndes those very welcome letters, parcels and newspapers. Her warm friendship with Professor Gordon Haight of Yale University began at this period. He was rapidly becoming the greatest living expert on George Eliot. This friendship was conducted by means of a long series of letters across the Atlantic, chiefly concerning George Eliot and her circle, but also with the war in Europe and life in England. M. B. L. only had the pleasure of actually meeting Professor Haight and his wife on one occasion, when they visited England after the war.

As time went on the course of Marie's life can be better traced in her letters than in any other way, for they have a directness and actuality that bring vividly back those long years of war.

M. B. L. TO HER DAUGHTER S. L. M.

> *Brand Hall,*
> *Market Drayton*
> *January 2nd,* 1941

We may be going to have a cow! There are so many children in the house, that a prodigious lot of milk is drunk.

We have plenty to eat and can even get fish by train from Shrewsbury. I managed to get two cases of oranges. As you know, I have made a life-long study of food. The human body is an engine, and if not rightly stoked, won't work rightly. That fact few people seem to realise.

Osbert Sitwell is a clever manager: he has wonderful unusual vegetables. We are asking him for the names of some of them.

I am writing a short story for Mary King Patterson called *Tiger, Tiger, Burning Bright*[1]. Elizabeth has found me a good secretary so it is going well.

M. B. L. TO MRS KING PATTERSON

Brand Hall,
Market Drayton, Shrops.
February 1st, 1941

Now let me tell you certain facts which will, I know, interest you about the London Zoo. One night, eighteen high explosive bombs fell on that comparatively small space, as well as hundreds of incendiaries. Astonishing to relate, not a single animal was killed. The oldest building in the Zoo—the charming little camel house—was utterly destroyed, as it had a direct hit, yet the camels had walked out quite unconcerned. The cage of the ravens was also hit, but the birds flew off into a tree. You probably saw the photographs after they were released for publication in the United States.

I saw Dr Vevers, who is, I presume, under Dr Huxley[2]. He was most kind and helpful, and I was taken round and shown everything. As you will see, I was particularly attracted by Jezebel and her mate! Next door to them are a pair of lions which have been—to my surprise and amusement—adopted by the Vic Olivers (Winston Churchill's second daughter and her husband). It was news to me that a private person could adopt an animal. You will see that I have worked in this adoption. To do the Vic Olivers justice, they cannot have done this as a publicity stunt, for I have never seen a word about it in any paper, and I read them all.

M. B. L. TO HER DAUGHTER S. L. M.

Brand Hall,
Market Drayton, Shrops.
March 26th, 1941[3]

My heart is full of dear Daddy today. I miss him—I am tempted to say strangely, and more as time goes on. How I wish we had gone to Lisbon in Autumn of '39. Though I did not realize it, he was failing

[1] This refers to a short story by M. B. L. called *Tiger, Tiger, Burning Bright* which was published in the *New York Daily News* and later in a volume of short stories, *What of the Night?* Pubs. U.S.A. 1943.
[2] Dr Julian Huxley: Secretary Zoological Society of London 1935-42.
[3] 1st anniversary of the death of F. S. A. Lowndes.

even then. And, as you know, he was *very* fond of the little house at Wimbledon. But it was a bad winter—deep snow, and he *would* go up to London and to the office when he felt bored—and by bus. One such expedition undoubtedly hastened his death. I am however *thankful* he did not live to see the *Times* bombed. His room destroyed. As you know, the splendid church of St Bride's, Fleet Street, where was held his beautiful memorial service, now has only its spire left. Human nature can get accustomed to anything. But he would never have become accustomed to the destruction of beauty.

We went to Oxford yesterday. Elizabeth had a Union of Catholic Mothers' meeting. I went to Chrissie[1]—you know her husband is very famous now that Agriculture is coming into its own. He looked very cheerful. He is doing a Penguin *and* a child's book on farming. Did I tell you we had 3 Free French Officers to dinner? I did enjoy it and they enjoyed the delicious dinner and some champagne I had brought from Wimbledon.

The president of Trinity[2] (Oxford) with whom Daddy was in constant touch, is going to Portugal with a note of introduction to you. He is going to present your PM with some high Academic distinction.

HESTER FULLER TO M. B. L.

March 31st, 1941

I am very sad about Virginia Woolf[3] though I can never forgive her description of my mother in that book of hers. I think she was unbalanced always, but she was a much finer character than her sister Vanessa. With her Stephen's family inheritance of honesty and integrity, she should have known better. Personally I believe V. killed herself because she realised that all she and her sister stood for and made a rule of life—a creed for after life—fell into smithereens in the face of this world crisis.

[1] Christabel Orwin: niece of F. S. A. Lowndes, m. C. S. Orwin, Director of the Institute for Research in Agricultural Economics, Oxford University and Bursar and Fellow of Balliol.

[2] J. R. H. Weaver: President 1938-54. Dr Salazar was given an Hon. Doctorate by the University of Oxford. The ceremony was held in the mediaeval University of Coimbra. F. S. A. L. had been at Trinity.

[3] Virginia Woolf: d. of Sir Leslie Stephen K.C.B. m. Leonard Woolf 1912. Novelist. She had drowned herself earlier this month. Mrs Fuller's nephew, James Ritchie, was missing from May 1940. This intensified her rejection of the Bloomsbury pacifism.

Cumberland Lodge,
Windsor
May 27th, 1941

Lord FitzAlan told me that when the news of the *Bismarck* was told by loud speaker in the Army and Navy stores everyone there *embraced!* Customers and Assistants! He is very anxious with regard to Crete. Vicomte de Bellaigue[1] came at 12.45 and stayed till 2.30. He said *very* little about Susan, though very, *very* gratefully—but he told me the whole odyssey of his *amazing* escape. I met Noel Coward, with whom I am lunching on Tuesday.

DIARY

June 15th, 1941

I have been shocked on reading an article entitled *Virginia Woolf* by Hugh Walpole. It was described as being one of the last things he wrote before his death, and the Editor actually added he was glad to print it not only because of the portrait it gave of Virginia Woolf, "but for the delightful self-revelation of its author".

The article included an unpleasant attack on Somerset Maugham's great book *Of Human Bondage*, and odious remarks on four women writers. According to Walpole, "Literary Ladies, from Rhoda Broughton through Katherine Mansfield and Rebecca West[2] to Gertrude Stein have worn, from time to time, the robes of priestesses engaged in throwing fragrant incense on their own altars".

I have known two of these women very well. Rhoda Broughton was one of the people I have most cared for in my life. I saw her constantly, almost every day, when she was in London. Never once did she mention any novel of hers to me. Neither did she ever allude to a novel of hers in the many letters she wrote to me.

I had long intimate conversations with Katherine Mansfield while she was in the South of France, and our meetings were followed by several brilliant letters from her. She never made any allusion to her work in our talks.

---

[1] Vicomte Pierre de Bellaigue: belonged to the Free French and saw S. L. M. and her husband when he escaped through Lisbon.

[2] Rebecca West: Novelist and critic, m. 1930 Henry Maxwell Andrews.

Rebecca West I have known since she was quite a young woman, and again I cannot remember any mention made by her of her writings. Indeed I recall being touched at seeing the colour rush into her face when I once told her that I regarded her short study of Henry James[1] as one of the best critical books in the language.

I am sorry I never met Gertrude Stein, but I have come across many allusions to her in contemporary memoirs and letters, and I don't remember a single reference to her ever having mentioned the work, which clearly is, I can't help thinking, much more to her than is their creative writing to most women writers.

All this being so I couldn't help feeling amused at Walpole observing in the same lamentable article on Virginia Woolf "As to throwing incense on her own altar, that was not at all the thing at this first tea-party. Virginia Woolf was ironic about her own work, and delicately humorous about others." Immediately afterwards Walpole put on record her "gay and ribald treatment" of some episode in E. M. Forster's *Howards End*, and he adds a nasty hit at Aldous Huxley.

The article confirmed my opinion that though Virginia Woolf was if not a great—a most original and remarkable writer, her work was often injured by a cruel and malicious touch, partly owing, no doubt, to certain facts concerning her youth, which must have soured her nature. No writer of my time not even Thomas Hardy or Conrad lived in such an atmosphere of adulation.

M. B. L. TO HER DAUGHTER S. L. M.

Brand Hall,
Market Drayton
September 16th, 1941

Your letter of 5th just came. Uncle H. left today. I fear he will dislike *Arcadia*. He lives in a world so remote from reality, and has no idea of what people say, believe, and *invent*. Nothing will change him, of course. He is quite unaware how famous, in a sense, he is, both here and in America, and the interest taken in his personality. Did I tell you that three separate Americans went to La Celle[2] to

---

[1] *Henry James*: by Rebecca West. Pubs. 1916.
[2] La Celle St Cloud: home of Louis Belloc, where his children M. B. L. and her brother were brought up. See *The Young Hilaire Belloc* by M. B. L., edited by Elizabeth Iddesleigh. Pubs. 1956 in U.S.A.

see the place and ask questions about him. I have twice been asked to provide material for my Mother's life. Oh! how glad I am I had enough energy left to do this book. It was a great labour, because I had too much material, all of which had to be gone through, selected, rejected, etc.

M. B. L. TO HER DAUGHTER S. L. M.

Cumberland Lodge,
Windsor
September 28th, 1941

I am having a delighful visit here. Yesterday Lord Hugh Cecil[1] came to lunch. He was nearly killed by the bomb which destroyed Savile House opposite where he lived. He asked after you. What a happy time we had with him that afternoon! He was very amusing, said it was a mistake not "to muddle through", as the British have a genius for improvisation, and so can meet each difficulty as it comes, and overcome it. It is like June and we sit out all afternoon.

Before I came here, I went to a most interesting cocktail party at Grosvenor House given by the publisher—Hamish Hamilton. All the writers in London were there, beginning with H. G. Wells. Also Brendan Bracken[2] with whom I had a long talk. I think he will do that really difficult job very well. Especially the American end.

M. B. L. TO HER DAUGHTER S. L. M.

28 *Crooked Billet, S.W.*19
October 10*th,* 1941

The book has made a wonderful start and went out of print *before* publication. Unhappily, having told me they were printing 5,000 Macmillan's had only printed 2,000. They are, now, reprinting 4,000! They *say* 2nd edition will be ready in 10 days, but that seems to me almost impossible. I have very good terms. 15% the first thousand, 20%

[1] Lord Hugh Cecil: Provost of Eton 1936.
[2] Brendan Bracken: 1901-1958. M.P. Then Minister of Information. Had been Chairman of *Financial News*, Managing Director of the *Economist* and Editor of *The Banker*. 1st Viscount Bracken, cr. 1952.

up to 4,000 and 25% after that. It is a 15/- book and is beautifully produced.

I work here about 10 times quicker than at Brand Hall. Since I arrived, just a fortnight ago, I have done a short story, and got on with a thriller. I *hope* Mary King will take it.

Here, Mrs Orchard[1] tho' 78 does me very well, I have Lady Maclagan coming here to lunch today and Dame Una next Friday. I have seen Thornton Wilder[2] and given him your address. He loves the book. I am dining with Alec Woollcott tomorrow. I find the Landsdowne Club *very* useful, as I can get parcels left there to be called for. I now have a bill at the famous poulterers, Bailey of Mount St. I get game, not too dear. He sends it to the Club, and Bliss picks it up while I am at dinner.

Of course you will see review of *Arcadia* in the *Times* of today (10th) and in current Lit. Supp. It is heartbreaking that it is out of print, a very heavy loss to me.

DIARY

October 20th, 1941

One of the strange things in England is the divorce between the press and ordinary opinion. In the last few days the papers have devoted many columns to Lord Gort's[3] despatches, but what they print about them is entirely unlike what people are saying all over the country. Only in one paper is there a hint that Gort was not able before the war to get the Expeditionary Force ready.

Again I've not seen a single paper mention the name of Hore-Belisha, yet he was far more responsible than Gort for the state of unpreparedness. What shocked people most, oddly enough, was not the lack of tanks, as the lack of ammunition. And yet a great many people must have known it. My son told me that each of his men had only fifty rounds.

The real truth—and that again, though I've heard it said several

[1] M. B. L.'s former cook-housekeeper, Frances Baird, had married and she now had this elderly, but excellent maid at her cottage.

[2] Thornton Wilder: American author. *The Bridge of San Luis Rey* 1927, *Our Town* 1938 and *Skin of Our Teeth* 1942, all won the Pulitzer Prize.

[3] Lord Gort: 1886-1946. 6th Viscount. V.C. Was Commander-in-Chief of the British Expeditionary Force in France.

times, had never been printed—is that the War Office, and Gort himself, believed in the Maginot Line. All the papers play up the theory that the King of the Belgians is a fine fellow. But whatever he did, fine fellow or nervous coward, he was largely responsible for all that happened during those eventful days.

That again, after the first two or three days, has never been in any way plainly said in the press.

The best account I've seen of Winston Churchill and the way he works appeared today. It was written by an American journalist. It was interesting to me because he does not occupy the rooms beyond the drawing room in No. 10 Downing Street, which was turned into a bedroom by Mrs Chamberlain. He evidently prefers what was Asquith's bedroom overlooking the garden. I feel a great interest in that house. When I knew it and went there so often the rooms were extremely beautiful, for Margot had brought there some fine pictures, and each room looked very, very different to what it did when Mrs Chamberlain came and altered everything, putting chintzes and modern furniture where there had been old furniture. The only room that remained unchanged under the Chamberlain regime was the dining room.

The account of Churchill's marvellous powers of work impressed me very much, as it proves his brain is unimpaired. An old friend of his told me that he works less hard now than in the old days when he was working simply and solely for money. His output then could only be described as "terrific". The war has enabled him to give up the hard and incessant writing.

Some one said to me the other day—someone who knew him well—that she often wondered what would happen to him after the war. She added, curiously, as I thought, "At any rate the British people will never treat him as the French did Clemenceau". I said nothing to that, and yet I wonder very much what his after-war life will be like. Another friend of his—a man—said that he hoped Winston would die in harness. I did not like to remind him of the astonishing change which has taken place with regard to the general view now held of Churchill. During the years when he was in the wilderness I was often the only one in a considerable company to say a good word for him. It was grudgingly admitted that he wrote very well: that he was very clever, but always he was labelled as 'dangerous', 'impulsive', and the last man who ought once more to play any part in public affairs.

Then in 1940 he was treated as a saviour. If people said a word of criticism concerning any action of his, he or she was regarded as a traitor. Apparently he accepted the adulation lavished on him with simple good humour. In former days he was often blamed for the way he spoilt his children, and as to that I always defended him. His children all loved him. He had far more influence on them than if he had been cross, severe, censorious, and what so many parents are, without meaning to be so, unkind.

Curiously little is said of his wife. Yet she has been all through the most wonderful helpmate, from the beginning of their married life. I often think of the time when I first knew her. It can truly be said of her that she walked in beauty like the night, for she was very dark and quite exquisitely lovely. It must have been a throw-back in the Hoziers, for though they were all good-looking, none of them have that wonderful outstanding beauty that she had. She was not supposed to be clever, yet she had great character which was shown in her breaking her engagement to the man who is now Sir Lionel Earle[1]. The fact that she did so, exasperated and angered the whole of that formidable Stanley clan.

The talk of the moment concerns the engagement of Ava Wigram[2] to Sir John Anderson. All those who know her cannot but be glad that she has found happiness. I know nothing of Sir John Anderson, except that he has been Home Secretary, and invented the Anderson Shelter. But since the engagement I've heard very varying opinions. Some people think that if anything happened to Churchill he would be the next Prime Minister. He must be very able, or he would obviously not have obtained his present position. He was, however, one of the Chamberlain men. He has been a widower for nearly twenty years, with a grown up son and daughter.

I cannot imagine anyone who would be more suitable to be his wife. Ava will make an excellent political hostess. I believe she would have married a Frenchman after she became a widow, but for the war. She was on terms of friendship with many members of the late French Government.

[1] Sir Lionel Earle: 1866-1948. G.C.V.O. Held many high posts in the Civil Service.

[2] Ava Wigram: d. of J. E. C. Bodley and widow of Ralph Wigram C.M.G. of the Foreign Office. m. 1941 Sir John Anderson, later 1st Viscount Waverley, c. 1952.

Renishaw Hall,
Derbyshire
October 22nd, 1941

Osbert lunched with the Devonshires yesterday (they now live in a house they have built in the park at Chatsworth). He heard that a bomb fell on the Carlton Club, while a number of men were dining including Harold Macmillan. He, Osbert, thinks the whole Club has been wrecked. He was told *half* London would be obliterated, but that by December there will be an enormous increase in the Air Force.

Margaret Rawlings[1] tells me that her late 4 days in London were *hell.* A bomb in Praed Street, Paddington (her flat is near there). Church at end of Westbourne Terrace gone, a bomb close to Charles Morgan —in Holland Walk. St James, Piccadilly, gone. Bond Street a wreck. I don't believe the Abbey *can* survive. Another bomb, or rather a land mine in front of Buckingham Palace. Ava Wigram's house in North Street bombed. Barton Street seems to have escaped. I am glad Daddy did not live to see this destruction. I dreamt of him for the first time. War was over and I was suggesting we should take half No. 9 Barton Street. How I wish I could. It is so strange, after 50 years, having no home of my own.

I am very happy with Edith—she is a very remarkable woman and so good—Do get *Two Generations*[2] by Osbert—It is *most* interesting. I hear poor Hannah Gubbay spends 10 *hours* every night in her dugout near Trent. What a will to survive that shows. You would laugh at dugout here (I have not been into it) entered by hole close to front door. I should think *very* dangerous.

DIARY

November 1st, 1941

I had an interesting experience yesterday. I dined with H. G. Wells to meet Alexander Woollcott. He had a large party, Lady Juliet Duff, a very clever man who is in the Food Ministry, Russell Page of the B.B.C. who looks after the French broadcasts, and of course Baroness Budberg[3] who really looks more enchanting than ever. She doesn't

[1] Margaret Rawlings: noted actress, m. Sir Robert Barlow.
[2] *Two Generations.* Pubs. 1940.
[3] Baroness Budberg: Author and translator.

make up at all. Her hair is grey, she is fat, but every man who sees her is in love with her. To my mind she shows great character in refusing to marry Wells, because it would make her his slave more than she is at present.

I really couldn't help laughing when I saw Juliet Duff lean down and more or less cuddle up against Wells, Juliet being phenomenally tall. She said to him "Don't kiss me because I have a cold".

It was a very nice dinner, soup, duckling, and a delicious savoury. There was some very special brandy at the end, which Wells said he kept for me. Wells spoke with bitterness of the *Times* for not printing his letters, but he admitted that the letter he wrote last was abusing the government for having shut up—according to him—a lot of Fascist Poles in some kind of camp. He seemed rather muddled about it. If there are any Fascist Poles they would surely remain in Poland. I think the truth is that they are anti-Russian Poles, which is a very different thing. He even seemed doubtful where the camp was.

I felt very nervous as time went on, for we did not sit down till a quarter past seven, and we were supposed to start for the Criterion Theatre at eight, there to hear *Les Trois Amis*[1]. At last, however, I said we must go, and I then heard, with horror, that Bush house was the place we were going to, Alec and I and Mr Russell Page.

Bliss got us there pretty quickly, however, and then began a most strange experience. We went through a great empty building down in a lift to what seemed the bowels of the earth. And then we walked for quite ten minutes through empty rooms and corridors out into the open for a yard or two, then into what has been given over as a studio to the Free French, very uncomfortable and stuffy.

Les Trois Amis sat round a table and talked. Suddenly they were joined by a fourth, a well known actor of the *Théâtre Française*. He came to say that he held Marshal Pétain in reverence, and couldn't bear to hear him perpetually abused. I thought it admirably done, particularly that bit, for the three other men spoke as they should do about old Pétain, not in the vulgar, stupid way in which the B.B.C. always mentions him. Yet their account of the way he is going on was far more devastating than anything ever said in English.

After some time we started back. Halfway through this underground place we came into a room where they deal with the news, and a very

---

[1] *Les Trois Amis:* Anonymous group who broadcast in French from London.

strange looking man with a twisted face was introduced to Alec, who at once said "You dined with me last time I was in London". They had some talk, and then after we had reached the lift Alec told me that he was Vyvyan Holland, the son of Oscar Wilde, whom I had last seen as a child. According to Alec he has had the twisted face ever since he and his mother and other brother were turned out in the snow in a Swiss hotel when it was discovered who they were. I was extremely surprised to hear this story, which was quite new to me.

Then I tried hard to get away to come down straight to Wimbledon, but Alec was determined I should go back to the Dorchester, so I did, for Alec's nice secretary, Mr Brown[1] was there. Mr Russell Page insisted on coming too. The minute we got in drinks were ordered. They did not come. I didn't tell Mr Brown the elementary fact that if they gave a tip they would have come at once!

Mr Brown telephoned again in a very lackadaisical manner, and was told that the drinks were coming, and they did come. He had asked for some ice. A lump came, as big as a rock. Mr Brown disappeared, and broke it up in some mysterious way, for it is very difficult to break ice. I said "How wonderful that Mr Brown got the ice broken!" Alec observed, "Didn't you know that he had once been an ice man?" which I think Mr Russell Page really believed.

M. B. L. TO HER DAUGHTER S. L. M.

28 *Crooked Billet, S.W*.19
November 7th, 1941

I had a delightful visit to Mrs Maguire, close to Horsham. She has acquired there a pretty modern *small* house, only one guest room. What I enjoyed was her clever talk, and the people she asked to lunch. Also she took me to Field Place, where Shelley was born. I kept thinking of Granny—and how happy going there would have made her. I saw the smallish room where he was born. The Lady Shelley of that day must have been moved in there. It can't have been her real bedroom. It is a small manor house, the dining-room untouched since his day—so I judged, too, the drawing-room. The rest of the house a good deal knocked about. It now belongs to the great brewers, the Charringtons.

I am having my last week in London, dining with Juliet Duff. On

---

[1] Mr H. Leggett Brown: Woollcott's devoted secretary and a Radio Agent.

Wed. dining with the Film Agent, David Henley, Thursday with Raymond Mortimer[1], my new friend of *The New Statesman*. As you know the difficulty for me of Wimbledon, is getting to and from London. I shall only come once *next* week, to lunch Mrs Lamberton Becker's daughter Beatrice Warde[2]. She is going to the USA after doing a very *valuable* work for England called *The American Outpost*.

I am trying to get a French cook for the Brand or a Swede. An English cook is determined to have a kitchen-maid, and I don't know what we should have done, had we not had the invaluable Tahitian Free Frenchman, provided by one of our Free French friends.

I registered for my rations, sugar, bacon, butter, etc. at Fortnum's, where quality is *excellent* and where they give me anything like biscuits, etc. when they have them. I shall have my rations sent me by letter post registered to the Brand. A saving of worry to darling Elizabeth and a benefit when I get extra things of the *un*rationed kind, such as one lb. of excellent pork sausages once a week.

M. B. L. TO MRS KING PATTERSON

Brand Hall,
Market Drayton
November 27th, 1941

My dear Mary,

I think I told you that Susan has got a little boy[3], just three months old. She writes us very funny letters about the baby. I think it was a great surprise, for she had been married nearly three years. But she is the first mother I have ever known who, within two or three days of the baby's birth, was already writing about her next baby!

I have had a very sad year, and I miss my dear husband more, instead of less. But I am feeling happier now—and, unlike most people, I don't believe the war will be very long. I believe Germany will collapse, as she did last time.

[1] Raymond Mortimer: C.B.E. Noted writer and critic. Chairman of Contemporary Art Society.
[2] Beatrice Warde: b. U.S.A. Typographer. Wrote *The Crystal Goblet*. M. B. L. was her godmother when she became a Catholic during the war. She was received into the Church from Brand Hall.
[3] Paul Lowndes Marques.

M. B. L. TO HER DAUGHTER S. L. M.

28 Crooked Billet, S.W.19
November 28th, 1941

It will amuse you to hear that during a talk I had with Mr John Wilson, the famous head of Bumpus, he said "Three lords came in to get your book[1] one after the other". At first I couldn't think what he meant, and he repeated crossly "don't you know what a lord is?" By the way, I am sending you Osbert Sitwell's new book from Bumpus, *Open the Door*, a book of short stories which has been splendidly reviewed.

I have got a new fur coat. £25, wholesale. My other was disintegrating, but I am having it cobbled up. My new one is like Elizabeth's Canadian skunk, a rich dark brown.

M. B. L. TO MISS MARY LOWNDES[2]

Brand Hall,
Market Drayton, Shrops.
December 15th, 1941

My dear Mary,

I was exceedingly interested in your letter which amused me very much. The way in which permits have been given has raised a good deal of indignation, and a little while ago, meeting Brendan Bracken, who is an old acquaintance of mine, and a very capable intelligent man, I spoke to him about it, pointing out what harm those sort of people did their country. He more than agreed, and said that he wished more Americans would come over here, and less English go over there. Of course all the permits to the wrong people had been given before his time. I cannot help wondering what will happen now to all those idiots —for idiots they are. I hope and believe they will all be sent home; certainly those of military age, both men and women. They will have to come whether they like it or not.

I have long held the view that the coming of America into the war, in the way which she has done now, would immensely hasten the col-

---

[1] *I, Too, Have Lived in Arcadia.*

[2] Miss Mary Lowndes: 1863-1947. Cousin of F. S. A. Lowndes. She had retired from being Headmistress of Rosemary Hall School, Greenwich, Connecticut, U.S.A.

lapse of Germany. A significant proof of this to my thinking, was the effect on the Berlin stock exchange.

As I think I have already told you, I get news of France mostly through the Free French, for no day goes by without someone escaping to England. Also, Susan sees a certain number of them in Lisbon. The conditions in Paris are indescribably terrible.

Conditions are a little better in the country, because there the people can grow their own food. Germany made a terrible mistake in her own interest when she took all the wine this year. Had she been wise, she would have said: "Now look, here is all your wine, produced by yourselves. You are short of everything else, because of the British blockade." Instead of that, they seized all the wine and took it to Germany, or rather, I believe, to Russia for their troops. The working class of France largely live on wine; the rough kind, which is extremely cheap, and is, after all, a species of food. I think they miss wine and coffee more than anything else. They have neither now.

I have brought out a book called *I, Too, Have Lived in Arcadia*, of which, if you see the *Times*, you may have noticed the review. It has been astonishingly successful. Published on October 7th, it is being reprinted now for the third time. Macmillans are giving me good royalties. That is not the same with my American publishers.

I did not tell my brother I was writing the book. He is very reserved, and quite indifferent to what people think of him. Among the recent fan letters I have received, one writer says he understands that H. is descended from Danton or Robespierre!

Elizabeth and I have learnt that our local District Nursing Association has no gas and air machine for mothers in labour. I am giving them one. The cost is so small. The Matron is delighted and says it will "make all the difference to the mothers and to us midwives". André Millet's[1] wife Jacqueline is going there, she expects twins. This is why we know about this excellent Maternity home. Both André who is in the Fleet Air Arm and his wife come and go here. Elizabeth has lent them her cot and all the baby clothes.

I can't tell you what a happiness it is to me to see the Fighting French. All most remarkable men. Harry met André when he was on leave. I much regret the abuse of old Pétain. He ought to be left to history. All the Free French I meet, who of course are followers of de Gaulle,

---

[1] André Millet, M. B. L.'s cousin, was killed later in the war.

regret what is published about Pétain. I much fear there will be violent revolution in France after the War.

M. B. L. TO HER DAUGHTER E. I.

Renishaw Hall,
Nr. Sheffeld
December 21st, 1941

Osbert is convinced the war will last for years and years. He talks of the Germans as if they were super-men. He longs for Churchill to go, yet has no alternative to offer. It is an odd frame of mind. He constantly asks me what I think and when I reply, shakes his head crossly. He is very angered because it has come to his knowledge that the Treasury is allowing his father to get £100 per month and £200 extra every three months. Too bad, when one considers the ill feeling aroused in the U.S.A. by the penniless rich emigrés. I am being taken to see devastated Sheffield. This will interest me very much.

Both Osbert and Edith are very witty, which is agreeable. Also kind-hearted, but extremely censorious, with violent feelings of hate against many writers, and especially "poets who are puffed". I understand that, for she is really very, very good. Were she a man, this would be recognised.

I see the news is "out". The Americans are determined to run the Pacific side of the war, a fact which naturally enrages the War Office and especially the Admiralty. The P.M. has gone over to smooth out this delicate situation, it is unsmoothable. I hope the hideous cold in the U.S.A. won't kill the mission. Though I should not miss Lord Beaverbrook, but he is indestructible.

M. B. L. TO HER DAUGHTER E. I.

28 Crooked Billet, S.W.19
April 2nd, 1942

I had a very interesting talk with Stanley Morison[2] last night, heard all the *Times* news. Of course they will be overjoyed if I will help in

---

[1] Sir George Sitwell: 4th Baronet who was living in his Castle of Montegufoni in Italy.

[2] Stanley Morison: member of staff of *The Times*. Typographical adviser to the University Press, Cambridge, *The Times* and the Monotype Corporation.

any way over the obituaries. He thinks that if Cripps[1] pulls off India, he may oust Winston fairly soon. There's been a great row at War Office. Winston coolly intended sending Grigg[2] to the Lords and putting his own son-in-law Sandys[3] in Grigg's place. Grigg refused with rage. Churchill is also anxious to get good job for young Randolph.

I have seldom had more interesting talk with anyone. Stanley Morison's account of Winston Churchill was most curious, Winston even pursued and rang Grigg up at a private dinner, not knowing it was the Editor's dinner. Morison does not like Warren Fisher[4]. He said he had come to the *Times* office last week hoping they would make a row, but of course they played for safety.

M. B. L. TO HER DAUGHTER S. L. M.

*28 Crooked Billet, S.W.*19
April 15th, 1942

Well! I have taken number 1 Barton Street, Mrs Herbert's house. The ground floor is quite nice—a very good sitting room, and in a large alcove will be dining table, and six small chairs. I have the house on a yearly tenancy. There is a very pretty little paved garden with a fig-tree. Unhappily a row of steps leads to front door. I am thinking of having them made *black*. My trouble will be getting a *good* servant, even if, as I fear, I have to have daily char. Wages have risen incredibly. I shall have to pay £2 a week if the woman can cook.

Luckily so many people who had big houses now live in hotels, or what good cooks *hate*, live in their country houses with relations, children, and so on. I know of one where there are three sets of nursery meals! Also good cooks love *London*.

A lot of people now have hens in their back yards. Even Charles has some, as paying guests with a neighbour. I was amused to hear that there are even some fowls living on the roof of one of the houses in Grosvenor Square.

---

[1] Sir Stafford Cripps: 1889-1952. Solicitor-General 1930-31.

[2] Rt. Hon. Sir James Grigg: Permanent Under-Secretary of State for War 1939-42. Secretary for War 1942-45.

[3] Rt. Hon. Duncan Sandys: Financial Secretary to War Office 1941-43. Parliamentary Secretary Ministry Supply 1943-44. Minister of Works 1944-45. Married Diana, daughter of Sir Winston Churchill.

[4] Sir Warren Fisher: 1879-1948. Permanent Secretary of Treasury, Head of Civil Service.

1 *Barton Street,*
Westminster, S.W.1
June 5th, 1942

René Millet[1] and his Portuguese-U.S.A. Princess Wife, dined here last night. He is 33, and extremely intelligent. Escaped from Germany into Russia, where he had a hellish six months in prisons until Hitler attacked. So he is under no illusions as to the Russian character. He says a second front now is very unlikely. But there are persistent rumours that it is coming, that the P.M. promised Stalin that even if it failed, it would be worth while as it would provoke such risings all over the Continent as to make German occupation impossible.

M. B. L. TO PROFESSOR GORDON HAIGHT[2]

1 *Barton Street,*
Westminster, S.W.1
July 3rd, 1942

Dear Mr Haight,

I wonder how you view the situation? I am convinced Civilian Germany will collapse, as she did the last time. To me the fact that Rommel was made to come to the microphone to talk to Berlin after his victory (the fall of Tobruk) is most significant. I expect peace-feelers to follow very soon. My views are not shared by any of the clever people I am now seeing, but I recall the last war—and how up to the week when the German High Command asked for an armistice the government had no belief in a German collapse. The army chiefs expected a great campaign in the spring and summer of 1919. I don't suppose Foch shared that view. I suspect he knew.

I hear dreadful accounts of France—all old people and delicate people, are dying—especially, I gather, in the unoccupied districts. In the occupied, the Nazis keep anyone alive who can work—for them. As to conditions in Civilian Germany, news does seep through, as a certain number of neutrals, Scandinavians, for instance, do come and go.

[1] René Millet: cousin of M. B. L. He had married a Braganza princess.
[2] Professor Gordon Haight: of Yale University. Expert on George Eliot. Author of *George Eliot, a Biography.* Pubs. 1968.

1 *Barton Street,*
*Westminster, S.W.*1
August 19*th,* 1942

It is so strange to be back, the only inhabitant in this, to me, beloved little street. No bomb dropped here, though behind it many fell. Five one night alone in Smith Square. This is a very pretty little house, all dark panelling with a tiny garden, so people like it better than No. 9. I am glad to be back in London, indeed it was really necessary for my work. But I shall go to Salop now and again in the winter, for it is very lonely for Elizabeth. She is only allowed enough petrol to go once a week to Church, and once to do Welfare work in Market Drayton and the same day to get food for her household of 13/15. I have a room here I can give her, and now that Harry is in War Office he comes to dinner with me once a week. I am blessed in having an excellent Cook/Housekeeper, who likes my having people in to meals. Of course it is less easy than it was, but now that game is in, I find it possible.

All my French grandmother's great-grandsons of fighting age, are in the Free French Forces, three here, one in Syria. I had Admiral Muselier[1] here this week, intensely interesting to me, indeed I see as many Frenchmen as I can.

The older ones miss their children so dreadfully. They are a very remarkable lot of men. The French are, I think astonished no use is made of de Gaulle's immense technical knowledge. After all his book taugh the Germans most of what they know about tank warfare and the war of movement.

M. B. L. TO HER DAUGHTER E. I.

1 *Barton Street,*
*Westminster, S.W.*1
August 27*th,* 1942

I dined last night with an airman friend who was extremely interesting. He seemed worried about the Duke of Kent's[2] accident and

---

[1] Admiral Muselier: de Gaulle's Naval Commander.
[2] H.R.H. the Duke of Kent had been killed in an air-crash on August 25th, 1942.

231

said it should not have occurred, that the pilot should have been much higher in the sky. He told me a most curious secret, that an exactly similar accident had befallen a whole Air Mission going back to Russia. Every man was killed and apparently Russia thought it had been done on purpose. This was at least a year ago.

He was extremely interesting about the whole question of the R.A.F., the bombing of Germany, and so on, and gave me what I presume is the R.A.F. view of the Dieppe affair.[1] He naturally confirmed my idea that the time will come, not so very far off either, when there will be no armies in the world, only armies of the air and navies. One thing he did tell me which cheered me, was that before leaving Dieppe, everything that could have been useful to the enemy was destroyed. He is in the R.A.F. Intelligence.

M. B. L. TO PROF. GORDON HAIGHT

1 *Barton Street,*
*Westminster S.W.*1
August 31*st,* 1942

My dear Professor Haight,

Perhaps one reason why I hold what you call an optimistic view of a collapse in Germany, is because I do not see how otherwise it can end, while Hitler has this strong steel-like grip on his miserable people. I always felt certain that civilian Germany would be frightfully shaken by bombings, and only this week I heard, on what I consider absolute authority, that the workers there are beginning to shirk going into the munition factories at night, and that though they have marvellous shelters.

You can force men and women to do almost anything except work. The Nazis themselves admit that production has gone down very much. But they naturally do not give the reason which I have just told you I have heard is the real reason. In this country the workers go back to a factory immediately after it has been bombed; they appear to be what in the old days would have been called fatalists. When the siren went at 5 o'clock one afternoon last week, not a single individual went to a shelter. One week, recently, we had a warning (about 3 a.m.) every night. I listened. I did not hear even one pair of footsteps pass my house.

---

[1] The Dieppe raid had taken place on August 9th, 1942.

232

I also believe that the entry of America into the war has had an increasingly frightful effect on German *morale* and on German imagination. It is surely plain that every middle-class German must regard your country as the promised land, if not for himself, then for his children. Germans have done so well and are so highly respected in America. This *must* make them ache to see the War end before a lot more Germans have been killed in battle by Americans. They hoped against hope no American bombers would ever go over Germany.

ALEXANDER WOOLLCOTT TO M. B. L.

Bomoseen, Vermont
August 31st, 1942

Dear Marie,

During this past week it has been a deep and sad pleasure for me to go through the file of letters which Alice Duer Miller had written me during the more than twenty years of our life as neighbours. It is not one of the thick folders in my files for most of that time we were together or just about to be. There are many allusions to you scattered across the years for she enjoyed you and held you in great affection. Sometimes it is difficult to determine whether the allusion *is* to you, for Alice's treasured cook was also named Marie. Thus, in a letter written from Hollywood back in the winter of '36-'37, I find these two sentences: "I don't know when I shall be coming home—but in about three weeks more, I should imagine. Marie and Harry seem so happy together I should hate to interfere with them." I think that *must* refer to the time you were queening it in her quarters in New York while she was toiling away out on the Coast.

Of course she made the kind of exit anyone would have expected who knew how wise and honourable and self-disciplined she always was. I think I told you that as early as June 12th, three days before I left for my own operation in Boston, she wrote me that her days were numbered. So as not to disturb the party, she whispered to me behind her fan that she would be leaving soon. And in a hasty confidential note written to me early this month, when writing was beginning to be a chore for her, she told me she could not help hoping the time would not be long. Well, in her sixty-eight crowded and triumphant years she had only six months of disability.

233

*28 Crooked Billet, S.W.*19
September 16*th,* 1942

People are rather melancholy—expecting raids, etc. I think the Government is over-doing its regimentation of the people. The more so that nothing seems to be properly carried out. Last night, at 9, a very nice gentlemanly *young* man (not 30) arrived to know who lived here, if my servant was over 60 (she *is*) who was my next of-kin, I gave Charles. I gave him a cup of coffee and a cigarette. I said you and Harry had two rooms and came when you could. Of course, *our* interview went off *very* well. But you can imagine how *enraged* a certain class, far the largest, would have been at such a call, at such a time, He practically told me that even in *this* quarter almost everyone on whom he called was most unpleasant and resented his questions. He ought, he admitted, to have gone over the house—I pitied him—he looked very delicate.

Woollcott's love for Alice Duer Miller was certainly *very odd.* They had nothing in common, and he never saw her before she was 50. Of course she did not like me. She was so used to reigning quite alone in his heart—I really hated being in her beautiful flat and longed to leave it. I did so a week earlier than had been arranged. I did get fond of Harry Miller, he is in fact very like a certain type of English squire. Of course he hated spending Alice's money. She had bought him a "seat" on the Stock Exchange but in partnership, so he could do nothing silly. He had a farm he *had built with his own hands.*

M. B. L. TO HER DAUGHTER E. I.

*28 Crooked Billet, S.W.*19
September 24*th,* 1942

The following I should like you to regard as private. I think it extremely curious and I fear it is true. This is the strange, extraordinary story I heard last night. Four days before the attack on Dieppe, there seems to have appeared in *The Daily Telegraph* a large advertisement of some woman's dress. It was called *Dieppe Beach Model,* and there were details in the advertisement that made it quite plain what was going to take place.

Now my view, odd as it may seem, is that this was a sinister joke on the part of the German High Command. They had obviously received every detail from their spies, the news being conveyed via Dublin; so I believe they thought out this scheme of "pulling the leg" of those whom it concerned. The Germans have always been fond of rather elaborate jokes, and I think this one would have specially appealed to them. Oddly enough I remember that advertisement, as I now take in the *Telegraph*. I thought it such a queer thing to call it *Dieppe Beach Model* at this time of year. But as you know they have fancy names for clothes.

M. B. L. TO HER DAUGHTER E. I.

28 *Crooked Billet, S.W.*19
November 19th, 1942

Last Tuesday Cynthia Asquith gave a most extraordinary party for her new daughter-in-law, in what I think must have been an empty house, for the seating arrangements were very peculiar; most of the people sat on window seats. To me it was like a gathering of ghosts of the past. The bride is a singular, and indeed a beautiful girl, very tall and slight, with a fringe. Margot, who wore a highwayman hat, said to Cynthia: "Your new daughter-in-law is very plain but no doubt a good girl!"

Margot sat down all the time, and, what I thought very pathetic, not a single person spoke to her except myself. She sat by the door of the room where the reception took place, and opposite her was the buffet. On the buffet there were lobster patties, and queer looking Maid of Honour cakes, also jugs of beer and coffee. Everyone had come expecting a fork luncheon, and the bolder spirits, including myself, hoped for a little champagne.

Eddie Marsh, who is seventy today, was the only really happy looking person there, so delighted to be back, away from his relations in Cambridge. After a while he went and squatted at the feet of Lady Desborough[1]. What really surprised me was seeing Sir Kenneth Barnes[2], the brother of Violet Vanbrugh. I suppose, by the expression on my face, he thought I had forgotten who he was, and he reminded me that I had met him last week—the day before Violet's death—at Lady

[1] Lady Desborough: w. of 1st and last Baron Desborough. Famous as a political hostess.
[2] Sir Kenneth Barnes: 1878-1957. Principal of the Royal Academy of Dramatic Art 1909-55.

Mountbatten's. He was the only person there connected with the theatre. I thought this strange, as in Barrie's day Cynthia Asquith knew all the theatrical people.

Viola Meynell[1] was the youngest person there except the happy couple. Her father was ninety yesterday. Dear Mrs Hartley and her husband, Leslie's mother and father, were there too. Suddenly I saw a strange looking woman. I thought "Surely that cannot be Sibyl Colefax?" and then I heard her unmistakable voice.

I had forgotten dear Rhoda's wise saying, "kindness brings its own punishment": I felt stricken with pity, and said to Sibyl I would give her a lift. She looked so terribly ill I was certain she would go straight home. But she made me stay on nearly half-an-hour more than I had promised the taxi man who had brought me. At last she perched herself on the armchair (the only one except the one Margot sat on) of Lady Desborough. So what with Eddie squatting at her feet and Sibyl (whom I thought she much disliked) poor Ettie was completely hemmed in. She made efforts to get at me, as she cherishes a great affection for your uncle, and wanted to talk about him, but neither of the two would budge. I kept feeling as if at any moment the ghost of Barrie might walk into the room.

Margot at once, and in this quite her old self, asked me to lunch, but in a vague kind of way. She said she was very dull, back in her old house. I shall ask her to lunch with someone, I think Stanley Morison. She was the one there for whom I felt most concern. But I really felt sorry for them all excepting Cynthia and her husband. What amused me, and which I suppose was induced by disappointment at the re-freshments, was the fact that quite a number of the people who spoke to me mentioned Cynthia's large legacy from Barrie.

M. B. L. TO HER DAUGHTER E. I.

1 *Barton Street,*
*London S.W.*1
December 31*st,* 1942

Baffy Dugdale's[2] husband came to tea and was extremely candid as to the Balfours one and all. He evidently disliked his in-laws. I

---

[1] Viola Meynell: author, d. of Wilfred and Alice Meynell.
[2] Mrs Edgar Dugdale, daughter of Lieut. Col. Eustace Balfour and Lady Frances Balfour, m. Major Edgar Dugdale who wrote the *Life of Arthur James Balfour* two vols. Pubs. 1936.

was extremely amused. He so liked my Scotch cake, he longed to buy a half pound from me but I refused. We had an interesting discussion about the Prime Minister, he thinks he will want to make the Peace. I said I thought Russia would get into Germany, this distressed him.

CHAPTER XIII

1943-1945

Visits to the country houses of her friends continued to be a great pleasure both to Marie and to her hosts, for she was an admirable guest. Working at her current book all morning in her bedroom and then enjoying their company for the rest of the day, without the fatigue of long expeditions which petrol restrictions had made impossible during the War.

M. B. L.'s elder daughter and her family moved to Parfetts House at Eversley Cross in Hampshire, which Marie much preferred to Shropshire.

The War finally came to an end. There was little of the rejoicing that marked for a short time the close of the First War, and Marie realised that the world had entirely changed. Her gloomy fears that she would be turned out of her Westminster house were fortunately unfounded and she went on living there.

M. B. L. TO HER DAUGHTER S. L. M.

1 *Barton Street,*
*Westminster S.W.*1
January 19*th,* 1943

I am so happy today as Elizabeth is coming up with the two boys. Stafford goes to school on Thursday morning and Edward[1] sees some doctor; though he appears quite well, and has long periods of being quite well. He reminds me strongly of your Uncle Hilary when he was a child, excepting that he is not nearly so delicate. He is, to my mind, an amazingly clever boy; his mind works in a remarkable way, but so did that of your uncle.

Shane Leslie spent an evening with me, which was very amusing; his book of Cardinal Vaughan's Letters to Lady Herbert[2] has made a mild sensation, and is having very nasty reviews in the Protestant press. She was a silly woman, in fact, that is the first thing people tell one who knew her—even kind Lord Fitz[3] said it to me. I found the religious part extremely dull, and it is by far the greater part. Since the book came out, someone who was in Rome at the same time as Lady Herbert, the Cardinal and some other goody-goody lady, gave me a funny account of how the two ladies fought for his attention—he being much too busy to worry about either of them!

[1] Hon. Edward Northcote: M. B. L.'s grandson.
[2] *Letters of Cardinal Vaughan to Lady Herbert of Lea.* Edited by Shane Leslie. Pubs. 1943.
[3] Lord FitzAlan.

1 Barton Street, S.W.1
February 27th, 1943

Dearest Mary,

It was indeed a kind thought of yours to send me those cuttings about dear Alec Woollcott[1]. His death is a real grief to me. He was endlessly kind to me, and over so many years. I am happy to feel that during his visit to London in the fall of '41, I saw him nearly every day. I managed to procure a book that is extremely rare—some letters connected with Dickens—and on the last day of his visit, I had the good luck to find in a bookseller's catalogue, a most amusing letter from Dickens about some improper French book. I gave it to him as a parting gift, to his great delight. We had dinner with H. G. Wells together.

Since his death, I have received a parcel from him containing an odd assortment of things—razor-blades (valuable to my son and son-in-law), lipstick, which I was able to give to a lady who yearned for some, and last, not least, two half-pounds of butter. Strangely enough, it was the only parcel he ever sent me, with the exception of, at intervals, a peculiar kind of maple sugar, which seems to be a speciality of Vermont.

When he died, I sent a cable to his secretary, asking for details, but have heard nothing. I do so wonder what will happen to all his things. One of my gifts which amused and interested him was a group, consisting of the Prince Consort and Queen Victoria, taken just after their marriage: it was in some sort of pottery, and very charming, the only one I have ever come across. I got it in a Brighton curiosity shop.

He felt terribly the death of Alice Duer Miller. To me, their friendship was inexplicable: they were so much more than different: but she was certainly the only woman he ever genuinely loved.

M. B. L. TO PROFESSOR GORDON HAIGHT

1 Barton Street, S.W.1
March 25th, 1943

I was so interested in your letter. Apropos the damage done to the House of Commons, I can tell you a curious story. During the last war,

---

[1] Alexander Woollcott had died January 23rd, 1943.

a noted fortune-teller told a friend of mine that she saw the House of Commons more or less destroyed by a bomb, masses of masonry on the floor, and so on. At the end of the war, my friend observed: "You see, nothing has happened to the House of Commons. That woman is a fraud." I said: "But, my dear, some day or other that *might* happen!" She was indignant, for, of course, at that moment the "War to end War" was just over.

I hope that, some day, certain of the very extraordinary things that have happened in *this* war will be put on record. One of interest to me can now be told. The first bomb which fell on London was on a fine afternoon, about four o'clock, spring of 1940. It came, so to speak, out of the blue, and went through a big building, in the centre of which a committee meeting was being held. Eight men were present. They were all killed. I had known one of them, a distinguished man[1] for many years. My girls had gone to balls in his house. I knew his wife's family very well. So when his death was announced in the *Times* with an obituary, but no word as to how he died, or where, I felt much puzzled and distressed too. I learned the strange truth about a fortnight later. The building in which he was killed was a philanthropic institution, and was of no military importance whatsoever.

I do hope you will have received a copy of my book, *What of the Night?* If you are kind enough to read on till you get to *The Molotov Bread Basket*, you will find an account of the effects of blast. I took great trouble to find out all about blast: I failed, for no one really knows what blast comes from: it is a most freakish thing: it may kill a roomful of people, or it may kill a man standing by another who remained unhurt. It seems to travel like a reverse letter L, everything living in its path being destroyed. It is singular that a human being killed by blast shows no effects, and looks as if he had died a quiet, natural death. One of my girl's friends[2] who had just become an Air Raid Warden, heard the sirens, and was going through her apartment door when a bomb dropped, not on the building but next to it. Blast killed her, and she looked as if she had fallen asleep.

---

[1] This was Lionel Hichens: b. 1874. Member of the Carnegie U.K. Trust. He belonged to several public bodies. m. Hermione y.d. of Rt. Hon. General Sir Neville Lyttelton, G.C.B., G.C.V.O.

[2] Miss Dorothy Baldwin.

1 *Barton Street, S.W.*1
May 9th, 1943

Only a line, darling, to say Rose Macaulay[1] telephoned to me yesterday just as I was starting for Pope's Manor, a lovely house Mrs Meyer Sassoon has taken 'for the duration'. She is coming to see me Friday to tell me all about you *all four*. She says Paul is like you and baby[2] more like Luiz. She was *so* nice.

M. B. L. TO PROFESSOR GORDON HAIGHT

1 *Barton Street, S.W.*1
May 10th, 1943

My mother might have been the stepmother of Mrs Sidney Webb[3] and so also the step-grandmother of Sir Stafford Cripps! Mr Potter[4], a friend and contemporary of her father, was left as a widower with nine daughters; and he asked my mother to marry him after what seemed to her an extremely short interval. When as a young woman, I used to meet Mrs Sidney Webb, I wondered if she knew of that passage in her father's life.

My mother might also have been stepmother to another and extremely different type of famous Englishwoman; i.e. Isabel Burton, the wife of Sir Richard Burton[5]. She met that lady's father not long after she became a Roman Catholic. He was an Arundell, a member of one of the oldest Catholic families in England. I don't know where or how they met, but probably through the then Dr Manning.

I think you would agree that, as a rule, a woman always attracts the same kind of man; I mean taking it broad and long. The astonishing thing about my mother was that she attracted such extremely different

---

[1] Rose Macaulay: died 1958. Author and critic. She had been staying in Lisbon to gather material for her book *They Went to Portugal,* pubs. 1946, and spent much of her time with M. B. L.'s son-in-law and daughter.

[2] Ana Lowndes Marques: M. B. L.'s granddaughter.

[3] Mrs Sidney Webb: 1858-1943. m. Rt. Hon. Sidney Webb with whom she wrote many works on sociology.

[4] Mr Richard Potter: chairman of the Great Western Railway and President of the Grand Trunk Railway of Canada.

[5] Sir Richard Burton: 1821-1890. Explorer and orientalist, translated *The Arabian Nights.*

types of men. I had a whole collection of letters to her from a racing man, who called a horse after her! When not on the turf, he was a barrister, and his letters are addressed from Chambers in the Temple.

M. B. L. TO HER DAUGHTER E. I.

1 *Barton Street, S.W.*1
May 20th, 1943

I find it difficult to know what it is best to do. If the alerts go on every night, it is plain I must get away, for it means that some nights I get practically no sleep. I thank God I don't feel frightened. Last night I slept really well from 11.30 to 7.30 yet there were two warnings. I was so *fearfully* frightened in the last War. It is strange that I don't care now. I am only frightened of broken glass.

It is clear that the bombs are dropped anywhere now. They have, so far, managed to keep any from falling on the centre of London, but I don't know how long they will be able to do that.

The unfortunate suburbs catch it. Even Charles, who is, as you know, very brave, looked worn out when he came to see me this morning. Streatham, where a bomb destroyed some small houses last night, is really only about a minute by a plane from Wimbledon.

Incidentally, getting food is becoming more difficult every minute. I have Father D'Arcy[1] tomorrow, and Mr Lees-Milne[2] Saturday. I have secured some gull's eggs, but, so far, nothing else.

M. B. L. TO PROFESSOR GORDON HAIGHT

Brand Hall,
Market Drayton, Shrops.
June 14th, 1943

I have just sent the page proofs of my new book[3] to Harold Ober, my agent. It will be published by Dodd Mead some time in the fall, over here in August. People won't like it as they did *Arcadia* for it lacks that element of romance so dear to the reader's heart. It covers nine years of my life—from when I was 17 and went back to France, till my marriage. I shall be more than content if it dispels certain false ideas about the

[1] Rev. Martin D'Arcy, S. J. Philosopher. Author. Wrote *The Nature of Belief.*

[2] James Lees-Milne: the architectural historian. Architectural adviser to the National Trust.

[3] *Where Love and Friendship Dwelt.* Pubs. 1943.

French—ideas more prevalent in England than in America. During the 18th century, France and England were very close. But first, I take it, the Napoleonic Wars, and secondly, without doubt, the pro-German atmosphere of the Court caused 19th century Britain to move away mentally, *culturally* and sentimentally from France. Carlyle played his part, and later Wagner. Also in the political sphere there were many admirers of Bismarck—Lord Rosebery hated France in an active sense. I often feel cynical amusement when I hear the things *now* said of Bismarck and Germany. After all, he started the Blood and Iron regime.

You are right as to G. E.[1] essentially, as her letters to my mother prove, a simple, unaffected woman by nature—being made into a kind of pompous idol. I wonder if you know that when the London Library was founded, Leslie Stephen[2] said the only *fiction* to be admitted should be the novels of G. E.? Someone at the meeting observed, "Ruling out Fielding, Richardson, Sterne?" (Jane Austen wasn't thought much of then). "Certainly," replied Sir Leslie quickly. Now, though, the L.L. only buys *one* copy of a novel they have thousands of them in French and English; the members, as one of the attendants said to me lately, queue up for them! I suppose to forget, for a short time, their War work.

M. B. L. TO PROFESSOR GORDON HAIGHT

*1 Barton Street, S.W.*1
August 21st, 1943

Many of the sayings, I should think always true, attributed to the Prime Minister, are too personal to be sent in a letter, as he has a mordant wit. I was amused at his reply to someone who wanted him to allow a lot of children to be admitted to some party where he was to be. "I suppose they take me for a Giant Panda?"

This has been going the rounds:

> There was a young lady of fashion
> Whose husband adored her with passion;
> So she merrily said,
> As she skip't into bed,
> "Well there's one thing Lord Woolton[3] can't ration!"

[1] George Eliot.
[2] Sir Leslie Stephen: 1832-1904. Editor of the *Dictionary of National Biography*.
[3] Lord Woolton: Minister of Food 1940-43. Minister of Reconstruction 1943-45.

PROFESSOR GORDON HAIGHT TO M. B. L.

464 *Yale Station*
September 21st, 1943

There is a curious confirmation of your remark about the impropriety of representing the passions in Victorian days, in a review of *Jane Eyre* by an American clergyman, who writes the most unbelievable things about it. Somewhere in my notes I have an extract from a letter by some fairly moderate Englishman, denouncing *Adam Bede* for its extreme sensuality! I think we have strayed too far in the opposite direction; after all, with the Victorians one could supply what was lacking; but with some of the contemporary trash, the picture of human life is even more disproportionate in its exaggeration of passion. Was it not Lady Mary Wortley Montagu who said that there were fig leaves needed for the mind as well as for the body?

PROFESSOR GORDON HAIGHT TO M. B. L.

464 *Yale Station*
October 3rd, 1943

Dodd Mead sent me *Where Love and Friendship Dwelt* the first day it was published, and I read it with the most intense interest. It is completely absorbing to me, crammed with most fresh and intimate observations of literary people and of life itself. I am happy to see that the reviewers recognize its importance too; I enclose the article from the *New York Herald-Tribune,* which even if the publishers have sent you a copy of it, you will be glad to have.

The chapters I found most exciting were those on Verlaine and de Goncourt, and Zola, which are exceedingly vivid and give me the feeling of being present, that is the test of real writing. But the more domestic parts of the book are of deep interest to me too. What you have to say of the French institution of *l'ami de la maison* was very curious to me, for I think its like is seldom seen in America and perhaps even in England. Mlle de Montgolfier, I suppose, is a sort of representative of it in the Belloc family.

M. B. L. TO HER DAUGHTER S. L. M.

Cumberland Lodge, Windsor
December 20th, 1943

A good many people believe the rocket-bomb is coming, but a famous airman laughed at the idea of its being a real danger to London, and said that Hitler's secret weapon was Smuts!! His ill-advised speech made a great stir. I'm glad he has gone. I remember the days when people refused to meet him at dinner at Lord Haldane's on the plea he was a strong pro-German. When one lives to my age, one recalls many odd things!

People thought—Oh! how falsely—that I was making heaps of money, because I was happy and cheerful owing to my dear kind husband, dear kind children, and good health. *Also* because I was interested in everything and everybody. My love of reading I regard as my crowning mercy from God. Only 2 or 3 times in my life have I been too anxious to read. Anxiety owing to my children not being well—nothing else.

M. B. L. TO HER DAUGHTER S. L. M.

Parfetts, Eversley Cross
May 4th, 1944

We are most curious to know what you and Luiz will think of Chesterton's life[1]. I don't think as well of it as does Elizabeth. It gives in my opinion a false picture of his wife. She suited *him*, but was narrow-minded and penurious. He knew hardly any other writers—only Uncle Hilary and Maurice Baring. That tells its own tale, for he was a friendly creature. Think what my life would have been if I had only known people in 'society', and Chesterton didn't even know, as I have always done, men and women in the political world. They lived a very narrow life, and she was always trying to stop him spending money. However, it is an *amusing* book, largely because there are so many quotations. Also Frank Sheed[2] has done admirably an account of the Marconi scandal.

M. B. L. TO HER DAUGHTER E. I.

Rockbourne, Hampshire[3]
June 4th, 1944

I had a curious interesting time with Edith Olivier[4]. She evidently loved Rex[5] deeply. She talks of him constantly, her eyes full of tears.

---

[1] *Gilbert Keith Chesterton*: by Maisie Ward. Pubs. 1944.

[2] Frank Sheed: Maisie Ward's husband, is believed to have written the chapter on the Marconi scandal.

[3] Home of L. P. Hartley: Author and critic. His novel *Eustace and Hilda* won the James Tait Black Memorial Prize in 1947.

[4] Miss Edith Olivier M.B.E. d. 1948. Author. Mayor of Wilton, Wiltshire, 1938-41.   [5] Rex Whistler.

What a very singular woman! She has an *immense* acquaintance with people who write to her constantly. Read me a long intimate letter from Lady Gage (where Rex was quartered for some time) full of anger that Lord David Cecil's "tribute" was not put in the *Times*.

In Wilton village I got a packet of *pre-war* typing paper—finest quality! I suspect dear—for my bill, including little items was 9/-. But the paper splendid.

Algernon Cecil very affectionate. He is indeed a most singular being! He should be Julia's[1] P.G. He is curiously credulous, still thinks poor Eugenie caused the war of 70-71. Brushes aside Bismarck, as of little account. He regards Churchill as "a warmonger". Every minute I expected him to assert Churchill started this war—I think he does partly believe it. Next to Russia he fears America. He is remote from ordinary humanity so it is strange indeed he is drawn to me! He is rather like Sir Willowby Pattern in *The Egoist*.

Algernon greatly fears Canada will end by being filled with French practising Catholics as the Catholics alone have children. He was really funny about the birth rate. Edith was one of 10, 8 are married, and have 4 children among them. A. says "How can people have children without a lot of domestic help?" He said to me "I suppose you had 3 servants when you married"—this after I had said we were really poor, and never thought of not having children.

But, I am becoming very fond of him, it is noble of him to stay with Blanche[2]. She is quite helpless, two nurses. It is most strange to hear him talk, Leslie is detached, I am painfully interested. Algernon shuts his mind against anything that wars with his views. I stand up to him in a gingerly way. When we are alone, while Leslie is working, he talks a good deal of the past and of people. When I get home I shall re-read his *Metternich*.

SIR OSBERT SITWELL TO M. B. L.

Renishaw Hall,
Renishaw, Nr. Sheffield
August 9th, 1944

Dearest Marie,

How very kind of you to send me Ernestine Evan's notice of my book[3] in *The New York Herald Tribune*. It has gone through 5 editions

---

[1] Julia: Hon. Mrs Rochfort Maguire.
[2] Miss Blanche Cecil: his sister.   [3] *Left Hand, Right Hand!*

between May 15th and July 15th. It comes out here in the autumn—but I suppose that means the spring.

Unless the war ends before October, I fear things will get much worse in London. What are your plans? Let me know if you think you will be able to come here. We long to see you. The only thing is, I might have to go away for a few days in October—in connection with the second volume of my Autobiography. Edith and I were going to Scarborough with John Piper[1] for him to do drawings of the town, but alas! we could not get into any of the hotels, and the only free time they have is in October, but I would willingly put this off rather than miss you.

Forgive a typed and rather dotty letter, but I find it difficult to concentrate because I was on the Bench all the morning, dealing with wretched little children who now get up to all sorts of mischief. Some of the cases are most surprising

Best Love
Yours ever
Osbert

I have a new pamphlet out today *Letter to My Son*. A. L. behaved oddly about it, so a new firm has published it but they won't send me my copies: otherwise one would go with this letter.

M. B. L. TO HER DAUGHTER S. L. M.

Parfetts House, Eversley Cross
August 12th, 1944

I have been having some delightful days at Compton Beauchamp, the lovely old house the Reggie Fellowes[2] have for the summer. They had their silver wedding on the 9th. Lord Berners who lives near and Meraud Guinness[3] were there. She sent you her love. The flying bombs upset her, so Daisy Fellowes took her in. She was really very nice— asked a lot after you. She is very clever in making herself clothes out of furniture materials (requiring no coupons).

[1] John Piper: Painter and writer. Trustee of Tate Gallery.
[2] Hon. Reginald Fellowes: s. of 2nd Baron De Ramsey. m. Marguerite, d. of 4th Duc Decazes and widow of Prince Jean de Broglie. M. B. L. became very attached to them both and saw a great deal of them.
[3] Meraud Guinness: m. 1929 Alvaro Guevara 1894-1951. He painted the portrait of Edith Sitwell in the National Portrait Gallery. She had passed through Lisbon and had seen M. B. L.'s daughter Susan.

I brought a chicken. I find Fortnum and Mason a great boon. Everyone *hopes* for olive oil and lemons from Algiers or Italy. Some red wine has come through but it is expensive and not nice. Elizabeth bought a half bot. of *British* brandy the other day. *Very* peculiar, but far better than nothing.

I am working hard at my book on my early married life.[1] My real difficulty is to make a selection. I have so much material as I knew *all* the writers and some, as you know, interesting. I am concentrating on Maurice Hewlett, Elizabeth of the German Garden, Masefield, Henry James, Hardy, Bennett, dear Rhoda[2] and so on.

It is curious how certain men so famous *then* are forgotten now. Or kept alive through films. Anthony Hope[3], Stanley Weyman[4], Mrs Humphrey Ward[5], Lucas Malet[6] etc. etc. How surprised *some* of them would be! The men more than the women. There will be some 'comebacks'. Barrie, I feel sure. Uncle Hilary never mentioned now. But his future place secure as a poet. His verse is *constantly* quoted in House of Commons, House of Lords, the *Times* and public speeches.

M. B. L. TO MISS MARY LOWNDES

Parfetts House,
Eversley Cross, Hampshire
August 29th, 1944

Your parcel just arrived—and general joy and excitement. Many warm thanks, my dear.

What astonishing things have happened, since I last wrote. I feel still anxious as to Paris. I hear privately that the Germans asked for a 3 day Armistice to get their 50,000 wounded out of Paris—then, within 24 hours, began fighting again. As I expected, a *jacquerie* has begun. One

---

[1] *The Merry Wives of Westminster*: by M. B. L. Pubs. 1946.

[2] Rhoda Broughton.

[3] Sir Anthony Hope Hawkins: 1863-1933. Author of *The Prisoner of Zenda, The Dolly Dialogues*, etc.

[4] Stanley Weyman: 1855-1928. Author of *A Gentleman of France, Under the Red Robe, The Red Cockade*, etc.

[5] Mrs Humphrey Ward: 1851-1920. Novelist. Author of *Robert Elsmere*, etc. Granddaughter of Thomas Arnold of Rugby.

[6] Lucas Malet: Pseudonym of Mary St Leger Harrison 1852-1931. d. of Charles Kingsley. She wrote *Colonel Enderby's Wife*, etc.

can't wonder at it. In fact, so far it has not been savage. I suppose everyone is weak, and suffering from acute malnutrition. Of course were I in
London, I should see people from Paris. As it is, I "listen in" to all the
broadcasts and read all the papers. I am aching to be in London and
would *now* willingly brave the Robot bombs! Some people believe that
before the end, the Germans will use poison gas over London. But such
is not their technique. Hitler might do anything but I don't believe that
now even his henchmen would obey him if it meant worse terms at the
end.

I cherish a secret hope of spending the 3 coldest winter months in
Lisbon. Susan could find me a tiny flat and I should get through a great
deal of work there. According to my Agreement, I shall have to turn
out of 1 Barton Street 3 months after the war in Europe is over. But as
my house is the only one in the street in good order—clean and cheerful
looking, I cherish a hope they may let me stay on. But the Ecclesiastical
Commissioners are the hardest landlords in, I should think, the world!

For the moment my little house is a source of income. But since flying
bombs, I thought it only right to halve the rent my *very* nice American
tenants paid.[1] They live there servantless! So make their own breakfasts,
and have all other meals out. Had they left, I should have had to go and
live there, for fear of burglars. Everything I have in this world, save a
few pictures, is there and very dear to me. The furniture, in fact, that
was in our little Wimbledon house. I sometimes wake up in the night
and wonder if everything that was at No. 9 Barton Street is really gone.
It is so vivid to me. I was indeed a fool not to move my precious things
from the Depository when the bombing began in '40. Though they
were not bombed and burnt till May '41. The last *great* raid.

L. P. HARTLEY TO M. B. L.

Rockbourne, Hants.
October 14*th*, 1944

Dearest Marie,

I *wish* you could have come on Tuesday, but I see it would have been
difficult, and I think you're right that A.[2] and Edith[3] might not have
altogether hit it off! I *do* hope you will be able to stay on into next week.
I long for some talk. A. and I have been reading some stories of Sheridan
Le Fanu's, antiphonally in the evenings—and he tells me today that he

[1] M. B. L. now had P. G.s for bed and breakfast.
[2] Algernon Cecil.   [3] Dame Edith Sitwell.

hopes to hear one from you much outdoing them in terror (he very much enjoys thrillers).

My book[1] is said to be coming out at long last on the 30th. Huntington thinks it will be sold out before publication, but he has such rosy ideas of my literary future. There is a wonderful picture of me on the cover, looking like an elderly and dissipated bloodhound exhausted after a long chase. It was taken by my sister Norah's dog-photographer which explains the canine look.

M. B. L. TO HER DAUGHTER E. I.

1 *Barton Street, S.W.*1
November 3rd, 1944

Daisy Fellowes dinner party was a marvel!! I sat between Duff Cooper and a delightful American Col. Whitney who is partner of this man who is buying *The Lodger* rights from Alfred Hitchcock! There were 8 in all. It was a good dinner. Duckling the main dish. A great deal to drink served in French way. Champagne at the end. I had deeply interesting talk with Duff, and after dinner he went and got me a touching letter from Desmond MacCarthy about Uncle Hilary.

I am working hard now at the spy story. It is worth doing, as it would mean such a *lot* of money *if* it comes off. I think I shall have to come to you if it is not taken as a serial. Did I tell you the Censor held up the Toby dog story in MSS of my book, because I mentioned a landmine! The story had, of course, appeared with landmine complete in a 7 million syndicate in the U.S.A.

M. B. L. TO MISS MARY LOWNDES

Parfetts House,
Eversley Cross, Hants.
November 30th, 1944

A long letter I wrote to you on Nov. 13th has just been returned as the U.S.A. Post Office could not read my bad handwriting. It is hopelessly out of date now. I am again writing with quill pens. A great relief, I will dictate my little news. In spite of the P.M.'s speech yesterday, I believe war will be over sooner than most thoughtful people now believe. Russia is pressing on again, I feel sadly disappointed at not being in London for a few weeks at Christmas. But my children are so impressed by the rocket bombs, someone they knew was near one that fell last

[1] *The Shrimp and the Anemone.* Pubs. 1944.

week. As you know, they travel quicker than sound, so no-one can take shelter.

Elizabeth and I lately found a number of old letters, written more than a hundred years ago, each with black stamps. These are now worth a pound each and I am joyfully selling them. I have also found a series of letters from Joseph Priestley written from Northumberland, on the Susquehanna, to a man in Philadelphia. I am sending these to an American friend who is a dealer. The charm of selling, is that in England one does not have to pay Income Tax on anything sold.

I am naturally very much cheered about France, and especially, (I may have told you this before) because the Château at La Celle St Cloud, which I have considered as dear to me as our own home, has been spared destruction, and the owner, my daughter-in-law's uncle, is back again there. It housed for four years the German G.H.Q. so it is a miracle it was not bombed, but it is as if really hidden in the old Royal woods, and is not very large. I am getting on with my new book.

DIARY

February 27th, 1945

In my view the frankness regarding public affairs and those who conduct them in France has been a most unfortunate thing for the French nation. It is curious that a country which has amongst its most often quoted proverbs—"all truth is not good to tell' should insist on hearing the truth.

I am now reading with passionate interest a book called *The War in Paris* which consists of a day to day diary kept by an educated Frenchman named Charles Braibant. The diary covers from the 8th November 1942 to the 27th August 1944; every day this man put down everything he heard, and he was apparently in a position to hear a very great deal. He does not gloss over anything; when he considers that the French behaved badly he puts it down. He is equally critical of the British and the Russians. This gives the book great value to me. Of all the war books it has interested me the most.

M. B. L. TO HER DAUGHTER E. I.

1 *Barton Street, S.W.*1
March 5th, 1945

I had good talk with Reggie Fellowes after Mass at Farm Street. He, like me, does not think war on point of collapse. Clemmie Churchill had been to see them, Daisy is at Compton Beauchamp, shutting up there. They are going to take a house at Sunninghill for the summer. I am going to be active regarding U.S.A. P.G.'s this week. My cook yearns for them.

M. B. L. TO HER DAUGHTER E. I.

1 *Barton Street, S.W.*1
April 8th, 1945

I had a most interesting evening with H. G. Wells and his beloved Baroness. Just us 3. He is so *very* clear and shrewd and, of course, he and I have, roughly speaking, known all the same people. He is tolerant and broad-minded. I *did* think him much *changed.* He looked very thin (diabetes). I rather wonder Baroness Budberg does not marry him, for he does so dote on her—and she does give up her life to him. She lives close to Eric Maclagan and Wells in the Regents Park! I do hope he will leave her enough to make her comfortable. He is *very* rich.

M. B. L. TO HER DAUGHTER S. L. M.

1 *Barton Street, S.W.*1
May 6th, 1945

I have now got a very nice paying guest, a Swede, who has become a naturalized American. He is very well mannered and quiet, and also very kind. Thus he is going to fetch me a cab this morning to go to Mass. I am going to Farm Street and then lunch with Christabel Aberconway[1] at the Connaught Hotel. This evening I have Osbert Sitwell to dinner. With a heavy heart I have paid thirty shillings for a guinea fowl, which would have been 4/6 before the war.

London is so full in view of the coming VE Day[2] that soon people will be sleeping in the streets. I think it will amuse you to hear that Lord FitzAlan and Magdalen[3] are coming to live in Marsham Street in a new block of flats, Lord and Lady Salisbury are there, and so are the Cranbornes. It is conveniently near the House of Lords.

I am giving in the manuscript of my new book *The Merry Wives of*

[1] Christabel Aberconway: wife of 2nd Baron Aberconway and d. of Sir Melville Macnaghten C.B.
[2] Germany surrendered on May 8th.
[3] Hon. Magdalen FitzAlan-Howard: only daughter of Lord FitzAlan.

255

Westminster on Tuesday next. I have been fortunate in Elizabeth having found the diary I began to keep about 1909 and which I kept all through the last war. It has been a great help to me. Of course some of the funniest things in it I don't feel I can put in the book, such as the following. Apropos of the life of Sir Charles Dilke by his adoring niece, Gertrude Tuckwell, "A member of the Thirty said that Dilke only cared for beds and blue-books, and that in this book the beds were left out".

I feel anxious as to what will happen *after* the war. I fear inflation is certain.

M. B. L. TO MISS MARY LOWNDES

1 *Barton Street, S.W.*1
May 13*th*, 1945

Very pleased to get your letter on V Day! I stayed at home during the two days. I am pleased the workers got two days "off". But it was most inconvenient for most people as no adequate arrangements had been made as to food. All the bread ran out etc. Thousands slept in the parks, luckily it was and is frightfully hot.

London has been so tremendously knocked about, living is so high that I am convinced there will be an exodus as winter draws near. Apart from the "pictures" and very expensive theatres, there is no form of entertainment. Once all the provincial sight-seers have satisfied their curiosity and the Americans have gradually slipped away I believe London will go dead for a time, though this is not the general belief. Now the town is crammed to bursting.

I've given in my book. It covers the first 18 years of my happy married life from 1896-1914 War. Has accounts of Hardy, and many of the writers of that time. I knew almost all well. I did not know Galsworthy well, I did not care for him and I never met Conrad. Hewlett was my greatest friend. I have a chapter on Henry James. I knew him for about 5 years. I have letters from all those writers.

I had lunch with Margot (Tennant, Asquith, Oxford) yesterday. I was truly fond of poor Elizabeth Bibesco. That is a real bond between us. Margot now lives with one servant in a beautiful old house in Kensington Square. I doubt if there has ever been a greater change in any life in my time. She is now disliked where formerly she was adored, yet she is exactly the same as she was 50 years ago. It is the world which has changed.

CHAPTER XIV

1945-1947

The General Election was held very soon after the end of the War. M. B. L. was intensly interested in it and her forecast of what the results would be, was more accurate than those of many of her contemporaries.

Towards the end of her life Marie Belloc Lowndes paid two visits to her daughter in Lisbon, the first for the birth of her youngest grandchild and the second in the following winter. Her interest in people and places made these visits to a new country a particular pleasure to her and she gives her impressions in a series of lively letters to her daughter in England.

The book ends with a characteristic letter to her younger daughter after her return to England. Marie quotes a verse which could serve as a motto to only too many letter writers, but which did not apply to herself. She rarely gave advice by post and seldom by word of mouth, though she was ever ready to listen to the troubles of her friends and to console them as far as was in her power.

M. B. L. TO MISS MARY LOWNDES

1 *Barton Street S.W.*1
June 1st, 1945

I feel intensely interested in coming Election. I *was* convinced Labour would sweep the board. I now begin to doubt it for the Caretaker Government, or rather its Chief, is being very clever stealing, as quickly as possible, the other side's thunder. I deplore the international squabbles, it seems to me odd of Great Britain, after the Greek affair, to take the Lebanese side in the near East. A friend who has just been a month in Paris, a clever woman who has a flat there, believes it will be years before France will recover from the German occupation, they took *everything*. Every cock or hen, every pig or cow in this countryside so well known to me. They cut down all the good trees, and pillaged every house, large and small, between Paris and the *banlieue* towns. An egg is still an unknown object, except when bought on the black market, which procures what it has on sale from the distant parts of the country, hidden in army lorries. Yet she says that as everyone is working hard the country may recover quicker than seems possible.

June 5th. Your most kind gift just came. Many many thanks. Food is beginning to be on the very short side. Rations, especially fats, are cut, and though there ought to be plenty of fish, as a matter of fact there is extremely little on sale. Difficulty it is said of transport. What is odd is that there is no "good fish" when any is to be procured. No

259

soles, turbot or so on, that is a real mystery for the black market can't get it all, but some one does.

I thought this Labour (Attlee) speech (delivered last night) extremely good. Opinions are very divided, though Churchill is embedded in all *hearts*, no *heads* can possibly admire the Conservative M.P.'s who have sat longer than almost any others and who are indeed a poor lot. When one remembers their delight at Munich, their complacency during that sinister winter of 1940, their howls against their late idol Chamberlain and slavish subservience to Churchill since the Peace, one can only feel deep contempt for almost all of them. Whatever happens I hope few of these will come back.

M. B. L. TO HER DAUGHTER S. L. M.

1 *Barton Street, S.W.*1
June 7th, 1945

Optimists believe Govt. *will* come back. *I* have got doubts of that. Human nature loves a change. The present people have only *one* asset —Churchill. But I notice, (among working people) that a very sharp line is drawn between Churchill—the hero who won the war—and Churchill the Tory boss! There is naturally much bitterness at this Government's record as to housing, coal, and the *very* high cost of living. Vegetables which used to be from 4d. to 1/- per pound now are 2/6d. to 5/- out of reach of *any* save *very* well off. Potatoes (controlled at I think 2d. a 1b) have vanished. I went to 5 shops and found *none*. So had to buy, as I had someone to dinner, broad beans at 2/6d a 1b. Fish *very* scarce still, though *there* I notice a *little* improvement.

No one dares give any guess as to how the Election will go. I alter from day to day. *So do the M.P.'s I see.* They each believe their seat is safe, which amuses me very much.

I hope you are not overtiring yourself. It is folly to do that before one has a baby. Do *rest* a lot. I hope you have a good nurse for the children. Do you recall Daddy said at a time we were *very* hard up "I would not be a child's nurse for £5,000 pounds a year!"

M. B. L. TO HER DAUGHTER S. L. M.

1 *Barton Street, S.W.*1
July 21st, 1945

I can't help being interested at the seizing of empty houses. It will enrage my landlords! There is biggish empty *house next to this house.*

The one modern house (apart from the Runciman's) in the street. The one with bulging windows, hideous! Rent £300 a year. Rates on top. Everyone panting to know how Election went. We shall know on 26th, next Thursday.

I saw Lady Bonham-Carter lately, asked affectionately after you. She is doing war work round the corner. Looked *exactly* as she did 10 years ago. Poor Margot is *said* to be very ill. Her mind has been affected. She lives alone, with one charwoman-servant in a beautiful old house in Kensington Square. The *real* trouble with her, as with many others of her sort, is that they don't get enough to eat. They don't or won't bother about it. I get extraordinary meals when I *do* dine out. I *never* lunch out. The only good food I get is at home. English people don't realize the importance of food. They glory in being indifferent to it. No wonder they can't keep even one servant. Of course anything *not* rationed is either *very* expensive, or has vanished. *Eggs* are practically *non est*, unless one has hens or is in touch with a farm. Life will take a long, long time to become normal in *any* way.

DIARY

July 28th, 1945

I have never known the people with whom I am in touch, more amazed than at the result of the Election.[1] Those who are well off are trembling with fear, some even are afraid of a capital levy.

On the other hand, it seems as if certain people connected with the Government—one ought to say the *late* Government—cannot believe that they are really going out. Sir John and Lady Anderson gave a lunch party of ten. Three people came on here afterwards and told me about it. They said that no-one there seemed to realize what was going to happen.

J. H. Martin who called on me in the afternoon, thought it would have been better for his party (the Socialists) not to have come in just now. I asked him if it was true that they were already quarrelling among themselves; he admitted that this was so, and that a great struggle for power was going on between Morrison and Bevin, both wanting to be Foreign Secretary. He told me he thought Bevin would win, and I see today that has come to pass.

[1] In this post-war election Labour won 393 seats, the Conservatives 213 and the Liberals 12.

Parfetts House,
Eversley Cross
September 7th, 1945

I am going to Margot's Memorial Service on Tuesday at St Margaret's. What an amazing *oddity* she was. I recall her at the Christening of Clare's[1] twins in St Margaret's. The late King was very ill, but that day he was getting better. *If* he died, Margot was going to get a large sum from some U.S.A. paper for an intimate account of him. So she was quite openly vext when I told her (thinking she would be pleased) I had heard from the *Times* office he was better! She angrily denied it! She was a *terrible example* of the effect of always thinking of money and longing for what only money can buy. But I strongly blame her father for not leaving her a substantial addition to her marriage settlement. He was so enormously rich. He had £300,000 a year.

The real truth was that she was a child of nature. She could not conceal what she was feeling, and she was wholly lacking in the capacity to behave with what may be called the hypocrisy without which life could scarcely be carried on.

DIARY

September 10th, 1945

I have been re-reading with painful interest Margot Asquith's autobiography, it was almost as if I heard her voice. As I read my heart ached, for had she shown the proofs to any ordinary honest friend, that friend would have advised her to take out what in all amounted only to a page or two: the few lines concerning the Robert Louis Stevensons at Davos, and a passage in the book which deeply hurt and offended someone whose heiress had married one of Asquith's sons by his first marriage. Had this lady not had a considerable nobility of nature she would most certainly have altered her will. Mr Asquith did not read the manuscript, a fact which is stated plainly in the preface.

Long after the book was out, some word or two by Mr Asquith emboldened me to ask him why he did not read the proofs of his wife's book. He looked at me quite straight and said "I made a mistake there."

[1] Hon. Mrs James Beck: d. of 1st Baron Glenconner. Her twin son and daughter were born in 1929.

When I was staying at the Wharf for a weekend; the book lay on a table. I opened it. Margot ran across the room and took it from me. "Please don't look at that book", she cried, "it has lost me all my friends". Considering her brilliant mind and the intense interest she felt in human nature, it is strange indeed that she did not realize the effect some passages of her memoirs would have on certain people whom she regarded as her nearest friends. Undoubtedly nothing published in my time has aroused so violent a feeling of anger.

M. B. L. TO HER DAUGHTER S. L. M.

1 *Barton Street, S.W.*1
September 13*th*, 1945

Charles Morgan spent a long time with me yesterday. He is now writing another long novel (having a short one done). His son is (temporarily) in the Coldstream. Their daughter[1] is very attractive, like her mother. Of course C. M. makes large sums from his work. He sold the film rights of his last book for £8,000.

How strange is the part money plays in life! I often think of it. It means at once so very, very much and so very, very little, as regards happiness in civilized human communities. I suppose spendthrifts, *for a little* while, and misers, *all life long*, get the most pleasure from the possession of money. I have known all sorts in my now long life.

M. B. L. TO HER DAUGHTER E. I.

Trematon Castle[2]
Saltash
September 25*th*, 1945

Well! I had a touchingly warm welcome. Great joy at provisions *and* port. But it was a water-only meal of a strange kind. Good soup, stuffed eggs (made by Violet Trefusis[3]) and Apple Charlotte with very good cream. Violet's maid unpacked for me beautifully. She said dolefully "My lady calls me 'Jones'. But my name is Matilda"—so I

---

[1] Elizabeth Shirley Morgan: m. 7th Marquess of Anglesey 1948.

[2] Trematon Castle: the house of Sir Claud and Lady Russell where M. B. L. often stayed. Sir Claud had retired from the Diplomatic Service.

[3] Violet Trefusis: d. of Hon. Mr and Mrs George Keppel. m. Major Denys Trefusis M.C.

said "You shall be Matilda to me!" Violet is 52, looks and dresses like 28 and is fond of Old Chesnut Stories. She went, or says she did, to see the Queen and Princesses. Going to live (at the Ritz) in Paris— I do wonder what French people think of her!

I can't believe she is wholly *English*—the strangest mixture of truth and fantasy. She *cried* when describing her flight from Paris to Bordeaux with the Princess de Chimay[1] and two children in her small car. *Constant* heavy machine guns, especially *first* day when they went to Caen—no other road being open. They broke their flight at Milly Sutherland's[2] house, apparently deserted. *But* then they found her in an upper room— dressed, and with all the jewels she could put on her person, waiting for death; as a huge ammunition dump close by was to have been blown up. It was—but not before they had forced her to leave. It was the strangest narrative to which I have ever listened, and it lasted about 2 hours.

She is a fascinating talker, *and* companion. To me it is extraordinary that of the *many* women who have spoken to me of Violet Trefusis, not one gave me even the smallest inkling *of what she is like*. Even as a talker, she is *extremely* individual—I expect this irritates people, for she likes "holding the floor." V. is no adorer of Winston as she knows he set her mother against Hore Belisha—who is *now* making a "retreat" in a monastery. *I* tell her she ought to marry a Frenchman. Her love of France seems to me one of the honestly *true* things in her astonishing nature.

In the middle of dinner a man rang her up—she was gone a good 10 minutes—only consolation of host was that the man rang up, she did not make the call. She makes a great many. I do wonder who her father was. She *really* has *la joie de vivre*. I suppose that quality in her mother enchanted Edward VII. Sir Claud and I had long, learned discussion re. Berkeley-Fitzhardinge pedigrees, etc. etc. Violet pretended she had known them all. Sir Claud goaded, exclaimed "They lived over a 100 years ago." She replied "I mean those living now". He said "There are now none".

I have same room with enchanting view over Tamar river, really arm of sea. I go to Church at Laundry Convent. Sir Claud loves them,

---

[1] Princess de Chimay: d. of Lord Ernest Hamilton. m. 1922 Prince Alphonse de Chimay.

[2] Millicent, Duchess of Sutherland: 1867-1955. d. of 4th Earl of Rosslyn, widow of 4th Duke of Sutherland. Her house was at Juigné-sur-Loire.

as they do his shirts so beautifully. We go to lunch at the Abdy's[1] a treat for Violet. I think I shall enjoy it, as they have lovely pictures etc. But I would rather have stayed quiet today. I shall try and do the story for Mary King.

DIARY

October 3rd, 1945

I have twice had the melancholy experience of seeing the contents of a house where I had been very happy and had spent delightful days put up for sale. The first time the sale took place at 19, Portman Square, where lived the famous Victorian collector, Henry Yates Thompson. I happened to pass the house as the sale was going on. Fortunately for me it took place in July 1941, at a terrible moment of the War. I left three bids, all I could afford. I was very anxious to acquire a large, Wedgwood plaque of my great-great-grandfather, Joseph Priestley. It was one of a pair[2] the other being of Priestley's friend, Benjamin Franklin. I had sat at dinner opposite these plaques I think I may say innumerable times, from before my marriage till the death of Mr Yates Thompson.

The other object for which I left a bid was the well-known though not at all common statuette of Thackeray. It is specially dear to me because it is singularly like my husband—in fact there was a time in his life when it might have been done from him. This statuette went for one pound. Had I known what was going to happen, and the prices things would fetch later in the war, I would somehow or other have procured a hundred pounds and bought many other things at that sale.

Yesterday I went down in the hope of buying some little object which would recall happy days at Lympne, Philip Sassoon's country house where I always stayed once or twice every year. The house outside looked like an 18th Century manor house. The inside was fantastic and, in my eyes, most beautiful. I felt certain I could find something in the sale which would be fairly cheap, for though he had there many valuable pictures, mostly watercolours by Sargent, and some splendid carpets and rugs, there were many small tables, chairs and so

[1] Sir Robert Abdy and Lady Diana Abdy—their house was Newton Ferrers, Callington.

[2] Priestley was a friend of Wedgwood and the oval plaques bought at this sale for £20 are 13 inches in height.

265

on, which in an ordinary sale before the war would have fetched only a few shillings each, but I learned with astonishment that everything was fetching enormous sums.

The prices were the more surprising to me because it was clear that Hannah Gubbay had put aside certain things I remembered which had stood on the writing table in the charming library. This was also true of certain pretty, small pieces of good furniture in the same library. It was strange and painful to me to see the drawing-room furniture piled up for sale. A carpet, not unlike one I myself bought the first year of the war in 1940, for thirty pounds, had fetched £600!

By far the most interesting and beautiful thing in the house has had to be left there—a series of paintings by Rex Whistler on the walls and ceiling of what had been the only unattractive room in the house. When I first went it was a billiard room, but Rex had turned it into a place of great and it may be said, fantastic beauty. He so painted the ceiling that the room appeared to be a tent, and on the walls were strange landscapes.

M. B. L. TO HER DAUGHTER S. L. M.

Rockbourne, Hampshire
November 2nd, 1945

I feel, sometimes, as if I had lived a thousand years. So great are the changes since I married 50 years ago on 9th of next January. The greatest change is condition of working people. A *very* good thing. There was endemic poverty *then*. Apart from professional philanthropists, *no one* pitied poor people or indeed gave them a thought. Because my mother did so, she was regarded as odd. Of course there were a good many professional philanthropists, but ordinary people kept well away from them, unless like dear Maude Stanley[1] they really cared and *they* never mentioned their work. Incredible hardness of heart was universal among ordinary gentlefolk. That is made clear in all the diaries and letters of that period. There was a fearful gulf between the well-to-do and those who were *not*. I was the only person in a large circle who had only one servant. And *I* had a children's nurse. The less well-to-do, I knew, *all* had two servants—at least. I think that *now*

---

[1] Hon. Maude Stanley: 1833-1915. d. of 2nd Lord Stanley of Alderley— founded *The London Girl's Club Union*.

people go to other extreme. Keep *no* servant and live in restaurants. Quite well-to-do young couples do that. A horrid way of life. I wonder if you liked *Brideshead*[1]. Parts of it very remarkable, though I thought the Catholics in the book quite unrealistic, like cats with 2 heads. Of course he has known none of the type he describes. The same *kind* of mistakes were made by E. M. Delafield[2] in her early anti-Catholic novels. They were filled with fantastic *imaginary* figures of the old Catholic world.

M. B. L. TO HER DAUGHTER E. I.

Hotel Florida, Lisbon
December 27th, 1945

I don't *like* flying though it was best flight for long time against head wind. Susan and Luiz met me at airport, their flat charming, but really too small now, though she seems quite content. Ana, a very pretty small neat little fair girl, full of energy, far more than Paul. Susan wears the astrakhan coat[3] with glee, how glad I am I failed to sell it and it is just right for her figure, so I persuaded her not to have it altered.

There is a lot of fruit and drink here. It is still a very cheap country, obviously extremely prosperous. Splendid shops. I feel rather poorly, otherwise all is well, shall D. V. finish story for Mary King and send to Miss Bellis[4] to type by the end of week.

Susan, I gather, may go into hospital January 7th. Determined to do all she can before then. I wish they had small house of their own outside Lisbon. They may but prices huge now. Full of British here to avoid tax and have lots to eat. Large turkey 12/- etc. butter dear or bad. Bread rationed but plenty all the same. Luiz delighted with all you sent him, also children. I have begged Susan not to come here till after lunch and I am dining in the hotel, but her energy is astounding. I was like that once as you know. She is getting me a secretary for two-three mornings a week.

[1] *Brideshead Revisited*: by Evelyn Waugh was published this year.
[2] E. M. Delafield: 1890-1945. d. of Count Henry de la Pasture and Mrs de la Pasture who wrote *Peter's Mother* and the *Unlucky Family*. m. Arthur Paul Dashwood 1919. Wrote many novels and *Diary of a Provincial Lady*. Pubs. 1930 and its sequels.
[3] M. B. L. had bought this coat for £100 in 1930.
[4] Miss Bellis: M. B. L.'s excellent secretary.

267

M. B. L. TO HER DAUGHTER E. I.

Hotel Florida, Lisbon
December 30th, 1945

I think of you constantly, longing to know you are all right after your nightmare journey to help me get off. I feel much better today after good night. I suppose they have now killed the turkeys and cocks who screamed and crowed all my first night.

Susan and I had happy time yesterday, I buying a hat, today I drive with 'Ann Bridge'[1] the Ambassadress. I feel Susan is doing too much, but she likes it. I think my being here gives her pleasure, as she is most anxious I should stay as long as possible. The food is cheap and delicious, huge tangerines at 1d each. How I wish you both and darling children were here for a week. I think Harry would be amused.

All property going up daily, owing to huge influx of British mostly. My plane had several emigrés, who made no bones about it. Mostly elderly men on pensions. It was rather sad to me to hear their delight at getting away from England. I felt most of the men will end as drunkards, rolling down the lovely Portuguese roads, for there is nothing for them to do. When in Susan's flat, I read to encourage her to lie down, but she is out a lot, it is the party centre of the world! So far I have escaped them.

M. B. L. TO MISS MARY LOWNDES

Hotel Florida, Lisbon
December 31st, 1945

It is astounding, to me, to be in a prosperous country. Lisbon is like Paris before 1914. Splendid shops, wonderful cheap fruit. I am having *pitiful* letters from Paris. Few can afford any kind of warmth. Most people live in bed.

I know well the British Ambassadress here—Mary O'Malley. She is generosity itself. She took me for a wonderful drive yesterday, and told me of the large sums she makes in the U.S.A. Macmillan's have now taken her on. Little Brown having turned down her new book as being

---

[1] 'Ann Bridge': w. of Sir Owen O'Malley K.C.M.G., British Ambassador to Portugal 1945-47. Her first novel, *Peking Picnic* 1932, won *The Atlantic Monthly* prize.

anti-American. She believes in telling people their *verités vraies*. That did not work out well for Mrs Trollope *or* even Dickens. A friend of mine, Una Pope-Hennessy, has just done a book on Dickens. But there is still a good deal of mystery surrounding his life. I believe he had *many* illegitimate children. One son of the kind got a large sum out of Sir Henry Dickens, for a long series of love letters which were burnt in the presence of my informant. I am so horrified at the idiotic lies told about people concerning whose private lives I know a great deal. Last example, an amazing book on George Eliot, makes her out a gorgon and G. H. Lewes a saint.

I must now get up and go to the Irish Friars Church[1] which was protected all through the Revolution by Edward VII. The only Church left open, then, in Lisbon. The beauty of this town gives me great pleasure. Also that no cat is ever killed or hurt[2].

M. B. L. TO HER DAUGHTER E. I.

Hotel Florida, Lisbon
January 1st, 1946

I thought of you seeing off Catherine and Hilda[3] yesterday. It will be great fun for them. I think all your children have the power of enjoyment. I have always had it, if well. Daddy not always. Things had to be "just so" for him to feel satisfied. Also he became easily bored.

What a fascination just the knowledge of the possession of money has for some human beings. When Hannah de Rothschild's father died, Lord Rosebery jilted a charming American girl, to whom he had just become engaged. This made a sensation. He waited a little while, then asked Hannah de Rothschild. Of course in those days engagements were not publicly "announced". Still less put in the papers. She had always cared for him—He was the *jeune premier* of that generation. His letters to Queen Victoria are *very* good. Far the best of any stateman's letters published in her life. She began with a strong prejudice, ended by finding him fascinating. His failure as Prime Minister deeply

---

[1] Corpo Santo Church, Lisbon, served by friars from the Irish Dominican Province for over 300 years.
[2] The Portuguese consider it unlucky to kill a cat, so stray cats in public gardens and parks are given food by well-wishers.
[3] Lady Catherine Northcote and Lady Hilda Northcote. M. B. L.'s granddaughters.

269

troubled and surprised her—he could be *very rude*, a fatal peculiarity in a public man. The Rothschilds all hated him. He called Aylesbury "The New Jerusalem".

M. B. L. TO HER DAUGHTER E. I.

Hotel Florida, Lisbon
January 9th, 1946
My wedding day 50 years
ago

Susan looks blooming, I've not been able to examine baby[1] as she is always asleep when I go to the British Hospital at 4. She is suckling nicely now, was rather averse at first. She looks big and well nourished, I've not heard her cry. Susan not allowed to see visitors for a week, very good thing.

Yesterday the very nice schoolboy nephew[2] lunched. He does so with some member of the family every Tuesday. He kept Paul and Ana in stern order, talked excellent French to me, to Paul's disgust. He adores stamps, you might send me, say 6. He is a fine, healthy looking, very dark haired boy. I went to see some friends of Susan's, a splendid house, fine pictures, not a book about. A regular small ladies tea-party. There is great wealth in Portugal, huge commercial fortunes, and immense benefits from not having been in this War. I am seeing a good deal of diplomatic society. Lunching today with the U.S.A. Crockers[3], son of that dear woman who was so kind to you and me in New York.

Susan is splendidly fed at hospital. I saw her doctor, Dr Pedro da Cunha, he looks 25, but has eight children.

There are excellent reading rooms at the British and French Institutes. Taxis seem to me the only really cheap thing in Lisbon. Luckily Susan's flat is rent controlled, the Government is very efficient in some ways. I like Luiz's Aunt very much, and I am glad she is looking after things in the flat. Paul now goes to a Nun's infant school every morning for 2 hours. Luiz is out all day. Dinner late, but good when it comes. I am gradually escaping thraldom of the elderly English

[1] Antonia Lowndes Marques: M. B. L.'s youngest grandchild.
[2] Antonio Henrique de Oliveira Marques: now a distinguished historian.
[3] Mr and Mrs Edward S. Crocker: He was then Counsellor at U.S. Embassy in Lisbon. Later U.S. Ambassador to Iraq.

270

widow whom Susan found to take me out whilst she is in hospital. She takes me today to French Institute, where she can't imagine why I want to go. If I were young she would sadly suspect that I have a lover.

She is astonished that I want books. She thinks reading a kind of queer vice. "If you can't remember what you read, why trouble to read?" she observed crossly yesterday, when I foolishly told her I wished to re-read *British Agent*[1]. The one intelligent person I am in touch with is Dutch.

This town interests me very much, it is beautiful, picturesque and strange. Their "Rue de la Paix," is full of big jewellers, food, clothes shops, all dear. I spend nothing, save on taxis and fruit, tangerines and apples. I am honorary member of the Lisbon Ladies Club with a good library.

It is very *curious* little Colony—I imagine rather like life (among the British) in a West Indian Island. What touches me is that (apart from drink), they are all so respectable. A *big* C. of E. congregation. Not many English Catholics. There are survivals of the British-Portuguese links. But the only cosmopolitan society is composed of diplomats. They live in *beautiful* old houses and form a world to themselves.

M. B. L. TO MISS MARY LOWNDES

Parfetts House,
Eversley Cross
May 1st, 1946

Everything is as usual with us, and I am spending a few days at the Lansdowne Club in London. I do that now and again, and I am eagerly looking forward to being once more at No. 1 Barton Street. I hope to move back there at the end of May, and then I let off the second floor, consisting of two bedrooms and a bathroom, to two men. I give them bed and breakfast for £5 each a week, and in the old days I should have felt myself very rich on the proceeds. As it is I now pay £3 a week to my housekeeper, and £1 a week to her helper, and there seem to be endless incidental expenses. I hope this time to stay there for four months, as I am bringing out my new book—*The Merry Wives of Westminster*—in July.

---

[1] *Memoirs of a British Agent*: by R. H. Lockhart. Pubs. 1932.

I have been reading the *Life of Lady Beaconsfield* with great interest and pleasure and was amused to come again across the story of the man who had asked her how and where she had discovered a certain Cabinet secret, and she replied with simplicity, "In bed". It reminded me of a dear French friend who once said to me that the best place to hear a secret was when one's head was lying on a pillow.

DIARY

July 29th, 1946

I am going off to Faringdon to stay with Lord Berners[1] who is a most clever and singular being. I have read his account of his very strange childhood[2]. He is now writing what I hope will be an equally strange account of his boyhood. He is a kind, good friend to me. I much enjoy staying with him as there are generally interesting people of the writing type.

DIARY

August 9th, 1946

A man next to me at dinner talked of the attack which had just been made by Hannen Swaffer[3] on Charles Morgan. We agreed what a fine writer he was. Morgan has been doing a series of articles for the *Sunday Times* in which he expressed a fear which I believe every type of person has long felt, of the increasing desire on the part of the Government to control the actions of the private individual. I read Charles Morgan's remarks not only with very great interest, but with entire approval. I have always remembered that one of the first things my mother said in my presence stuck in my infant memory: the old saying, "Better England drunk and England free than England sober and in chains!" And such I can truly say has always been my sentiments.

These, however, are not the sentiments of the Labour Party, and Charles Morgan's thoughtful and mild remarks have driven the Socialist press to frenzy.

To me there is something melancholy in the thought of how throughout the ages credit for some great and valuable benefit to humanity has gone to the wrong man or group of men. I have never seen any

[1] Lord Berners: 1883-1950. 14th Baron. Writer. Noted eccentric.
[2] *First Childhood*: pubs. 1934.   [3] Hannen Swaffer: Dramatic critic.

allusion to what is surely true, that among those few who helped to win the Battle of Britain, a place should be found for the man who was long dead when it took place. That is Lord Northcliffe. From the day Northcliffe saw the brothers Wright try out their flying machine at Biarritz, he realized what may be called the potentialities of flying. He spent large sums of money on prizes for air races round Britain and more important to him, his time and energy in encouraging the science of aeronautics.

M. B. L. TO HER DAUGHTER E. I.

West Coker[1]
September 22nd, 1946

I lunched alone with Lord Tredegar[2] and spent the afternoon with him as Violet was out. He is certainly the *oddest* man I have ever met while outwardly quite ordinary. His marriage is legally ended. He is toying with thought of proposing to *Lady Illingworth*. He has just been staying with her. He talks of women all the time. He has houses (or flats) in Rome, London, Paris and Bali—lives just now with his mother near Horsham.

He spoke at length, and kindly, of his first wife, Lois Sturt. *Says* he got leave from the Pope to have her cremated. He *has* a shrewd intelligent side—nothing bitter or spiteful, but I *do* think he is slightly odd. The Inland Revenue sent to his bankers recently for *all* his banking accounts to his natural rage, as his income tax is collected at source. Told me *all* about his money matters—If income tax is lowered to 7/6 in £1 he will be rich again! His mother lives in bed, *in the dark.* Her only affection is for a Pekinese who goes out twice a week for a drive, and is never allowed to walk, though quite well. Is always carried in a shawl, and has an attendant who only looks after him. Though a boy dog, he has never been allowed to see a bitch—this Lord T. thinks very cruel! He has an enormous number of acquaintances—I fear no *friends.* I doubt if he ever reads a book. According to him he has done *many* important, secret, war jobs. He has *la folie de la grandeur.* It comes out strangely at times, such as telephoning to the Pope most evenings.

Have you heard that his mother has the unusual gift, perhaps the

[1] West Coker: M. B. L. was staying here with Mrs Denys Trefusis.
[2] Lord Tredegar: 1893-1949. 2nd Viscount. Author.

273

mania, for making chaffinch's nests? She retires for some weeks at a time and then emerges with a perfectly constructed nest which would deceive an ornithologist.

M. B. L. TO HER DAUGHTER E. I.

Praça José Fontana 12-1,
Lisbon
Boxing Day 1946

My precious darling

How very *very* well I recall my first visit to Eton. Frances[1] filled with fears at the thought of a "Journalist". I only guessed that *much* later. Dear Charlie loved me from first second. She a good many seconds later—what interested her was my sympathy with the unfortunate and unhappy. Not much of that in England, *unless* the misery is on orthodox lines. Lack of imagination is a *great* asset. The greatest asset of the British people. "God was at Eton, so we can't be beaten", might well be Eton's *real* motto.

The floods at Eton were terrible. Amazing they kept the school there in the old days. When I was young a lot of the boys used to die. It is a most unhealthy place, now I suppose they do drain it. Boats used to paddle in the High Street. I remember the playing fields constantly under water. Queen Victoria used to drive there to see the fun.

The boys were supposed to exist for the benefit of the Masters. This was not realised by the fond parents, who were treated with distant, cold courtesy. The 4th of June was *their* day, their only day. Eton was indeed an eye opener to me when I first went there. First "the Castle" then "the masters" then a long way after, "the boys". In most of the houses the boys did not have enough to eat, hence the Tuck Shops. The Lowrys were one of the very few who gave their boys enough to eat and were regarded as Blacklegs in consequence by the other Housemasters. The boys used to queue up outside the Tuck Shops. I learnt a great deal, as I took the group of Catholics to Church, then in a slum in Windsor. It was very wrong of Catholics to send their boys to Eton. Of course almost always when the father was an old Etonian. So strong was the anti-Catholic feeling that very few parents would have their sons in a house where Catholic boys were accepted. I think Charles

---

[1] Frances Lowry: M. B. L.'s sister-in-law. m. her cousin Charles Lowry who was a Housemaster at Eton and later Headmaster of Sedbergh and then of Tonbridge.

Lowry had 3 or 4, all sons of old Etonians who had been at Eton with him. The Catholic Church is a pathetic little building. I recall how it was said to make Queen Victoria uncomfortable to send the Queen of the Belgians and other Catholic Royal visitors to that little Church. Windsor was a very low Church place. Many Scots trades people, who followed the Queen south; it seems a hundred years ago.

I am re-reading Ronny Storrs'[1] really very interesting book. I can't remember if you ever knew him. A Cust on his mother's side. He is very *very* clever. His hero, Harry Cust, whose naughty ways he imitated and emulated. His book is *very* good, first called *Orientations*, then wisely, *The Memoirs of Sir Ronald Storrs*, one of the best books of the kind ever written in my time. Best account of Kitchener, also of Lawrence of Arabia.

Storrs and his wife now live in Essex and I wonder what the Essex ladies think of him! I have always had what the French call a *faible* for him—partly because he is so clever. I hope he has a pension, for he was very extravagant. But she has money from her first husband. According to him he fell in love with her when at Eton and never looked backwards or forwards. She listens to such assertions with a wan smile. He makes them in front of her, as it saves time.

M. B. L. TO HER DAUGHTER E. I.

Praça de José Fontana 12-1,
Lisbon
January 9th, 1947

It is odd how certain words have vanished—no one now says "He is *near*" for "mean" or "She is on the close side"—same thing—or "She is the grey mare". The words "appealing" "fast", "a screw" have vanished—there were a good many Anglo-Indian expressions—all gone—a great many French words were used—Lady Burghclere the last to use them often—Pamela[2] *never* did—old Lady Leconfield did, now and again. All her generation spoke perfect French—all the men *read* French novels—of course these novels were supposed to be "naughty", only a few of them were. Sir Claud Russell has a good many French books—though his mother was French, he dislikes the

---

[1] Sir Ronald Storrs: 1881-1955. Served in Middle East in several official capacities. Governor of Jerusalem.

[2] Lady Glenconner, afterwards Lady Grey of Fallodon.

French. He has certain of their faults. His virtues are English—the *oddest* of his pecularities is never going to church. The Russells are supposed to be extremely eccentric. *One* of them, in Victorian days, was certainly a murderer. It was hushed up about 40-50 years ago— he killed himself after he had done this murder—that made it all square. I have longed to ask Sir Claud about this really very mysterious affair. It was widely known.

M. B. L. TO HER DAUGHTER E. I.

Praça de José Fontana 12-1,
Lisbon
January 13*th*, 1947

We are *so* excited at the thought of your coming here[1]. I think Susan will find a house fairly soon. There is *very* little choice.

I think Paul an exceptionally clever child—full of curiosity about everything and on the whole good tempered. He enjoys going to school. There are many "children's parties", among the English. Lisbon is very like the London of my childhood—socially speaking. What Susan *and* Luiz enjoy are the people "going through". The £75 limit stops the tourists—to a certain extent and, I suppose, keeps hotel prices down. But by taking a little trouble, it seems people can get monthly allowance from England. But a large sum would be, I fancy, difficult. The Portuguese of the better class are *very* prosperous— there are no *direct* taxes, from what I can make out. But I suspect that, as in the France of my childhood, everything is taxed that can be.

M. B. L. TO HER DAUGHTER E. I.

Praça de José Fontana 12-1,
Lisbon
January 21*st*, 1947

I have always noticed that to marry for money is foolish, unless the man can buy a big job with his wife's money. When they married, Margot's £8,000 a year meant nothing to Asquith, as he was Home Secretary. But it *did* mean a good deal later—though he was, in my view, unaware of this fact. In some ways Asquith was the most singular

[1] E. I. flew out later to fetch M. B. L. who had had a serious heart attack earlier in the month.

man I have ever known. There were so very many sides to him. He secretly disliked Eddie Glenconner. This to me remains a mystery. Asquith once to my astonishment, told me all he had *done* for Eddie, made him a peer etc., saying angrily Eddie had done nothing for him! It is an odd fact that I never saw either Pamela or Eddie at 10 Downing Street *or* Cavendish Square. I should like an honest talk about them all with Violet Bonham-Carter.

M. B. L. TO HER DAUGHTER E. I.

Praça de José Fontana 12-1
Lisbon
January 23rd, 1947

I hope you have good accounts of Hilda and Nicholas[1]. I suppose baby and Ana will get measles. Paul has it very lightly. Better at home than at school. I am getting on with my work. I lose count of time. I feel as if I was in a limbo, cheered by Susan's presence. She makes me very happy and comfortable. I tell her strange, true tales as a reward.

It is very sad reading the lives of people I knew, and hearing of their troubles or of seeing their troubles omitted. Having known all about them. The part money plays in educated life is a fearful thing. I have been reading the life of one of the British Ambassadors to U.S.A., Spring Rice. I knew his good wife well, daughter of Sir Frank Lascelles, Ambassador to Berlin where Spring Rice had been attaché. She came to see me at 9 Barton Street to ask if I could help her son to get into films, his one wish and dream. When her husband died in a moment, while on visit to the Buchans in Canada, she was left badly off. What astonishing ups and downs of such a life. How very, very strange life is. I wonder if Lord Peel has yet had a Catholic baby, I hope so, it is such a fine old name. His mother was a great heiress (wealth derived from carpet-making). His father said to his platonic love, when he was going to marry the carpet heiress "How awful to have to sit opposite to that face every morning for the rest of my life". Let us hope she breakfasted in bed. It was not the fashion then to do that. He would have been much disturbed at the thought of his grandson a Catholic.

Tonight we go to dinner party. I think host a bachelor. A very

[1] Nicholas Maxwell-Lawford.

funny novel might be written on life among Lisbon British. A modern Fielding might do it, even a Thackeray. I am working away. By the way did Daniel Macmillan tell you when my book is coming out? I should like to see proofs.

M. B. L. TO HER DAUGHTER E. I.

Praça de José Fontana 12-1,
Lisbon
February 20*th*, 1947

I always thought it odd of my brother to buy Kingsland as it *is* low— and he is so fond of hills and mountains. I suppose when he was looking for a country farmhouse, etc. he was taken by the *Mill* and nearness (in a sense) to Horsham. My heart so often aches for him. He had a wonderful life for, say, 15 years—perhaps only 10 years, if one leaves out the first war—but before '14, when Daddy and I were so very, very worried and hard up, Hilary had a glorious life—nothing like him had been seen in the high little world in which he lived.

Elodie[1] yearned for London, and the literary life. I feel certain that, clever as she was, she never had even "an inkling" of his dislike of "the literary life". In that he was like dear Laurence Binyon and, I suppose, many poets!

M. B. L. TO HER DAUGHTER E. I.

Praça de José Fontana 12-1,
Lisbon
March 30*th*, 1947

What false pictures are painted of human life—when I recall the utterly selfish life of Mrs Haldane[2]—regarded as a noble being by the friends of her *really* noble unselfish daughter, I feel enraged—I believe I was Elizabeth Haldane's nearest friend during the closing years of her life. She wrote to me frequently and in London used to see me very often. She did not care for any of Richard's English friends—she was fond of Violet Carruthers. She could make nothing of Lady Horner —but neither could Lady Horner make anything of *her*—Mrs Haldane *hated* Lady Horner.

[1] Elodie Agnes Hogan: 1868-1914. m. 1896 Hilaire Belloc.
[2] Mrs Haldane: 1825-1925. Born Mary Burdon Sanderson.

278

When Sir John had scarlet fever (the boy, aged I think 17, died) I believe Mrs Haldane was terrified lest Richard should marry her. I never thought so. I don't think she would have married again. Her one love was Burne Jones, *and* her children. I think Frances Horner fascinated Haldane. Elizabeth H. saw nothing in her. This was strange for she was fascinating up to old age. (You recall silly Canon Hannay[1], he *adored* her). I became *very* fond of her and intimate with her at the end of her life. She was *convinced* Asquith was the lover of that poor little Oxford widow—Frances had lived in a *very* immoral world in her youth. I suppose a rich Glasgow world, yet she adored moral Burne Jones. She once told me that had she been born 15 years later, she would have run away with B. J. I said "No, your children would have held you back", and she agreed.

M. B. L. TO HER DAUGHTER S. L. M.

Parfetts House,
Eversley Cross
June 30th, 1947

As to servants, it is really a question of money. English servants now expect enormous wages. Those who won't or can't give them, lead a dreadful life of discomfort, lack of proper cooking. It is a sad state of things, and will never be remedied. Luckily for me they all want to be in London and with 'one lady' or 'one gentleman'. Elizabeth was getting one of 70 and deaf. But she has now haughtily decided not to come. Very, very foolish of her, if she only knew, as Elizabeth is not only an angel of kindness, but here there is enough to eat. This is rare. I don't wonder masses of people are going to live abroad. Others settle down to starve in hotels or boarding houses. If I had the energy I would write a satiric book about it all.

The state of things amazes Americans—one couple told me they had just had with us the only good meal they had had in England. We gave them a very simple meal. It is a little easier in the country than in London. There, every restaurant or teashop is crammed. Everyone looks angry and hungry. There is little entertainment. It is an astounding state of things. Love of hospitality is dying a lingering death.

[1] Rev. Canon James Hannay: 1865-1950. Wrote novels under the pseudonym of George Birmingham.

Parfetts House,
Eversley Cross
August 4th, 1947

I can't tell you how odd everything is. I get on, so does Elizabeth. But many people don't know how to manage. The Ivy has suddenly shut for 3 weeks, and heaps of people who ate there always don't know what to do. Restaurants of all kinds will only have their "regulars" *or* have shut for a holiday with practically no notice.

The Government is being bitterly blamed. Yet I don't see what it could do. Thousands are trying to go to the continent. It is thought there will be an embargo on travel. Everything is being done to stop money leaving the country. Life is so uncomfortable. Far, *far* worse than at worst time of the First War.

Elizabeth and Harry and the children are spending the day, on the river. It is rather cold and windy this morning. But I remember what intense pleasure being on the Thames brought to your father and to me, when we could afford it. These trips were most expensive. Spending two or three days away cost a fortune, and I used to be amused and Daddy annoyed, because they always thought us an unmarried couple off on a 'spree'. I think this was because I was so gay and happy, and he was so kind and looked after me so well. We once had a terrible adventure, we nearly went over a weir and should have been drowned. I shall always remember with astonishment Daddy's terrible language. I was steering, and but for his language, I think we would have drowned; but I was so surprised and taken aback that I managed to turn the boat round!

Isn't this funny? It is a perfect example of humorous exasperation.

ADVICE

"Write, write, write a letter—
Good advice will make us better,
Father, mother, sister, brother,
Let us all advise each other".

Your loving
Mother

INDEX

281

288